The Power of Public Investment Management

DIRECTIONS IN DEVELOPMENT
Public Sector Governance

The Power of Public Investment Management

Transforming Resources into Assets for Growth

Anand Rajaram, Tuan Minh Le, Kai Kaiser, Jay-Hyung Kim, and Jonas Frank, Editors

WORLD BANK GROUP

ISBN (paper): 978-1-4648-0316-1
ISBN (electronic): 978-1-4648-0317-8
DOI: 10.1596/978-1-4648-0316-1

Cover photo: "Road Gang"—painting by Brad Burns, www.constructionfineart.com. Used with permission; further permission required for reuse.
Cover design: Debra Naylor, Naylor Design Inc.

Library of Congress Cataloging-in-Publication Data has been requested.

Contents

Boxes

Figures

Photos

Tables

Acknowledgments

As an effort to consolidate widely dispersed knowledge on public investment management, this volume represents a collective effort of a large number of practitioners at the World Bank, in governments, in various development organizations, at a number of universities, and in private consulting.

At the World Bank, Anand Rajaram, Tuan Minh Le, Kai Kaiser, Jay-Hyung Kim, and Jonas Frank initiated and led the global work on public investment management and coordinated the preparation of the volume. James Brumby, William Dorotinsky, Nick Manning, Linda van Gelder, and Deborah Wetzel provided guidance at various periods during the preparation of the volume.

The chapter authors are acknowledged as follows:

Chapter 1—*Building a System for Public Investment Management*: Anand Rajaram, Jonas Frank

Chapter 2—*A Unified Framework for Public Investment Management*: Anand Rajaram, Tuan Minh Le, Nataliya Biletska, James Brumby

Chapter 3—*Country Experiences of Public Investment Management*: Murray Petrie, Anand Rajaram

Chapter 4—*Approaches to Better Project Appraisal*: Graham Glenday, Kai Kaiser, Tuan Minh Le

Chapter 5—*Public Investment Management under Uncertainty*: Leo Dobes

Chapter 6—*Procurement and Public Investment Management*: Anand Rajaram, Joel Turkewitz, Nataliya Biletska

Chapter 7—*Public Investment Management for Public-Private Partnerships*: Jay-Hyung Kim

Peer review and substantive commentary by Paolo Belli (World Bank); Ian Hawkesworth (OECD); Kirsten Homman (World Bank); Jen Kromann Kristensen (World Bank); Petter Matthews (CoST), and Martin Rama (World Bank) is gratefully acknowledged. Commentary by Martin Darcy, Simon Groom, Richard Hemming, V. Krishnakumar, Joao Veiga Malta, Irina Luca, Gael Raballand, and Robert Taliercio was very helpful to strengthening individual chapters.

An overview of PIM practices across a large set of countries at different levels of development was critical to the knowledge that informs this volume and would not have been possible without the contributions of many senior government officials. Authorship of the following background country cases is gratefully acknowledged: Brazil (James Brumby, Marcos Mendes, and Tarsila Ortenzio Velloso); Chile (Hugo Arancibia and Nataliya Biletska); China (Christine Wong); Eastern Europe and Central Asia (Oleksiy Balabushko and Bernard Myers); East Timor (Murray Petrie and Habib Rab); Equatorial Guinea (Rafael Muñoz Moreno); the Republic of Korea (Jay-Hyung Kim); Lagos, Nigeria (Olugbenga Ebenezer Oyewole and Volker Treichel); Latin America (Jonas Frank); Lesotho (Tuan Minh Le, Marco Larizza, Morabo Morojele, Huong Mai Nguyen, and G. P. Shukla); Mongolia (Zahid Hasnain); Peru (Jonas Frank and Gustavo Guerra-García); Sierra Leone (Douglas Addison, Yusuf Foday, and Murray Petrie); Uganda (Asumani Guloba, Serif Sayin, Jorge Shepherd, and Jos Verbeek); United States (John E. Petersen and Ha T. T. Vu); Vietnam (Quang Hong Doan, Tuan Minh Le, and Duong Anh Nguyen); Western Balkans (Simon Groom); Zambia (Tuan Minh Le, Patricia Palale, and Gael Raballand); Zimbabwe (Tuan Minh Le, G. P. Shukla, Camilla Blomquist, Huong Mai Nguyen, and Tendai Mukurazhizha).

Additional background work that was helpful to the preparation of the volume included inputs by Ha Vu, Alfonso Sanchez, Zachary Mills, Verena Fritz, Jurgen Blum, Cem Dener, Francesco Grigoli, Young-Kyu Kang, Najibullah Motahedy, Saw-Young Min, Nicola Smithers, Grace Verances, and Lorena Vinuela.

Mary Anderson is gratefully acknowledged for her careful review and editing of each chapter. The enthusiasm, advice, and production support of Stephen McGroarty, Paola Scalabrin, and Jewel McFadden from the World Bank's Publishing and Knowledge Division was of great help in finalizing the volume.

The work on this subject benefited from a valuable partnership with the Korea Development Institute and the financial support of the Korean Trust Fund. In addition, the financial support from AusAid and the constructive engagement of Edward Archibald and Paul Keogh has been very helpful. We would also wish to acknowledge valuable opportunities to share the ideas contained in this volume and get feedback from diverse audiences at conferences organized by partners at the International Monetary Fund, the United Nations Economic Commission for Latin America, the Natural Resources Charter, and the Arab Fund for Social and Economic Development.

About the Authors

Nataliya Biletska is a Public Sector Specialist in the Governance Practice of the World Bank. She has worked on a range of policy and operational issues in public finance, including performance-oriented public financial management reforms, efficiency in public investment management, capability of central finance agencies, fiscal policy for growth and development, and revenue administration. Earlier, she held various positions at the national government of Ukraine. Her publications focus on public investment management, performance budgeting, and Medium-Term Expenditure Frameworks.

James Brumby is Practice Manager in the Governance Practice of the World Bank. He has worked on public management reform at state, national, and international levels for 30 years. Prior to joining the World Bank in 2007, he was Division Chief in the Office of Budget and Planning, Deputy Division Chief in the Fiscal Affairs Department at the International Monetary Fund, and Division Chief in the Public Management Group at the Organisation for Economic Co-operation and Development. He held various positions at the treasuries of New Zealand and the state of Victoria in Australia.

Leo Dobes is Adjunct Associate Professor at the Crawford School of the Australian National University, where he teaches a master's degree course in cost-benefit analysis. Following a doctorate (Oxford), he worked for almost 30 years in various public service positions, ranging from the diplomatic service to the Australian Treasury. In 1992 he established an Environment Branch within the Australian Bureau of Transport Economics, publishing a number of reports on the costs and benefits of mitigating emissions in the transport sector. His main current research interests are in the area of adaptation to climate change.

Jonas Frank is coleader of the World Bank's Decentralization and Subnational Finance Thematic Group, which has more than 300 members. He works on public finance with a focus on fiscal decentralization and public investment in the Governance Practice. In his capacity as Senior Public Sector Specialist in the Latin America region he primarily dealt with intergovernmental relations in a variety of institutional contexts. He also led the Bank's Country Office in Ecuador, where he engaged on economic and social development. Earlier, Jonas was Lecturer at the *Universidad Las Américas*, and Associate at the German Technical Cooperation (GIZ). He holds a doctorate in economics and social sciences with a focus on public administration, earned at University of Potsdam (Germany).

Graham Glenday is a Professor at Duke Center for International Development, Sanford School of Public Policy, Duke University, where he directs and teaches programs in international taxation, project appraisal and risk management, and budgeting and financial management. He has over 25 years of professional experience in consulting, research, and working in ministries of finance in public finance matters in over 25 countries. Formerly, he was Director, Public Finance Group at Harvard Institute for International Development, Harvard University, and also a senior official in the Department of Finance, Government of Canada. He graduated from University of Cape Town, Oxford University, and Harvard University, where he completed his doctorate in public policy.

Kai Kaiser is Senior Country Economist for the Philippines in the Governance Practice of the World Bank. Previously, he was colead of the Decentralization and Sub-National Regional Economics Thematic Group. He focuses on public finance, intergovernmental relations, and institutional reform issues. Prior to his current assignment, he was based in the World Bank's Indonesia country office in Jakarta and with the Public Sector Anchor in Washington, DC. His work on intergovernmental reforms and benefit sharing has led to his concentration on natural resources and development.

Jay-Hyung Kim is an Advisor to the Governance Practice of the World Bank and coconvenor of the PIM Community of Practice. He has been a Fellow at the Korea Development Institute since 1994, conducting research and advising on public finance, infrastructure and regional development, and public sector governance. He served as managing director of the Public and Private Infrastructure Investment Management Center of the Korean government from 2006 to 2012. Born in the Republic of Korea, Jay-Hyung Kim holds bachelor's and master's degrees in economics from Seoul National University, and a doctorate in economics from the University of Chicago.

Tuan Minh Le is Senior Economist at the World Bank. Prior to joining the World Bank, he worked at the Public Finance Group, Harvard Institute for International Development, Harvard University, and was Assistant Professor of Economics at Suffolk University. He has engaged in a broad range of teaching, research, policy consulting, and operations on public finance in Asia, Eastern Europe, the Middle East, and Sub-Saharan Africa. His publication focuses on tax policy design, revenue forecasting, tax administration, appraisal of development expenditures, and public investment management. He obtained his doctorate in public policy from Harvard University.

Murray Petrie is Director of the Economics and Strategy Group Ltd, and a Senior Associate at the Institute of Governance of Policy Studies, Victoria University of Wellington. Murray has worked for the New Zealand Treasury and, since 1998, has consulted extensively for the World Bank and the International Monetary Fund. His areas of specialization include public expenditure and public investment management, fiscal transparency, and the management of fiscal risks. He is actively involved in civil society and multi-stakeholder initiatives to promote fiscal transparency and the quality of governance. Murray has a doctorate in public policy from Victoria University.

Anand Rajaram is currently Practice Leader for Governance and Public Management at the World Bank and coconvenor of the PIM Community of Practice. Prior to this, he was Sector Manager of the Public Sector Reform and Governance Department for Sub-Saharan Africa from 2007 to 2012. He has led the work of the World Bank on fiscal policy for growth for the Development Committee of the Bank and the International Monetary Fund, from which the widely used PIM diagnostic approach is a spin-off. He was closely involved in the major fiscal and budget reforms in Turkey from 2000 to 2004. His country experience includes substantive assignments on Kenya, India, China, and Nepal as well as extensive experience across Africa. He holds a doctorate in economics from Boston University and a master's degree in economics from the Delhi School of Economics.

Joel Turkewitz is a Lead Public Sector Specialist in the Governance Practice of the World Bank. He has worked for over 12 years in the World Bank, serving as Program Coordinator, EAP Regional Governance Hub, South Asia Regional Procurement Reform Coordinator, Senior Procurement Specialist, and Senior Public Sector Specialist. He holds a juris doctorate from Colombia University School of Law and a bachelor's degree from Wesleyan University. Prior to joining the Bank, he was associated with the University of Texas School of Law and the Central European University. He has published articles on public sector performance and improving public spending in fragile and conflict environments.

Abbreviations

CBA	cost-benefit analysis
CEA	cost-effectiveness analysis
CHOGM	Commonwealth Heads of Government Meeting
CoST	Construction Sector Transparentcy Initiative
ERR	economic rate of return
EU	European Union
GAO	General Accountability Office
GATT	General Agreement on Tariffs and Trade
GDP	gross domestic product
GPA	Governments Procurement Agreement
HD	Harrod-Domar
IDA	International Development Association
IFI	international financial institution
IFRS	International Financial Reporting Standards
IRR	internal rate of return
IMF	International Monetary Fund
IPA	Instrument for Pre-Accession Assistance
IPSAS	International Public Sector Accounting Standards
IPSASB	International Public Sector Accounting Standards Board
IRR	Internal Rates of Return
KDI	Korea Development Institute
LIC	local investment corporation
MDAs	ministries, departments, and agencies
MOSF	Ministry of Strategy and Finance
MPI	Minister of Planning and Investments
MTEF	medium-term expenditure framework
NDP	National Development Plan
NGO	nongovernmental organization
NPV	net present value

O&M	operation and maintenance
OECD	Organisation for Economic Co-operation and Development
PEFA	Public Expenditure and Financial Accountability
PFM	public financial management
PIM	public investment management
PIMAC	Public and Private Infrastructure Investment Management Center (Republic of Korea)
PIP	public investment program
PIU	Project Implementation Unit
PPIAF	Public-Private Infrastructure Advisory Facility
PPP	public-private partnership
PRSP	Poverty Reduction Strategy Paper
SAFETEA-LU	Safe, Accountable, Flexible, Efficient Transportation Equity Act: A Legacy for Users
SANRAL	South African National Roads Agency Ltd
TPCM	Total Project Cost Management
UEMOA	West African Economic and Monetary Union
UNCITRAL	United Nations Commission on International Trade Law
UNIDO	United Nations Industrial Development Organization
VFM	value for money

Note: All dollar amounts are in U.S. dollars unless otherwise noted.

CHAPTER 1

Building a System for Public Investment Management

Public Investment Management: Why It Matters

Consider the perspective of a finance minister in any of a number of developing countries—particularly one that has received news of a large new resource discovery and is anticipating significant new fiscal revenues on the order of hundreds of millions, possibly even billions, of dollars. He or she recognizes the opportunity this windfall offers to finance critical infrastructure and human capital investments that would fundamentally alter the opportunities available for citizens of the country—opportunities that would offer the prospect of private sector jobs and growing incomes for millions of young employment seekers. But at the same time, the minister recognizes that there is no institutional capacity to make the necessary decisions on sound economic principles and there is a high risk of ad hoc and politically motivated investments that will not contribute to the development goals of the country.

Or consider the challenge facing a country with high levels of debt and limited resources for investment, where every dollar allocated to investment must be made to count and contribute to economic growth. Or even consider the situation confronting the governor of a state in a highly developed country that has faced a climatic disaster that has destroyed coastal homes and infrastructure on a massive scale. The government will need to make difficult decisions on taxation and borrowing to replace or rebuild the infrastructure to better guard against what may well be repeated extreme weather events forecast by global warming experts. Here, too, efficiently using resources for public investment is imperative.

There is a high-profile debate in many countries about the role of the state in managing economic development, and the ideological preferences of the citizens and political leaders have an important influence on where the balance lies between a dominant role and a facilitative and limited role. Apart from the extreme libertarian view, however, there is a common acknowledgment that government has a role in undertaking public investments that private enterprise alone would not provide because of the fundamental incentive problems due to nonappropriability and nonexclusion that are characteristic of public goods. The challenge then is to ensure that where public investments are required, they be undertaken with regard to efficiency and value for money, among other reasons to minimize the need for taxation, which may impose a distortionary impact on citizens, or the need for borrowing, which may impose a burden on future citizens.

Yet the experience of countries, both developed and developing, is that public investment decisions are often seen to be wastefully managed, subject to corruption and misappropriation, and a constant source of dismay and disappointment to citizens. For countries earning significant revenues from natural resource exports but with weak institutional capacity to invest in assets for development the risk of a resource "curse" looms large in the minds of policy makers and development partners. Under these conditions, investing in the effort to establish effective systems for managing public investment is likely to yield high returns.

Evolution of Ideas

The idea that governments ought to invest in public infrastructure and institutional assets to support production and trade is well established in the economic literature going back at least to Adam Smith ([1776] 2000), who noted the following in *The Wealth of Nations*:

> The sovereign has only three duties to attend to; three duties of great importance, indeed, but plain and intelligible to common understandings: first, the duty of protecting the society from the violence and invasion of other independent societies; secondly, the duty of protecting, as far as possible, every member of the society from the injustice or oppression of every other member of it, or the duty of establishing an exact administration of justice; and, thirdly, the duty of erecting and maintaining certain public works and certain public institutions, which it can never be for the interest of any individual, or small number of individuals, to erect and maintain; because the profit could never repay the expence to any individual, or small number of individuals, though it may frequently do much more than repay it to a great society.

Underlying Smith's vision was the idea that government provision of complementary public goods such as roads and bridges would facilitate the development and growth of markets and long-term economic growth. Private enterprise by itself would be unlikely to provide such public works, and that implicit market failure, without government provision, would constrain economic growth.[1]

John Maynard Keynes (1936) provided a complementary rationale for public investment as a tool of countercyclical fiscal policy, justifying public works programs during the Great Depression as a means to stimulate aggregate demand, catalyze the income and employment multiplier, and thereby restore the economy to full employment.[2] Ever since Keynes, governments have sought to justify deficit-financed public investment projects as a corrective response, both to serve as a countercyclical stimulus and to enhance the stock of public assets that could support private sector enterprise and long-term economic growth.

The models of economic growth that motivated five-year plans and industrialization strategies in much of the developing world in the postwar years were heavily dependent on high levels of public investment and estimates of aggregate and sectoral growth based on capital output ratios.[3] Countries invested not only in basic infrastructure for agricultural and industrial development (dams, irrigation canals, power grids, roads, and ports) but also, in some cases, in directly productive activities as state-owned enterprises grew and expanded into sectors where there was no justification (based on principles of public economics) for that role.

Public infrastructure has typically been the preferred form of fiscal investment given its justification as a public good with its broadly distributed benefits to the population. But the size and sign of the productivity of public investment is an empirical question that has stimulated a considerable literature, starting with the paper on *Public Investment, the Rate of Return, and Optimal Fiscal Policy* by Arrow and Kurz (1970). Aschauer (1989) showed that the stock of nonmilitary public infrastructure (such as roads, highways, airports, mass transit, and water and sewer systems) was a significant determinant of national income productivity in the United States and that the decline in productivity in the 1970s and 1980s could be attributed to the low rate of public investment. Subsequent work by Glomm and Ravikumar (1997), using endogenous growth models and including the effect of public spending on education, noted that estimates of the productivity effects of infrastructure were probably more modest than suggested by Aschauer but that a positive effect is generally expected. Rodrigue (2009) indicates that every dollar of investment in the interstate highway network during 1954–2001 in the United States contributed to six dollars of economic productivity.

The interest in public investment took a new and interesting turn in the early years of this century when a number of developing-country governments, particularly in South America, began to complain about the restrictions imposed on their capacity to undertake public investments by the macroeconomic stabilization framework recommended by the International Monetary Fund (IMF). In effect, governments facing macroeconomic pressures that tended to increase indebtedness and inflation were advised to follow restrictive fiscal policies that reduced government spending and borrowing. In many cases, these fiscal adjustments were achieved by cutting back on discretionary spending, with public investments typically bearing the brunt of such cutbacks. However, after a few years of politically difficult fiscal restraint, governments expressed concern that an exclusive focus on macroeconomic stabilization was shortsighted and that decisions to curb public investments for a prolonged period would result in sacrificing the potential for long-term growth.

Many developing countries face tremendous deficits in terms of provision of economic and social infrastructure, and the government is expected to be a principal actor in closing these deficits through public policy. Fiscal policies that were defined by a focus on the fiscal deficit alone did not acknowledge that the opportunity cost of delayed development may be detrimental even to fiscal stability. Easterly, Irwin, and Servén (2008) reviewed the evidence of fiscal adjustments undertaken by a number of countries through the 1990s and concluded that the cutback in public investment had in fact contributed to a decline in economic growth and that, from an intertemporal perspective, this may have been a suboptimal design of fiscal policy.

Rather than promoting fiscal sustainability, cutting public investment may lead to a weakening growth process with adverse, rather than positive, consequences for fiscal solvency. A better approach would be to adopt a longer-term perspective to the design of fiscal policy with a view to maximizing government net worth. Taking into account the evidence that the quality (speed and composition) of fiscal adjustment during an episode of macroeconomic stabilization has significant implications for growth, the World Bank (2006, 2007) proposed ways in which fiscal policy might be designed to promote growth and development while preserving macroeconomic stability. Some general principles should apply: cuts in public consumption are preferable to cuts in public investment, and a reallocation of resources from lower-efficiency uses to more productive uses is likely to be more long-term growth enhancing, other things being equal, than raising additional revenue or borrowing to finance the same productive expenditure. But these principles should be combined with an understanding of the specific country circumstances to customize fiscal policy design. The amount of "fiscal space" to finance new public investment would depend on the individual country context and whether there was room to reallocate resources to investment by improving the efficiency of public spending. Where the room to improve efficiency is limited, countries may seek to undertake investments through accessing external aid or implementing additional revenue measures.

Much of the argument for public investment relies on the belief that resources allocated to investment translate into an equivalent value of public capital stock, which, by lowering the cost of production or distribution, benefits the private sector and affects the overall growth process. This effect is typically measured by the rate of economic or social return from public investment. Social cost-benefit analysis is intended to define the expected rate of return on an investment, taking account of likely costs and benefits including any economic and social externalities.

But this rate of return will depend very much on the effectiveness of the management of the public investments, both in the budgeting and execution of the investment projects and in the subsequent operation and maintenance of the public asset created by public investment. Typically cost-benefit analysis assumes a frictionless process of project implementation. However, if the quality of public investment management (PIM) is low, and if resources are wasted or corruptly misdirected, it is likely that the realized (or ex post) rate of return will be low or negative even for projects that showed ex ante high rates of return. Without efficient management of public investments, investment spending is unlikely to be fiscally sustainable and would not promote growth and development.[4]

Challenges of Today

The 2007–12 global economic slowdown once more brought the spotlight on fiscal policy as an instrument to revive economic activity, although not in all regions in the same way. In the United States, this took the form of the expansionary policy of "fiscal stimulus" accompanied by the search for "shovel-ready" investment projects to invest in, whereas the high debt levels in Italy, Greece, Portugal, and Spain appear to have resulted in a greater emphasis on fiscal austerity and expenditure cutbacks in the European Union (EU). Nevertheless, uncertain economic prospects and tight fiscal conditions suggest that all countries will need to continue efforts for better PIM to get the highest value for money and the greatest growth impact of any public money spent. Given fiscal constraints that limit the overall *level* of public investment in most countries, attention to maximizing the *efficiency* through better selection and *management of investment spending* is a highly relevant policy topic.

Another set of countries faces an opposite fiscal problem, which nevertheless underlines the importance of PIM: as a result of the boom in commodity prices over 2002–12, natural-resource-rich countries are receiving large revenue inflows, and exploration is revealing new mineral and hydrocarbon deposits. Global resource rents from oil, gas, and minerals have more than trebled over 2003–11 to an estimated $3.7 trillion. Countries receiving these windfall revenues are well placed to expand public investment. Before the escalating political and military instability in 2014, Iraq—which had more than doubled its fiscal revenues between 2005 and 2011 because of the high price of oil and increased exports from its restored oil fields—planned to finance $100 billion of public investment over the 2010–14 national plan period (World Bank 2012b). In Africa, recognized oil and mineral resource exporters such as Angola, Chad, Equatorial Guinea, Gabon, Nigeria, and Zambia have been joined by countries with new discoveries of minerals and hydrocarbons such as Kenya, Mozambique, Tanzania, and Uganda that are likely to earn significant fiscal revenues from extraction in the coming years. Others such as Ghana and Sierra Leone have discovered new resources that are likely to substantially enhance fiscal resources available to governments. And newly formed countries such as the Republic of South Sudan, prior to the recent conflict, were counting on earnings from oil exports to provide the resources to jump-start development from very low levels.

All these countries require large investments in human and physical capital and economic infrastructure for economic development and poverty reduction. Using exhaustible natural resources to create productive capital assets is a welfare-improving transformation. Yet all these countries have extremely weak institutional capacity to ensure effective use of the resources for development: their PIM systems are weak or nonexistent, and the risks that they will not translate the revenues from exhaustible natural resources into durable developmental assets are large. Planned investment expenditures are often not undertaken despite enormous revenue resources, in large part because the government is unable to manage and execute its planned investment budget. Collier (2010) has underlined the critical importance of countries with natural resources investing in the capacity for PIM—to "invest in investing"—given the high value such capacity could bring to the effective management of natural resource earnings. Good PIM is a sine qua non for resource-rich countries, but it is also a critical capability for all countries generally.

The lack of good PIM capacity leads to myriad forms of resource waste. There is a wide range of bad practices that are economically and socially costly—from governments whose bureaucratic delays keep them from spending their investment budgets during the fiscal year to corrupt practices that divert public resources to private pockets. Cost and time overruns on public projects are widespread and highlight management challenges that are particularly salient for developing countries but are also prevalent in developed countries.

Flyvbjerg (2009) reviewed data from 258 transport projects in 20 countries across five continents and found that 90 percent of the projects experienced significant cost overruns. The average real-cost overrun for rail projects was about 45 percent; for bridges and tunnels, 34 percent; and for road projects, a little over 20 percent. The problem, though, is not confined to transport projects but is pervasive and afflicts most sectors, including defense and aerospace projects, power and water projects, urban and regional development projects, and increasingly information communication technology projects. Flyvbjerg attributes significant blame for such overruns to the tendency for project planners to systematically underestimate costs, a result of "optimism bias" that afflicts planners.

Because many public investment projects involve multiyear processes and significant planning, coordination, financing, procurement, and contract implementation challenges, it is not unusual for costs and completion dates to overrun even well-planned estimates. Budget allocations may be diverted by new priorities, key staff turnover can lead to loss of focus and momentum, and contractors may run into unexpected technical challenges. If such overruns are significant, they jeopardize the cost-benefit calculus that justified the project. But good management can limit such overruns.

The Construction Sector Transparency Initiative (CoST) is a multistakeholder attempt to assess the impact of greater transparency in implementation of public sector construction projects on the value for money derived from such projects. CoST developed and tested indicators relevant for such analysis (focusing in particular on competition and tender markets and on project time and cost overruns) and tested it on a pilot basis in collaboration with three to five procuring entities in each of eight countries. Figure 1.1 presents baseline evidence in terms of project cost and time overruns compared with the original project cost and completion time estimates from 145 projects in the eight participating countries (CoST 2011).

Figure 1.1 Average Construction Project Cost and Time Overruns in Selected Countries

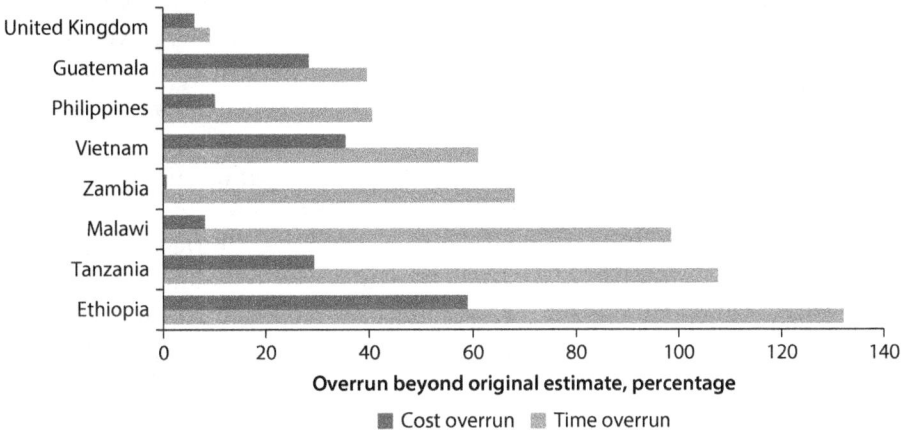

Overrun beyond original estimate, percentage

■ Cost overrun ▦ Time overrun

Source: CoST 2011.

The figure suggests that an advanced modern economy with relatively strong management and accountability systems, such as the United Kingdom, can better ensure value for money by minimizing the cost and time overruns more effectively than the typical developing country. But it is also clear that starting points and the institutional settings differ quite significantly across all the countries in the sample, and also across procuring entities within a country, requiring differentiated approaches to address the institutional shortcomings. Given these challenges, it is critically important to drill down on the causes of poor PIM.

Drivers of Inefficient Public Investment

The reasons why governments display relatively high inefficiency in undertaking public investments are manifold, and they reflect the particular character of a typical public investment project:

- Often, the project may be proposed or sponsored by a line ministry and be subject to review by a ministry of planning and a ministry of finance. Weak interagency coordination processes may lead to delays in both project evaluation and project oversight and implementation.
- Projects may also be driven by political considerations and therefore be subject to different criteria and timelines that, if widely applied, may disrupt established processes and diminish the credibility of ex ante project appraisal processes.
- Allocating resources to a project is typically a multiyear commitment, and that may pose particular challenges in a weak budget system with poor management of the annual budget.
- Large infrastructure projects often involve problematic site acquisition and resettlement issues, environmental safeguards, and complex procurement challenges that can result in significant delays and cost escalation.

To all this we must add the problem of corruption in public investment. Project complexity and weak management and accountability systems create the conditions for corruption to flourish, often to the point where large volumes of public money intended for public investment are diverted to private accounts with no public asset created and none of the expected benefits from the original project achieved. In the extreme case, powerful interests in government may treat the investment budget as an object to plunder with impunity, with no accountability or penalty for such behavior.

The risk of corruption is particularly salient for countries that rely on volatile revenues from natural resources, which create conditions of large revenue surges during periods of booming commodity prices or following new resource discoveries. Few budget systems have the fiscal rules and discipline to deal with such surges of revenue and are then at risk that powerful vested interests will divert the resources on the pretext of undertaking public investments to benefit the population at large. Where systems for ensuring accountability for use of public resources are weak (for example, lacking strong audit capability and legislative oversight with power to sanction the executive for waste and corruption), the likelihood that revenues from commodity discovery and price booms will be misallocated is extremely high and may contribute to the problem of the resource curse—with little development benefit to the population.

Given the problems noted above, the importance of developing PIM capacity cannot be overstated. The challenge is complex because every country is unique in its initial conditions and the nature of the problems it confronts. It is tempting but unwise to look at the example of developed countries that have evolved sophisticated management systems compatible with their specific political contexts and seek to emulate them in environments that are unlikely to be able to achieve such standards. Yet, there are clearly management *principles* that should be retained and adapted to lower-capacity contexts, and these can be termed the "must-have" features of a PIM system—features that help ensure that key risks are appropriately reduced through decision steps and controls that are within the government's capacity to implement.

Addressing these issues needs a systemic view and a careful diagnostic assessment. In a public investment cycle, weakness in upstream capability does affect later steps. From appraisal to ex post evaluation, each step can affect the quality of infrastructure. We will now turn to these issues.

A Unified Framework for PIM

This volume proposes a unified framework for PIM, which is developed in chapter 2. It is "unified" in two senses: (a) it provides a systemic view over each of the steps of the public investment cycle, ensuring there are no loopholes that can affect the quality of spending; and (b) it applies to both conventional projects and public-private partnership (PPP) modalities.

Figure 2.1 highlights the eight specific features that any "unified system" should try to establish and strengthen over time. These eight features provide a degree of assurance that there are no systemic gaps that would enable wasteful or corrupt decisions. They are considered to be "must-have" features, not with the intention of establishing a gold standard but to provide a logical and internally consistent system that even a low-capacity country should try to follow to establish basic disciplines for project selection and management. The framework presented in chapter 2 is an evolution and generalization of the diagnostic approach recommended in Rajaram et al. (2010).

This "unified framework" is based on the rationale that a system is only as strong as its weakest link. Ignoring any of the features opens the door to wasteful or inefficient investments: For example, in the 1980s, a number of countries invested heavily in building skills for cost-benefit analysis and even established units with responsibilities for project appraisal. However, without a mechanism to ensure that such analysis was effectively enforced (that is, without a gatekeeping function to screen out projects that did not pass appraisal), such capacity was quickly reduced to form without function, demoralizing the staff and atrophying the capacity for project appraisal. Equally, a well-appraised project can completely lose its justification if delays in implementation or poor operation of the asset change the cost-benefit calculus by raising costs and reducing benefits. A project that takes seven years to complete has a very different cost and benefit profile than the project that was appraised on the assumption that it would be completed in four years. Therefore, an evaluation function should provide feedback that should inform future project appraisals and lead to efforts to improve project implementation. Only through constant improvement can a good system for effective investment management be built.

The eight critical features of a PIM system are intended to provide countries with a systematic approach to creating the institutional capacity to manage investment. Even in low-capacity contexts, these features should be included as part of a long-term approach to institutional capacity enhancement. PIM capacity building should seek to ensure that:

- An investment choice is justified as a welfare-improving public policy;
- The actual investment project management is effective and leads to the completion of the project on schedule;
- There is efficient and sustainable operation of the asset created by public investment;
- There is a process of learning to improve future project selection, implementation, and operation; and
- Investment is undertaken through an allocation of risk that is more likely to ensure efficient and effective implementation of the project. Risk management is one of the key challenges when it comes to coordinating public and private investment modalities.

Applicability to Both Conventional and Public-Private Models

Governments have typically approached the issue of public investment as a problem of conventional public finance—of identifying resources within the annual budget that can be used to fund investments to improve the availability of public goods and services for which there is citizen demand. Public ownership, public financing (through general tax revenues, borrowing, or external aid), and public procurement constituted the principal model of public investment until two decades ago.

Most noticeably in the early 1990s, the public sector started partnering with the private sector in the financing, management, and maintenance of infrastructure. This approach has grown[5] and now offers an alternative to conventional public procurement. Motivating some of the initial PPPs were fiscal constraints on borrowing and taxation that limited the government's financial ability to undertake public investments. In other cases, low-capacity, resource-rich governments (including a number of African cases) have opted to do "resources-for-infrastructure" deals with extractive industry partners, effectively trading resources for private financing and construction of infrastructure.

But PPP schemes are problematic from a variety of perspectives:

- In many countries, PPPs have functioned as ad hoc, off-budget arrangements without an institutionally robust process for the review, assessment, and allocation of risks, decision making, and management that are required for any high-value, long-term commitment by government.
- The lack of an integrated approach to public investment has exposed governments to suboptimal risk commitments and potentially high values of contingent liabilities.
- In some cases, politically connected vested interests have proposed and pushed for PPP deals that a more objective assessment under a unified framework approach would have rejected. It is no surprise that PPP approaches have been controversial and have attracted criticism as costly and corrupted.

A key recommendation of this volume is the need for governments to ensure a unified PIM framework that covers both conventional procurement and PPP arrangements. This recommendation is based on a review of international experience: emerging good practice in the United Kingdom and Australia, two countries that pioneered the use of PPPs, illustrates the need to compare a proposed PPP with a public sector comparator project to ensure that the modality that offers the best value for money is chosen.

Considering these experiences and lessons, a unified framework would provide for a decision tree with alternative branches in terms of modality (figure 1.2). One early branch of that decision tree involves a choice about whether the project should be (a) solely a government responsibility and thus undertaken as a public sector project, or (b) undertaken in partnership with the private sector. A proper decision would require the preparation of two project

Figure 1.2 Deciding on Public Investment Modality in a Unified Framework

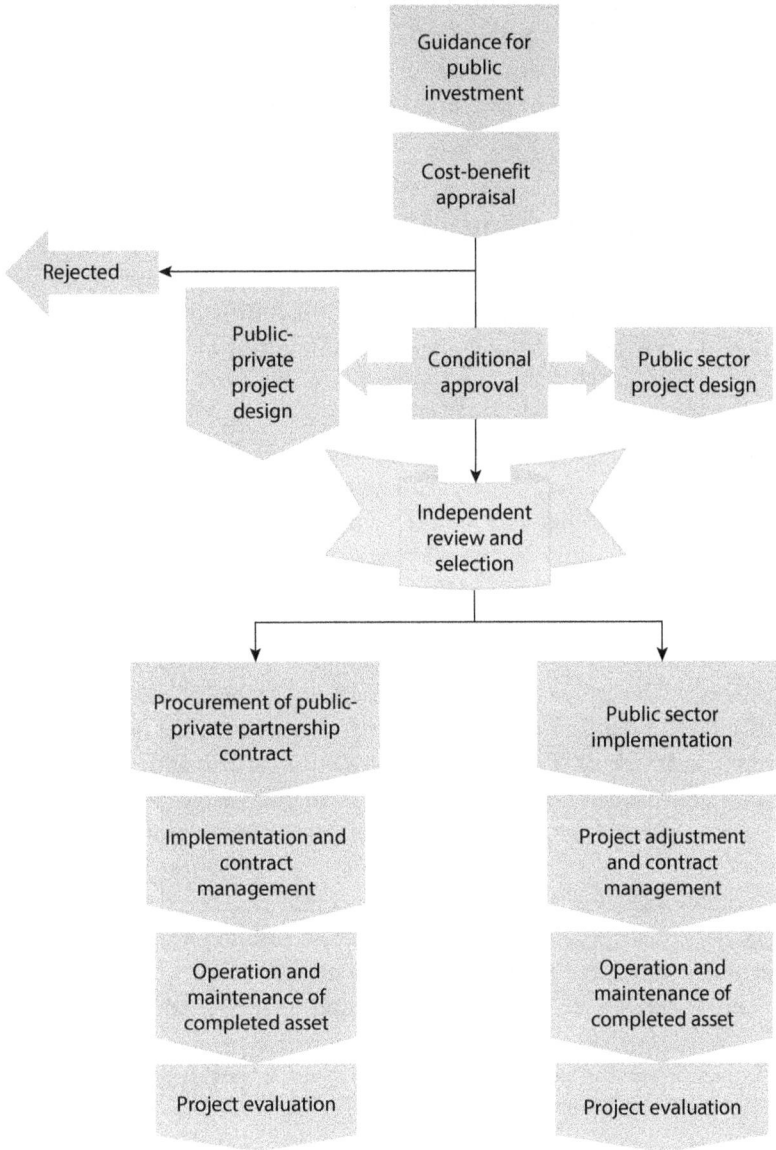

proposals—one as a PPP and the other as a public sector comparator—with the decision being determined by an independent review of the best value-for-money and risk-sharing arrangement. Once a choice is made on the basis of an objective and independent comparison of the two alternatives, appropriate management arrangements would have to be in place to ensure that the project is effectively implemented to achieve the anticipated net benefits. The arrangements for a publicly managed project are distinct from those for a PPP, with the latter requiring specific elements related to the fact that a private entity is contracted to achieve specific outputs and outcomes. In both cases, contract management would be required, but the nature of that challenge might differ.

Nevertheless, there are common PIM principles that apply to both, which are outlined in figure 1.2 and discussed further in chapter 2. Chapter 7 provides a detailed discussion of how best to manage PPP investments through each step of the unified framework.

Applicability to Diverse Economic Settings

As part of the global work on public investment, a series of country case studies were prepared in all regions of the world that, first, provided a useful (and hitherto missing) description of the range of existing PIM practices across countries. Second, the studies enabled the identification of the systemic weaknesses as well as practical steps to strengthen key features of the public investment system, using the diagnostic approach highlighted in chapter 2.

Some of the case studies were conducted directly by the World Bank or were included as references for country comparison. The case studies include Angola, Brazil, Chile, China, the Democratic Republic of Congo, Equatorial Guinea, Ireland, the Republic of Congo, the Republic of Korea, Lesotho, Mongolia, Nigeria (specifically, Lagos state), Peru, Sierra Leone, the Slovak Republic, Slovenia, Spain, Timor-Leste, Uganda, the United Kingdom, the United States, Vietnam, Zambia and Zimbabwe, along with regional summaries for Latin America and the Western Balkans (including Albania, Bosnia, Kosovo, Macedonia, Montenego and Serbia). The case study evidence provides robust confirmation of the relevance of the approach to a wide range of country circumstances while also confirming that country setting (reflecting different political and institutional histories) has an important influence on the actual functioning of PIM.

This volume classifies the country settings into five categories: (a) advanced economies; (b) emerging economies; (c) natural resource-dependent states; (d) aid-dependent states; and (e) fragile states. With a few exceptions, the mapping from country classification by country setting to the depth and quality of its public investment management system is consistent—more developed countries generally have better systems while fragile states have the weakest capabilities for PIM:

- *Advanced PIM systems.* The most effective PIM systems among the case study countries are in Ireland, Korea, the United Kingdom, the United States, and, surprisingly, given its emerging economy status, Chile. Although there is considerable variation in the institutional arrangements, modalities, and histories across these countries, in general they exhibit all of the eight must-have features and go considerably beyond that basic standard in nearly all respects. Emerging PIM Systems: These include countries such as Brazil, China, Peru and Vietnam with somewhat more diverse systems with uneven capabilities in PIM. While they display strength in some of the eight PIM features, they also have significant weakness in others, impairing overall performance and efficiency of investment. China and Vietnam represent PIM systems undergoing change as part of overall structural reforms and display better upstream project selection capabilities and somewhat weaker implementation and evaluation capacity.

- *PIM Systems in Aid-dependent states.* A distinctive feature of aid-dependent states is weak appraisal capacity as well as reliance on donors to design good projects. Weaknesses in project appraisal are, however, of less concern in a country where major donors generally conduct in-depth project appraisal. Further distinctive features are the division of the budget into recurrent and development budgets, with weak integration between them; weak implementation capacity; and inadequate funding for operations and maintenance of completed assets.

- *PIM Systems in New and prospective EU members.* It is clear from the case studies of countries such as Poland, Latvia, the Slovak Republic and Slovenia, that the external financing associated with EU membership and prospective membership has a significant impact on country PIM systems. Planning documents cover a fixed seven- to eight-year period aligned to EU budgetary cycles. However, challenges remain to fully integrate national strategies applying to both EU and domestically financed investment. Similar challenges exist regarding formal project appraisal, where appraisal of non-EU financed investment is underdeveloped. Nevertheless, alignment of planning periods helps to reduce uncertainty of external funding. Medium-term fiscal frameworks are in place but in an early stage of development, and in effect the selection of investment projects is still done in the annual budget round. Often special project monitoring and control structures are put in place, and a joint monitoring committee provides coordination with the EU. As in many countries in other settings, in the new EU-member states postproject reviews are very limited, and although supreme audit institutions provide basic financial oversight of implementing agencies, they usually do not provide value-for-money reviews.

- *PIM Systems in Natural resource-dependent states.* Countries rich in oil, gas, and mining resources face the fundamental challenge of translating prospective wealth beneath the ground into productive assets above the ground. However, owing to capacity and political constraints, together with volatile revenues and "boom and bust" cycles, many of these countries consistently fall short in terms of the quantity and quality of their capital spending. Investment guidance is limited given that government strategy documents may not apply to all public investment because of the important role that semiautonomous, state-owned national resource companies play in financing investment. There is typically limited capacity to conduct sound project appraisal, particularly when resource revenues and public investment spending are increasing rapidly. Abundant revenues weaken incentives to prioritize and carefully appraise projects. The lack of checks and balances on executive power typical in these countries results in a lack of demand for project appraisal and the politicization of public investment decision making. Dual budgeting, weak implementation capacity, and nonstandard modes of investment such as resources-for-infrastructure arrangements, are also features in these states.

- *PIM Systems in fragile states.* For obvious reasons, there are few functioning "systems" in a fragile state and usually public investments have suffered neglect in such states. But public investments are critical to restore public infrastructure. In the immediate postconflict period, PIM analysis, decision making, and implementation are focused on emergency reconstruction and are, at least to some extent, the responsibility of a parallel administration staffed by internationals (for example, in Bosnia and Herzegovina, Kosovo, and Timor-Leste). There is a difficult transition to manage from emergency to development assistance, the relinquishing of external authority and reactivation of local PIM systems, and the shift to more traditional forms of international involvement. After the initial years following the conflict, this typology comes to resemble in some respects the typical aid-dependent typology as donors help to rebuild PIM functionality—except where the country is also resource-dependent, in which case features of that typology will also be present.

Structure of the Volume

The analytical and case study contributions of this volume are meant to inform governments, the private sector, and international development agencies of the high returns from strengthening PIM systems so that resources are transformed into assets that support growth and development. To this end, the volume provides practical understanding of the weaknesses in PIM systems through application of diagnostic analysis across a wide range of countries. Following this introduction, the book is structured into six substantive chapters:

- Chapter 2, A Unified Framework for Public Investment Management, provides a simple but important unifying PIM framework by defining the eight critical or *must-have* features of the public investment project cycle. It covers both the typical investment project managed in the public sector and the project implemented through a partnership with the private sector in the form of a PPP. Although PPPs require specific institutional capabilities, the principles of the systemic approach apply broadly. As mentioned above, the emphasis is on the basic processes and controls (linked at appropriate stages to broader budget processes) that are likely to yield the greatest assurance of efficiency in public investment decisions. The chapter also proposes diagnostic indicators of inputs, processes, and outputs for an assessment of the functioning of actual public investment systems; they are aimed at providing objective measures of inefficiency that can help identify the decision nodes at which existing processes might be failing.

- Chapter 3, Country Experiences of Public Investment Management, summarizes the findings of case studies against this framework and develops a country typology of institutional approaches to managing public investments. The studies take a systemic approach (considering how components interact) and assess the whole public investment cycle under various institutional and capacity contexts. Different country groupings tend to have different patterns of weakness in the must-have features; different patterns of results in terms of the quality of public investment; and different feasible points of entry to improve the must-have features. The cases encompass advanced and emerging economies, the particular case of resource-rich settings, and finally aid-dependent and fragile countries.

- Chapter 4, Approaches to Better Project Appraisal, discusses appraisal as a key and critical step in the investment cycle. Effective appraisal can support appropriate choices of outputs and designs; reduce the risk of excessive construction and operation costs; and thereby prevent failure to complete or efficiently operate projects. A rigorous project identification system acts as the first screening mechanism to prevent inappropriate and inefficient projects from getting into the project cycle and gaining political support and momentum that can make them difficult to stop at later stages. With this background and motivation, the chapter describes the different methodological steps as well as institutional arrangements for appraisal; identifies a range of common failures in project appraisal; and, with a systemic point of view, provides several options and entry points for improvement—among others, by creating demand for improved project appraisal, by strengthening key stages of the project cycle, and by implementing budget system reforms to support project appraisal and capital budgeting.

- Chapter 5, Public Investment Management under Uncertainty, addresses the particular upstream challenges of public investment projects associated with the uncertainty of climate change. As a score of country-case examples highlight, projects need to be implemented as quickly as possible to avoid the physical deterioration implied in stop-and-go construction and, above all, to minimize the opportunity cost of resource use for other socially beneficial investments. These principles are based on the assumption of certainty in, among other factors, the availability of funding, the technical capacity and possibility to actually construct and implement projects, and the climatic conditions. But how does the project cycle become affected under uncertainty and risk? In an economically more globalized world, uncertainty is an important ingredient, particularly with regard to finance and availability of resources. This chapter uses the example of climate change to illustrate how the project cycle is affected, and would need to be structured, to factor in the phenomenon of uncertainty. The chapter discusses several risk assessment methods—their advantages as well as shortcomings—and, importantly, proposes how cost-benefit analysis can be structured to incorporate uncertainties into the economic appraisal. The chapter then centers the discussion on "real options" to delay full implementation of a measure until better information becomes available.

- Chapter 6, Procurement and Public Investment Management, makes the case for treating procurement planning, contract award, and contract management as critical parts of PIM rather than as a separate "procurement" process focused largely on contract award. Changes in global markets, in technologies, and in the ever-present risk of fraud and collusion make procurement one of the most complex and challenging aspects of public management. Yet procurement systems are often not explicitly considered in discussions of public investment. Conceptually integrating procurement with the PIM process adds scope for capturing the potential efficiency gains through coordinated management within this framework. This approach is well aligned with the growing interest in moving away from the older compliance-with-rules approach to a more performance-based approach to procurement. Countries could significantly improve PIM efficiency if the procurement process were integrated with upstream project planning and budgeting and if downstream contract and project management were also better coordinated. Admittedly, the required institutional capacities for such integrated PIM management are high, and many developing countries with limited capacities may initially fall short of the mark. Nevertheless, these capacities can be built up over time and activated through incremental and pragmatic reforms with a goal of efficient and effective investment.

- Chapter 7, Public Investment Management for Public-Private Partnerships, examines the key challenges of managing infrastructure projects undertaken through PPPs. Conventionally, in most countries, PPP investment has been treated separately from publicly financed investment and has not come under direct regulation as government expenditure. Because large parts of future government obligations on PPPs are long-term commitments (such as government payments for service purchase-type projects or as guarantee payments), it is important to examine from a fiscal perspective whether a government can maintain fiscal soundness and sustainability while promoting PPP projects. To this end, the chapter applies the unified framework for implementing both conventional procurement and PPPs. It takes the eight must-have steps associated with PIM and applies them to PPP-related issues. The chapter concludes that an immediate task needed to make the unified approach viable is to provide diagnostic tools that would enable systematic assessments for PPPs jointly with conventional PIM systems.

The focus of this book is on contributing to an understanding of the problem of PIM—a distinctive aspect of economic policy and budget management that requires and deserves special treatment and discussion and an acknowledgment of the special institutional arrangements and capabilities that are necessary to ensure good outcomes. This volume, together with the country cases mentioned above, provides both a broad conceptual treatment of critical aspects of PIM and a detailed examination of how a large number of countries actually undertake this critical function. The material is intended to enhance the knowledge base of practitioners and to encourage both adoption of good institutional practices and further applied research to strengthen PIM systems worldwide.

Given the high salience of public investment to addressing economic stagnation or catalyzing long-term development, this is a critical area for policy attention. The main message of the book is for policy makers and practitioners to consider the challenge of achieving effective public investment as a systemic challenge and to address each of the eight key steps as part of a unified approach to ensure that the effort to strengthen one aspect is not undermined by weaknesses in the others. At the same time, the book highlights where further analytical work is required to design systems that will limit the scope for collusion and corruption and enhance accountability for value. Public procurement is a particularly challenging area that requires more attention and that, unless it is systemically reformed, will remain a stumbling block for PIM. Because political interests often intervene to override PIM systems, greater attention is required to understand the political economy of public investment choices and devise transparency and check-and-balance arrangements to enforce accountability and limit the risk of rent-seeking behavior.

Notes

1. It should be recalled that a considerable amount of transport infrastructure (roads and railways) was developed both in England and in its colonial territories (such as India) in the 18th and 19th centuries through private investment in early forms of public-private partnerships. However, the development of national transport networks required national policies even if private companies undertook the construction.

2. Although Keynes's *The General Theory of Employment, Interest, and Money* (1936) is often cited, his earlier publication of *The Means to Prosperity* (1933) already contained specific recommendation of a countercyclical policy of public spending to offset the effects of a global economic depression.

3. The planning models in many countries were derived from the Harrod-Domar (HD) model of fixed coefficients production functions, with the accumulation of capital through investment determining the rates of growth of the economy. In India, the Mahalanobis model was an elaboration of an HD framework that guided the second Indian five-year plan (1957–62). See Kirkpatrick, Clarke, and Polidano (2002).

4. Pritchett (1999) cites the evidence from a number of countries where World Bank–supported projects worth many millions of dollars showed a wide range in ex post economic rates of return, including cases where the median return was zero. In such a case, either no capital asset is created or it is not operated to achieve a positive return.

5. In 2011, the value of new infrastructure-related PPP contracts worldwide was an estimated $42.9 billion, down from the peak 2009 value of $60 billion. More than half of the new PPP contracts were in two countries: Brazil and India (World Bank 2012a).

Bibliography

Arrow, Kenneth J., and Mordecai Kurz. 1970. *Public Investment, the Rate of Return, and Optimal Fiscal Policy*. Baltimore, MD: The Johns Hopkins University Press for Resources for the Future (RFF) Press.

Aschauer, David. 1989. "Is Public Expenditure Productive?" *Journal of Monetary Economics* 23 (2): 177–200.

Collier, Paul. 2010. *The Plundered Planet: Why We Must—and How We Can—Manage Nature for Global Prosperity*. New York: Oxford University Press.

CoST (Construction Sector Transparency Initiative). 2011. *Report on Baseline Studies: International Comparison*. Summary findings of CoST pilot baseline studies, CoST, London. http://gateway.transparency.org/tools/detail/43.

Easterly, William, Timothy Irwin, and Luis Servén. 2008. "Walking Up the Down Escalator: Public Investment and Fiscal Stability." *World Bank Research Observer* 23 (1): 37–56.

Flyvbjerg, Bent. 2009. "Survival of the Unfittest: Why the Worst Infrastructure Gets Built—and What We Can Do About It." *Oxford Review of Economic Policy* 25 (3): 344–67.

Glomm, Gerhard, and B. Ravikumar. 1997. "Productive Government Expenditures and Long-Run Growth."*Journal of Economic Dynamics and Control* 21 (1): 183–204.

Keynes, John Maynard. 1933. *The Means to Prosperity*. New York: Harcourt, Brace.

———. 1936. *The General Theory of Employment, Interest, and Money*. New York: Harcourt, Brace.

Kirkpatrick, Colin, Ron Clarke, and Charles Polidano, eds. 2002. *Handbook on Development Policy and Management*. Cheltenham, U.K.: Edward Elgar.

Pritchett, Lant. 1999. "The Tyranny of Concepts: CUDIE (Cumulated, Depreciated, Investment Effort) Is *Not* Capital." Policy Research Working Paper 2341, World Bank, Washington, DC.

Rajaram, Anand, Tuan Minh Le, Nataliya Biletska, and Jim Brumby. 2010. "A Diagnostic Framework for Assessing Public Investment Management." Policy Research Working Paper 5397, World Bank, Washington, DC.

Rodrigue, Jean-Paul. 2009. *The Geography of Transport Systems*. New York: Routledge.

Smith, Adam. (1776) 2000. *The Wealth of Nations*. Reprint, New York: The Modern Library.

World Bank. 2006. "Fiscal Policy for Growth and Development: An Interim Report." Background Paper (DC2006-0003) for April 2006 Meeting of the Development Committee, World Bank Group and International Monetary Fund, Washington, DC. http://siteresources.worldbank.org/DEVCOMMINT/Documentation/20890698/DC2006-0003(E)-FiscalPolicy.pdf.

———. 2007. "Fiscal Policy for Growth and Development: Further Analysis and Lessons from Country Case Studies." Background Paper (DC2007-0004) for meeting of the Development Committee, World Bank Group and International Monetary Fund, Washington, DC, April. http://siteresources.worldbank.org/INTPEAM/Resources/DC2007-0004(E)-FiscalPolicy.pdf.

———. 2012a. "Private Activity in Infrastructure Slowed Down in the First Half of 2011." PPI Data Update Note 68, Public Participation in Infrastructure Database, World Bank and Public-Private Infrastructure Advisory Facility, Washington, DC. http://ppi.worldbank.org/features/December-2011/2011-Global-update-note.pdf.

———. 2012b. *Republic of Iraq Public Expenditure Review: Towards More Efficient Spending for Better Service Delivery in Iraq*. Washington, DC: World Bank.

CHAPTER 2

A Unified Framework for Public Investment Management

Introduction

As noted in chapter 1, both developing and developed countries have a strong interest in ensuring that efforts to boost public investment are effective in achieving their objectives, whether in terms of a growth stimulus from creation of new economic infrastructure or in terms of greater equity through expanded access to public facilities. However, the argument to increase public investment spending is often weakened by evidence of its low efficiency in a number of dimensions, including the following:

- Political influence in project selection, often leading to wasteful "white elephant" projects with little economic or social value.
- Delays in design and completion of projects.
- Corrupt procurement practices.
- Cost overruns.
- Incomplete projects.
- Poor quality of completed infrastructure.
- Failure to effectively operate and maintain assets.

The impact of such failures in managing the selection and implementation of projects is to undermine the scope for public investments to enhance future economic prospects. In countries considering the case for expanding public investment, therefore, it is important that a prior assessment be made about the relative effectiveness and efficiency of the system of public investment management (PIM). Additionally, it would be desirable to identify the specific weaknesses that contribute to poor outcomes and to implement appropriate institutional and technical remedies that could correct such failures.

The approach taken in this chapter is to begin with a description of the "must-have" features of a well-functioning public investment system. Regarding those features, the emphasis is on the basic processes and controls (linked at appropriate stages to broader budget processes) that are likely to yield the greatest assurance of efficiency in public investment decisions. Mindful of the risks of recommending inappropriate institutional remedies and encouraging "isomorphic mimicry" that leads to functionally ineffective systems, the approach does *not* seek to identify best practice but rather to identify the bare-bones institutional features that would minimize major risks, be achievable in a lower-capacity context, and yet provide an effective systemic process for managing public investments.[1] This distinction deserves emphasis since much damage is inflicted by well-meaning transference of institutional arrangements to contexts where they are unlikely to function. While the approach is insistent on the "must-have" features, its application requires careful judgment on what would constitute an appropriate design of a functional system for the given capacity and context.

A second feature of this approach is the use of diagnostic indicators of inputs, processes, and outputs that would enable us to assess the functioning of actual public investment systems. These indicators should provide objective measures of inefficiency that can also help identify the decision nodes at which existing processes might be failing.[2] Thus, for example, an indicator of cost overruns relative to appraisal estimates may point to a diverse set of problems: unrealistic appraisal, poor project design, delayed project approval, inadequate budget allocations that cause delays in project implementation, corrupt procurement, weak contract management, or various combinations of the above that may need to be confirmed with more specific assessment. Similarly, a low rate of project completion often provides a robust indication that gatekeeping functions that prioritize project selection consistent with resource availability are not effectively enforced. Poor project planning and management and procurement delays may also contribute to this outcome.

Using this approach in the case study countries, we suggest a diagnostic "gap analysis" of the actual system relative to a basic PIM system to identify structural aspects of the public investment decision and management process that may be weak and in need of attention. The gap analysis will need to be supplemented by diagnostic indicators to identify the particular areas of weakness that are likely to contribute to low public investment efficiency. As with any diagnostic, good judgment regarding the underlying incentive and capacity problems will be necessary to supplement the gap analysis and diagnostic indicators. This framework has been "road tested" in a large number of countries and, as described in chapter 3, has been found to be a robust method to assess systemic PIM capability.

In principle, a good diagnostic would allow reforms to focus scarce managerial and technical resources on corrective actions where they will yield the greatest impact. The approach is based on a clearly defined institutional framework and recognition of the role of institutions, capacity, and incentives. It is broadly consistent with the approach taken in the Public Expenditure and Financial Accountability (PEFA) initiative, which addresses broader issues of public expenditure management.[3] Like the PEFA framework, the diagnostic uses well-defined symptomatic indicators that can be objectively assessed and that provide information to identify problematic areas. This identification will enable (and typically require) more detailed assessment to develop institutional remedies to the identified problems. Thus the approach can motivate governments to undertake periodic self-assessments of public investment efficiency and design reforms to improve government systems.

What is being proposed are principles that apply to the management of all public investments—a unified framework that applies regardless of the channel through which such investments are undertaken. The most common channel is for government to allocate resources through its budget process and have individual ministries, departments, or agencies implement their investment budgets. But increasingly governments have chosen to undertake large infrastructure projects through public-private partnerships (PPPs), often establishing extrabudgetary funding and separate institutions to manage such operations. And in countries that have received large inflows of natural resource revenues, a number have set up sovereign wealth or investment funds with the mandate to undertake public investments on behalf of the government. Regardless of the channel, the principles outlined in this chapter are worth following (with suitable adaptation) to ensure good outcomes from public investments.

The next section provides a schematic description of the eight must-have features of the public investment system. The section titled "Diagnostic Questions for Evaluating Public Investment Effectiveness and Efficiency" then proposes some questions and indicators that would help assess the functioning of the existing system. The final section concludes and indicates the next steps to implementing this indicator-based approach in particular country case studies.

Defining "Must-Have" Features for an Efficient Public Investment System

The schematic that follows, already referenced in chapter 1 but expanded upon here, identifies the eight features that logic and country experience suggest are essential features for achieving PIM efficiency. Each of these features is described and justified in the corresponding subsections.

Investment Guidance, Project Development, and Preliminary Screening

Broad strategic guidance for public investment is an important way to anchor government decisions and to guide sector-level decision makers toward national priorities. Such guidance may be derived from a national plan or other medium- to long-term strategic document that establishes economywide development priorities at the highest decision-making levels. The Poverty Reduction Strategy Paper (PRSP) may serve as such a document in some countries. In other countries, longer-term national vision documents may provide the necessary directional guidance. In many countries, the national plan may be supplemented by a sector-level or even subsector-level strategy that provides more detailed translation of the overarching priorities.[4] The existence of credible strategic guidance to public investment, which can be meaningfully interpreted at sector or subsector

The Power of Public Investment Management • http://dx.doi.org/10.1596/978-1-4648-0316-1

levels, is a basic requirement and may be referenced in annual budget preparation instructions.[5]

Beyond the strategic vision or plan, governments will need a formal process for project development. Line ministries and spending agencies initiating projects for public investment should prepare a project profile with basic project information, including the relevant strategic priority and program or subprogram, the specific problem to be addressed, the project objective, the main activities, the expected results, and the estimated budget. In addition, it is important at this stage that options for addressing the problem with and without a project are considered and that demand, supply, and gap analyses are undertaken.

First-level screening of all project proposals should be undertaken to ensure that they (a) meet the minimum criteria of consistency with the strategic goals of government, and (b) meet the budget classification tests for inclusion as a project rather than as a recurrent spending item. A project that fails to meet this consistency test should be rejected, making further evaluation unnecessary. As part of the first must-have feature of a PIM system ("Guidance," as seen in figure 2.1), an appropriate institutional arrangement must ensure that all major project proposals are screened so that resources are not wasted in more-detailed project appraisal. This function may occasionally rely substantively on responsibilities delegated to line ministries and spending agencies.

Formal Project Appraisal
Projects or programs that meet the first screening test should be subject to the appraisal of their viability, which requires feasibility analysis. Its objective is to

Figure 2.1 The Key Features of a Public Investment Management System

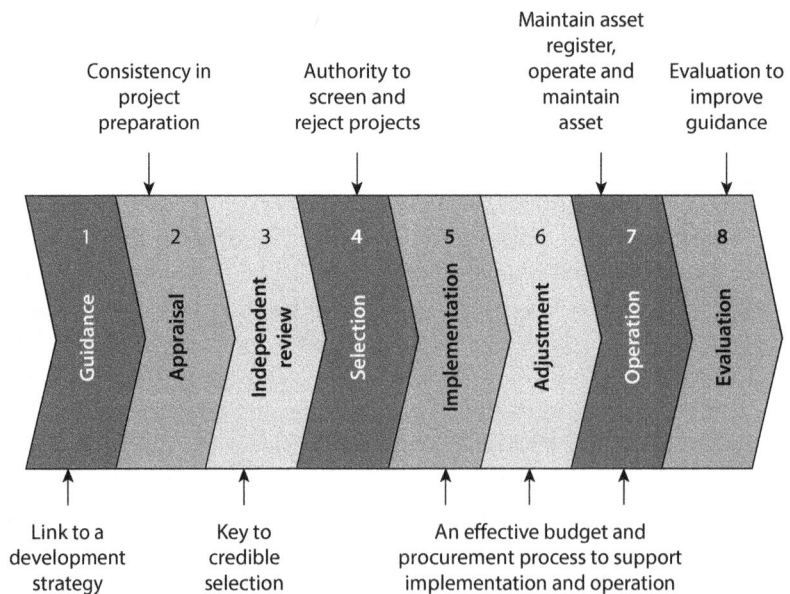

answer the essential question of whether a spending agency or line ministry should proceed with a project once it is established that it is consistent with government priorities. This process requires a regulated set of project preparation steps such as prefeasibility and feasibility studies (including preliminary design and environmental and social impact assessments) that must be completed and independently evaluated before a project can be approved for funding.

The prefeasibility study helps to identify relevant alternatives before undertaking a full-fledged feasibility study and to find out early on whether a proposed project is feasible. The feasibility study (summarized in table 2.1) takes prefeasibility analysis further by compiling all relevant data, refining project outputs and outcomes, outlining and analyzing in depth the selected alternative for achieving project objectives, and undertaking various background assessments including environmental and social impact analysis. Identifying an optimal option for preliminary design helps to narrow the scope of a project.

As part of feasibility analysis, projects or programs should undergo more rigorous scrutiny of their cost-benefit estimates or cost-effectiveness. The project selection process needs to ensure that projects proposed for financing have been evaluated for their social and economic value. To do so effectively, governments should have formal and well-publicized guidance on the technical aspects of project appraisal appropriate to the technical capacity of ministries and departments. The guidance should describe techniques of economic evaluation that are appropriate to the scale and scope of the project—with larger projects requiring more rigorous tests of financial and economic feasibility and sustainability. The project appraisal process should consider project proposals of different scales and take into account the key macro, sectoral, and project-specific uncertainties such as inflation, cost overrun, change in output, and key input prices over the project life. New investments should occur only when rehabilitating existing assets is not as cost-effective as undertaking investment in a new asset.

Further, the value of ex ante project evaluation depends very much on the quality of the analysis, which, in turn, depends on the capacity of staff with project evaluation skills. Upstream investment in training in project evaluation

Table 2.1 Key Components of Feasibility Analysis

Prefeasibility study	Feasibility study
Data gathering (geographic, climate, socioeconomic, and technical)	Compilation of all relevant data
Identification of project alternatives	Alternative technologies for project
Major risks (including institutional and budgetary)	Detailed estimate of costs and benefits for a selected alternative
Comparison of alternatives (engineering, socioeconomic costs and benefits)	Preliminary design
Recommended project alternative	Detailed risk assessment
Preliminary estimate of project costs and benefits	Detailed sustainability assessment
Regulatory requirements	Environmental impact assessment
Identifying information for social impact assessment	Social impact assessment

techniques is an important aspect of an effective public investment system.[6] Whether the government has an established process for training staff in project evaluation techniques would be a useful indicator of capacity creation. Quantifying the number of staff in government who have project evaluation skills would be another relevant indicator. Identifying whether such staff members are in line positions that effectively use their skills is another related indicator. In many countries, technical assistance is used to train staff in skills that are then not effectively deployed. Nonetheless, attention must be paid to create systems and incentives concurrently to assure that the acquired project evaluation skills are actually applied. Having sufficient numbers of trained personnel is a necessary but not sufficient condition to improve practices of formal project appraisal.

It is worth noting that a full-fledged feasibility assessment that employs complex techniques of cost-benefit and cost-effectiveness analysis is often poorly developed and implemented in low-capacity environments. Therefore, the emphasis should be on basic elements of formal project appraisal, including whether

- The need for a project is well justified;
- The project's objectives are clearly specified;
- Broad alternative options to meet the project's objectives are identified and comparatively examined[7];
- The most promising option is subject to detailed analysis;
- Project costs are fully and accurately estimated; and
- Project benefits are assessed qualitatively as likely to justify the costs.

It is helpful to maintain a portfolio of the appraised projects. Such a portfolio can help not only to track how many projects have been selected but also to revisit rejected projects later if and when underlying project circumstances change so that they become likely to generate net positive benefits. Hence, all appraised projects should be recorded in a project database ranked by priority for budget consideration.

As emphasized in chapter 1 and earlier in this chapter, it is desirable to have a unified PIM framework, including the selection of projects. Projects involving nonstandard procurement (such as PPPs and bundled "resources-for-infrastructure" projects) should be subject to the same appraisal process as standard public investment, and the costs and benefits of such projects should be compared against a public sector comparator project.

An important step after a project has been selected and before it is included in the budget is development of a detailed project design to ensure that the project is accurately costed and can be tendered and implemented (a "ready-to-go" check). This reduces the risk of implementation delays due to delayed procurement planning—a surprisingly common problem in project implementation. Additionally, land acquisition should be completed before the project is handed over to a contractor for implementation. Moreover, to facilitate project implementation, the project design should also provide a full risk assessment, performance indicators, and an implementation strategy that an implementing agency should use.

Independent Review of Appraisal

It is always sound practice to subject project appraisals to an independent review. Optimism bias among those developing project proposals—reflected in underestimated costs and overestimated benefits—is well documented and can skew investment decisions. Where departments and ministries (rather than a central unit such as the ministry of planning) undertake the appraisal, an independent peer review might be necessary to check any subjective, self-serving bias in the evaluation. This function can be performed by the ministry of finance or by a designated specialized agency. Having such capacity in a university or a policy research institute with an arms-length relationship to government would enhance the credibility of the independent review of project appraisal. In countries where donor-financed projects are significant, upstream aid coordination can help channel resources to priority areas but should be subjected to the same appraisal stages as government-funded projects. In this context, clarity of specific responsibilities is important. A multiplicity of players with unclear accountabilities can overburden the appraisal system. A formal set of delegations is necessary to keep minor projects from clogging up the appraisal. The experience of the United Kingdom is a relevant example for rigorous appraisal (box 2.1).

Box 2.1 Excerpts from the United Kingdom's "Green Book"

The Green Book: Appraisal and Evaluation in Central Government[a] constitutes HM Treasury's guidance for public sector bodies on how to appraise proposals before committing funds to a policy, program, or project.[b] As this excerpt from the preface states, "Appraisal, done properly, is not rocket science, but it is crucially important and needs to be carried out carefully. Decisions taken at the appraisal stage affect the whole lifecycle of new policies, programmes and projects. Similarly, the proper evaluation of previous initiatives is essential in avoiding past mistakes and to enable us to learn from experience."

- Chapter 2, "Overview of Appraisal and Evaluation," summarizes the key stages that subsequent *Green Book* chapters cover in detail.
- Chapter 3, "Justifying Action": "The first step is to carry out an overview to ensure that two pre-requisites are met: firstly, that there is a clearly identified need; and secondly, that any proposed intervention is likely to be worth the cost."
- Chapter 4, "Setting Objectives": "The second step is to set out clearly the desired outcomes and objectives of an intervention in order to identify the full range of options that may be available to deliver them."
- Chapter 5, "Option Appraisal": "The third step is to carry out an option appraisal. This is often the most significant part of the analysis."

box continues next page

Box 2.1 Excerpts from the United Kingdom's "Green Book" *(continued)*

- Chapter 6, "Developing and Implementing a Solution": "Following option appraisal, decision criteria and judgment should be used to select the best option or options, which should then be refined into a solution. Consultation is important at this stage, regardless of whether it has taken place earlier. Procurement routes should also be considered, including the role of the private sector. Issues that may have a material impact on the successful implementation of proposals must be considered during the appraisal stage, before significant resources are committed."

- Chapter 7, "Evaluation": "[The] main purpose [of evaluation] is to ensure that lessons are widely learned, communicated and applied when assessing new proposals."

Source: HM Treasury United Kingdom 2003.
a. *The Green Book*, first published in 2003, is currently being reviewed in response to changes in the public sector and the evolution in the theory and practice of appraisal.
b. The current edition of *The Green Book* and supplementary documents can be obtained through the U.K. Government's website: https://www.gov.uk/government/publications/the-green-book-appraisal-and-evaluation-in-central-government.

Project Selection and Budgeting

It is essential that the process of appraising and selecting public investment projects is linked in an appropriate way to the budget cycle even though the project evaluation cycle may run along a different timetable. There is clearly a two-way relationship between the budget cycle and the project selection cycle. The fiscal framework and the annual budget need to establish envelopes for public investment (on an aggregate or sectoral basis) so that a sustainable investment program can be undertaken.[8]

The keys to efficient investment include good investment choices, active management of the asset portfolio (including through disposals), and a budgetary process that ensures recurrent funding to operate and maintain existing assets. The latter is especially important for donor-funded projects that create assets while operation and maintenance costs are assumed to be borne by government. Efficient investment also depends on whether the recurrent budget adjusts to reflect the impact of the capital projects. For instance, additional costs may be incurred to maintain and operate existing assets; in these circumstances, how to fund these costs should be considered. Forward costs of investment projects, and their funding, should be reviewed systematically by both sector ministries and the ministry of finance during budget preparation.

Project selection is perhaps the most critical stage of the investment management process because it is often one of the most contentious stages of the investment cycle. Political patrons for the project typically exert a lot of pressure on selection agencies and committees and will seek high-level political intervention to overlook any unfavorable technical analysis. Ministries and departments that stand to benefit from the project will also look for ways to strike deals to ensure the project is selected. Private lobbyists and contractors hoping to win the right to construction contracts will work through both bureaucratic and political channels to influence selection of the project.

It is difficult in many countries to ensure an airtight technical process that can resist these various pressures. Therefore, it is a critical requirement that there be a strong gatekeeping function that limits damage to the credibility of the selection process and, at a minimum, ensures that wasteful "white elephant" projects are rejected. Having legislative backing for a strong gatekeeping function may help ensure that vested interests do not undermine this critical stage of the investment process. Transparent disclosure of the basis for project selection may also limit attempts to influence the selection process. The need for a clearly identified and institutionally robust role of gatekeeper is perhaps the most important "must-have" feature of a PIM system. If that role is not clearly established and sustained, it is difficult to keep financial discipline from unraveling, resulting in inefficiencies and waste in the public investment process.

Project Implementation

Projects that have been objectively appraised and selected for investment should be scrutinized for implementation realism. Project design should include clear organizational arrangements and a realistic timetable to ensure the capacity to implement the project. It is critical to establish and develop effective measures such as efficient procurement plans as well as guidelines and institutional capacity to manage and monitor project implementation. Ideally a government should establish a total project cost management system and multiyear budgeting for complex projects, anticipating the budgetary needs through the period of project implementation.

As discussed in chapter 6, procurement is typically a difficult but important element of project implementation and needs to be addressed as part of the overall PIM process. Managing the total cost of projects over their life requires an accounting system that captures and reports all project costs rather than accounting by separate contracts or stages and tracking against annual appropriations. Multiyear budgeting facilitates allocation of funds for project implementation over a project's life cycle. Project proposals, especially for a large infrastructure project, should also present organizational arrangements for running the project once the construction is finished. Implementation problems can at times be related to poor project selection and budgeting but are often due to procurement challenges.

Project Adjustment

The funding review process (typically part of the annual budgeting process) should have some flexibility to allow changes in the disbursement profile to take account of changes in project circumstances. For instance, if delays in project implementation escalate costs, the funding requests would have to reflect those cost increases. If events transpire to escalate a project's costs to the point where it is no longer incrementally beneficial, there should be a device through the funding approval process or the monitoring process to ask project sponsors to recast the project or even to halt disbursements. This approach suggests that funding should be carried out in tranches, with the tranches relating to the discrete phases of the project. In countries that are capable of managing such a process, each funding request should be accompanied by an updated cost-benefit analysis and a reminder to project sponsors of their accountability for the delivery of the benefits.

These funding mechanisms can reinforce the nature of the monitoring process, making it active rather than passive. Governments need to create the capacity to monitor implementation in a timely way and to address problems proactively as they are identified. Monitoring project implementation would minimally involve comparison of project progress relative to the implementation plan. Implementing agencies should be required to submit progress reports to identified monitoring agencies, which then may need to audit both financial and physical implementation.

Facility Operation

Once a project is completed, there should be a process to ensure that the facility is ready for operation and that services can be delivered. This process requires an effective mechanism for (a) handover of management responsibility for future operation and maintenance of the created assets, and (b) adequate budget funding of service delivery agencies to operate and maintain these assets. But the completed assets may still lie idle if they are not suitable for service delivery. Thus it is also important to verify the extent to which the newly completed facility requires post-completion adaptation or ancillary investment before the assets can be used.

In addition, asset registers need to be maintained and asset values recorded. Ideally, countries should require their operating agencies to compile balance sheets, on which the value of assets created through new fixed capital expenditure would be maintained. Whether there is accrual accounting or not, agencies should maintain asset registers that are exhaustive in their record keeping and, where necessary, legal title to property is affixed.

Active monitoring of service delivery is a desirable element of ensuring that the new assets serve the purpose over their useful life. This suggests that the quantity and quality of service delivery associated with facility operation should be tracked through time. Moreover, agencies responsible for service delivery should be held accountable for results.

Basic Completion Review and Evaluation

Finally, a desirable but often missing feature of government systems is a basic completion review and ex post evaluation of finished projects. Basic completion review should apply to all projects in a systematic way. It consists of an examination by a responsible agency or line ministry sometime after project completion, comprising (a) whether the project was finished within the original (or amended) budget and time frame, and (b) whether the outputs were delivered as specified. As a supplement to this basic completion review, a supreme audit institution should periodically conduct a compliance audit of a sample of investment projects.

Ex post project evaluation should focus on the comparison of the project's outputs and outcomes with the established objectives in the project design. It is usually carried out two to three years or more after project completion on a highly selective basis. Good practice suggests that the project design should build in the evaluation criteria and that learning from such ex post evaluations improves future project design and implementation. We include this as a must-have feature to underline the need for governments, even in a basic way, to ensure that there is some learning and feedback from projects that will create a positive dynamic for systemic improvement over time. If the evaluation shows that procurement processes, for example, led to costly delays, it should spur the agencies to address that upstream problem as a systemic corrective.

The two examples of ex post evaluation in box 2.2—the U.S. General Accountability Office's (GAO) review of the U.S. highway program and the Auditor General's report in Uganda—illustrate good practice of a constant process of identifying ways in which the system of public investment can be strengthened. In the GAO case, the review identified state-level practices that

---

Box 2.2 Two Examples of Investment Program Evaluation

U.S. GAO: Audit of Highway Program

In 2011, the U.S. government spent $39 billion on federally funded highway projects. At the request of a member of the U.S. Congress, the GAO undertook a 2011–12 performance audit of the highway project completion process. The report noted that the four phases of completing highway projects—(1) planning, (2) preliminary design and environmental review, (3) final design and right-of-way acquisition, and (4) construction—can sometimes take a long time.

In 2005, the U.S. Congress had enacted the Safe, Accountable, Flexible, Efficient Transportation Equity Act: A Legacy for Users (SAFETEA-LU), which established provisions to help expedite highway projects, including streamlining some portions of the environmental review process: it allowed states to assume greater environmental review responsibilities under certain conditions and delegated some authority from the federal government to states. GAO surveyed state transportation departments' (DOTs') views on the benefits and challenges of these provisions and also took note of other initiatives that states had implemented to expedite the completion of highway projects. The GAO report noted that a number of the SAFETEA-LU provisions were not being used because more effective solutions were available to the states.

The GAO nevertheless recommended leaving the federal provisions in place while concluding the following (U.S. GAO 2012): "Completing major highway projects involves a complex process that depends on a wide range of stakeholders conducting many tasks. The long time frames to complete highway projects are often caused by factors outside the control of state DOTs, such as a lack of available funds, changes in a state's transportation priorities, or litigation. These factors can be project specific and may not be controllable by legislation, or by federal or state initiatives."

box continues next page

Box 2.2 Two Examples of Investment Program Evaluation *(continued)*

Uganda: Auditor General Report on CHOGM Investments
Claims that costs of infrastructure contracts associated with preparations for a November 2007 Commonwealth Heads of Government Meeting (CHOGM) in Kampala, Uganda, were excessive and the work of poor quality led the Auditor General's office to commission an engineering audit to establish the facts and recommend corrective action. A follow-up audit reviewed the procedures followed by the Ministry of Works and Transport and the completion of work by contractors and identified a number of problems to be addressed by both the ministry and by individual contractors.

The reports of the Auditor General are public, and thus stimulated public discussion and debate, including in Parliament—providing some assurance that systems of accountability are functional and could, with improved compliance, lead to improvement in PIM systems.

Sources: Government of Uganda 2008, 2009; U.S. GAO 2012.

improved the completion of highway projects, enabling good practices in one state to be known to others. The findings of the Ugandan Auditor General pointed to specific weaknesses that required attention by relevant agencies. Both cases illustrate the importance of evaluation as a method to identify and address existing problems. Both also point to the important role of legislative oversight over the expenditure process.

Although the rigor of any of the PIM steps outlined in this chapter will need to be adapted to country capabilities, the emphasis here is on ensuring that attention is paid to the various aspects of good decision making, even if it is initially a rudimentary discipline.

Diagnostic Questions for Evaluating Public Investment Effectiveness and Efficiency

The following questions might provide the basis for a diagnostic assessment of the efficiency of a PIM system, presented in order of the system's eight must-have features.

1. *Investment Guidance, Project Development, and Preliminary Screening*
   - Is there well-publicized strategic guidance for public investment decisions at the central, ministerial, and provincial levels?
   - Is there an established process for screening of project proposals for basic consistency with government policy and strategic guidance? Is this process effective?
   - What proportion of projects so screened is rejected?
2. *Formal Project Appraisal*
   - Is there a formal cost-benefit appraisal process for more detailed evaluation (whether at the line ministry or the central finance agency level) of public investment project proposals?

- If yes, is appraisal mandatory for all projects or only for projects above a certain monetary value? Is project appraisal undertaken only for specific sectors and, if so, which sectors? What proportion of public investment projects is formally appraised for costs and benefits?

3. *Independent Review of Appraisal*
   - Are project appraisals formally undertaken by the sponsoring department or by an external agency? What is the quality of such appraisals?
   - What proportion of such appraisals is rejected or sent back for amendment?

4. *Project Selection and Budgeting*
   - What proportion of the public investment program (PIP, the collection of projects that are formally approved for budget allocation and implementation) is donor-financed? Are donor-financed projects subject to the same or different rules for appraisal and inclusion in the budget as government-financed projects? If the rules are different, describe the difference.
   - Does the government review project appraisals undertaken by donors? Are appraisals screened by an external agency or department for quality and objectivity of appraisal? Are such reviews credible as an independent perspective?
   - Are donor-funded projects ever rejected on the basis of cost-benefit analysis?
   - Is final project selection undertaken as part of the budget process or prior to the budget process? Does the government maintain an inventory of appraised projects for budgetary consideration? Are public investment projects selected and funded through extrabudgetary channels?
   - What is the role of the legislature, including special legislative committees, in the selection of public investment projects? Does the legislature's involvement cover both budgetary and extrabudgetary channels?
   - Is there an effective process to control the gates to the budgeted PIP? Is there an established but limited process for including projects for emergency or politically imperative reasons?
     - What proportion of projects enter the PIP by "climbing the fence," thus avoiding the gatekeeping process?
     - What proportion of projects that "climb the fence" is donor-financed?
   - What is the average value of new projects relative to the
     - Ongoing PIP?
     - Projects completed (use three-year moving average)?

5. *Project Implementation*
   - What is the completion rate of the PIP (annual average over the past five years), defined as the annual public investment budget divided by the estimated cost to complete the current PIP?[9] How does this completion rate differ across key sectors—education, health, water supply and sanitation, roads, and power, for example?
   - Do ministries undertake procurement plans in line with good practice (for example, using competitive tendering)? And, if so, do they implement procurement plans effectively?

6. *Project Adjustment*
- Has the government rationalized its PIP in the recent past? Did the rationalization improve the PIP's prioritization? Did it result in the cancellation or closure of ongoing projects—and if so, what percentage of the PIP was cancelled or closed? Indicate whether projects were merely "deferred" rather than cancelled.
- Are project-implementing agencies required to prepare periodic progress reports on projects? Do these reports include updated cost-benefit analyses? Are the sponsoring departments accountable for changes recorded in either costs or benefits and for the delivery of net benefits? What mechanisms exist to ensure that this occurs? Is this record of investment management used in subsequent budget discussions with the ministry of finance or ministry of planning? Does the government have a decision process to close down projects which have shown significant cost overruns or time delays which render them uneconomic?
- For a representative subset of the PIP, what is the average percentage cost overrun (in inflation-adjusted terms) on major projects in key sectors?
- Are projects commissioned to private contractors and, if so, are contracts awarded on the basis of competitive bidding? Are international firms permitted to bid on contracts? Is there any evidence of procurement contributing to cost escalation or fraud? Is cost escalation or fraud specific to some sectors, and is there evidence of cartel or collusive bidding for contracts?

7. *Facility Operation*
- Are there long delays in completed projects becoming operational? Is this a general problem, or is it limited to some sectors or projects?
- Is there a process for handover of management responsibility for future operation and maintenance of the created assets to service delivery agencies? Do service delivery agencies have adequate budget funding to operate and maintain these assets? Is service delivery associated with facility operation tracked through time? Are agencies held accountable for the delivery of services? Do facilities charge for access, and are such fees earmarked for facility operation and maintenance? Are facilities understaffed or overstaffed, and are complementary inputs provided for?
- Does the government maintain an asset register or inventory of public sector property such as equipment and vehicles? Is legal title to assets maintained? Are assets valued according to sound accounting principles, such that the accounting definition of an asset is met, depreciation is deducted from the asset value, and, where feasible, asset values are updated to reflect changed prices?

8. *Basic Completion Review and Evaluation*
- For a representative subset of the PIP, what is the delay in project completion relative to initial estimated time, and what is the deviation from the original (and amended) budget on major projects in key sectors?

- Is the actual net present value (NPV) of completed projects measured, and is a project end evaluation undertaken to review the nature of differences relative to the estimated NPV at appraisal? What alternative methods, if any, are used to undertake ex post evaluation of completed projects?
- Does the government undertake financial and performance audits of completed projects? Do the authorized agencies act on the findings of such audits? Are value-for-money audits undertaken, and are their findings made public? Do legislative bodies such as public accounts committees take appropriate actions when fraud or waste is uncovered?

Table 2A, provides a structured layout for an assessment of PIM and the likely efficiency of public investment.

Conclusion

Effective PIM systems require not only the alignment of capacities and incentives to improve project design and selection (features 1–4) but also credible commitments and long-term investment in technical and administrative capacity to improve project implementation (features 5–8). The typology presented in table 2.2 combines these two dimensions in a simple two-by-two matrix to describe typical country cases.

The cross-country evidence in this volume shows that while a larger number of countries in the sample have sought to adopt some of the required features to improve project implementation, the best-performing countries have been able to ensure both effectiveness and efficiency through good project selection and design and good implementation—which has progressively moved their PIM performance to the top left cell of table 2.2 (cell A: good design and implementation). They have done this in part by ensuring that their PIM systems included all eight must-have features, including the ex post evaluation feature, which is critical to periodic reassessment of the system and can spur further improvements. For countries starting with poorly functioning systems, the ex post evaluation feature is an important diagnostic tool to identify weaknesses and undertake gradual improvements to achieve a high-performing public investment system.

This book provides guidance to practitioners relevant to forming a pragmatic and objective assessment of the quality of public investment efficiency in a context where governments are seeking to mobilize additional fiscal resources

Table 2.2 Project Selection, Project Implementation, and Outcomes

Project selection	Project implementation	
	Well executed	Poorly executed
Good projects	A	C
Poor projects	B	D

for investment. An indicator-based approach provides a basis both for objective assessment and for highlighting weaknesses that should be addressed if the use of fiscal resources is to enhance public sector assets and economic growth. The use of indicators must be accompanied by good country-specific judgments on the functioning of institutions and the underlying incentives for public sector performance. Quite often, political economy considerations may constrain or block efforts to limit fraud or waste in public investment. As indicated by the examples in box 2.2, transparency is often of great value in highlighting wasteful expenditure and thereby creating public support for accountability in the use of public resources.

Annex 2A: Assessing the Effectiveness and Efficiency of Public Investment Management

Table 2A Stages, Institutional Arrangements, and Diagnostic Indicators of Public Investment Management

Stage of public investment	Key feature	Desirable institutional arrangement	Diagnostic indicator(s)
Guidance			
Investment guidance, project development, and preliminary screening	Projects or programs are subject to (a) actionable strategic guidance and (b) adoption of first-level screening of all project proposals relative to this guidance.	Published development strategy or vision statement that has unambiguous authority	Assess "realism" of strategy relative to resource availability—is it actively used to prioritize budgetary decisions?
		Various: centralized approval by planning or finance ministry (or delegated) for developing proposals; explicit ministry-level justification with strategy	Evidence of inadequate process for screening proposals—major projects inconsistent with government strategy or vision
		Clarity of project objectives in terms of outputs and outcomes	Sampling of proposals
		Consideration of alternative approaches to objectives	Sampling of proposals
Appraisal			
Formal project appraisal (executed by appropriately skilled staff or consultants)	Projects or programs that meet the first screening test undergo more rigorous scrutiny of their cost-benefit or cost-effectiveness. (The value of ex ante project evaluation depends on the quality of the analysis which, in turn, depends on the capacity of staff with project evaluation skills.)	Publicized and transparent guidance, backed by effective training and deployment of staff for project design and appraisal (including stakeholder consultation in project design)	Quality of published guidance on appraisal; number of staff with training in project appraisal in line positions
		Application of guidance in project appraisal	Sampling of appraisals

table continues next page

Table 2A Stages, Institutional Arrangements, and Diagnostic Indicators of Public Investment Management
(continued)

Stage of public investment	*Key feature*	*Desirable institutional arrangement*	*Diagnostic indicator(s)*
Independent review			
Independent review of appraisal	An independent peer review checks any subjective, self-serving bias in the evaluation.	Independent checks to ensure objectivity and quality of appraisals	Rate of rejection of project appraisals (including donor-funded)
		Disciplined completion of project appraisals prior to budget	Evidence to the contrary— appraisals "hurried" to meet budget timetables or downstream project design issues
		Identifying and maintaining an inventory of appraised projects ranked by priority for budgetary consideration	Existence of a portfolio of appraised projects by ministries
		Clarity of roles between (a) projects that are minor and may be dealt with at the departmental level and (b) those that require additional scrutiny	Multiple actors that lack clarity about specific responsibility for proposals
			Issue delegations, allowing the central appraisal system to be free of considerations of relatively important projects
Selection			
Project selection and budgeting	The process of appraising and selecting public investment projects is linked appropriately to the budget cycle.	Transparent criteria for selecting projects with reference to policy objectives at ministerial level	Lack of transparent criteria
		Well-structured budget preparation process with scope to integrate investment and recurrent implications of projects	Disciplined budget calendar, with clear requirements for consideration of recurrent implications
		Effective gatekeeping to ensure that only appraised and approved projects are selected for budget financing	Small percentage of projects in the budget that evaded established appraisal and selection process
		Ensuring adequate financing for selected projects, including recurrent needs on completion	High value of new project starts relative to ongoing total capital budget and to finishing projects

table continues next page

Table 2A Stages, Institutional Arrangements, and Diagnostic Indicators of Public Investment Management
(continued)

Stage of public investment	Key feature	Desirable institutional arrangement	Diagnostic indicator(s)
Implementation			
Project implementation	Projects are scrutinized for implementation realism and then implemented with regard to efficiency.	Published guidelines for project implementation	Review quality of guidelines for clarity and requirements for efficiency and accountability
		Cost-effective implementation through procurement and contracting	Evidence of competitive project tendering
		Timely implementation in line with guidelines	Sample for delays in project implementation relative to appraisal estimates—sector-specific indicators
		Timely implementation reports on major projects	Large stock of incomplete projects—data by vintage of projects by sector (look into reasons: lack of technical capability, unrealistic timetable, or underfunding)
		Effective budgeting for selected projects	Review sample of reports for timeliness problems of procurement on major projects by sectors
			Compare capital budget to outturn for several years
			Existence of multiyear budget allocation system
			Evidence of underfunding of major projects relative to actual requirements (shortfalls in budget allocations, unpaid bills, disputes over payment, and so forth)
			Existence of total project cost management system to prevent imprudent cost increase
			Estimates of cost overruns on major projects—sector-specific indicators

table continues next page

Table 2A Stages, Institutional Arrangements, and Diagnostic Indicators of Public Investment Management
(continued)

Stage of public investment	Key feature	Desirable institutional arrangement	Diagnostic indicator(s)
Adjustment			
Project adjustment	Project implementation review has enough flexibility to allow for necessary adjustments due to changes in project circumstances that would either change the disbursement profile or require project termination.	Active monitoring	Estimated costs and benefits updated to reflect material changes in circumstances Consequences of changes in estimated costs and benefits included in operating budgets, where relevant Mechanisms that prevent continued expenditure on a project when its benefits (net of sunk costs) are not positive
Operation			
Facility operation	Process for ensuring that a facility is ready for service delivery should be in place, and asset registers are maintained and asset values recorded.	Service delivery	Evidence that the facility is completed and operational and providing services Evidence of adequate funding for service delivery agencies for operation and maintenance
		Asset registers	Service delivery associated with facility operation tracked through time Agencies held accountable for the delivery of services Evidence that complete asset registers maintained Records management system that facilitates valuation and custodianship
Evaluation			
Basic completion review and evaluation	Basic completion review and ex post evaluation of completed projects are conducted.	Formal institutional arrangements for basic completion review and ex post evaluation of projects and programs with feedback into future project designs	Timeliness of project completion Deviation from the original (and amended) budget Compliance audit by supreme audit institution for a sample of projects Where ex post evaluation exists, useful indicators may include • Share of public investment projects subject to ex post evaluation; • Quality of evaluation and recommendations; and • Evidence of response to the evaluation findings.

Notes

1. Pritchett and de Weijer (2010) in "Fragile States: Stuck in a Capability Trap?" note that countries sometimes adopt advanced-country systems without being able to achieve their performance and are often encouraged to do so by advice on best practice that does not factor in local capacity and context. The end result is an organizational form without the associated function, another way of describing "isomorphic mimicry."

2. An obvious comment that might be made at this stage is that the economic rate of return (ERR) would provide the most appropriate measure of public investment efficiency. Where available, the ERR would be a valuable indicator and should be used. But this is often not calculated or, in many instances, is only available as an ex ante estimate. Some studies (Florio 1997, 1999; Florio and Vignetti 2005) suggest that ex post ERRs are systematically lower because of optimism in ex ante estimation or poor project implementation. The approach taken here is to develop a range of indicators that include indicators about process and institutional failures, which then provides the basis for corrective actions.

3. The PEFA Program was founded in 2001 as a multidonor partnership between seven donor agencies and international financial institutions to assess the condition of country public expenditure, procurement, and financial accountability systems and develop a practical sequence for reform and capacity-building actions. For more information, see http://www.pefa.org/.

4. The United Kingdom requires departments to prepare Departmental Investment Strategies to guide investment decisions. Some countries produce plans for subsectors where the subsector is characterized by long planning and building cycles, such as for roads, hospitals, and schools. See Allen and Tomassi (2001) for a discussion of countries with transition economies (those moving from centrally planned to market-oriented economies).

5. Five-year plans in many countries proved to be noncredible to the extent that they proposed targets that were not grounded in realistic resource projections.

6. See Fontaine (1997) for a description of the sustained effort undertaken by Chile to train a number of generations of public officials in project evaluation techniques.

7. This may include consideration of whether the project should be directly procured by government or undertaken as a public-private partnership with appropriate risk and reward sharing with the private sector.

8. A medium-term budget framework can provide some forward visibility regarding resource availability and predictability for long-gestation investments.

9. To illustrate, if the residual investment to complete the current program is $1,000 and the annual investment budget is typically $100, the completion rate is 10 percent, implying 10 years to complete. A low completion rate may confirm a poor gatekeeping process that allows too many projects into the budget, or it may reflect cost escalation that causes the cost of completing projects to exceed initial estimates.

Bibliography

Allen, R. E. and D. Tommasi, eds. 2001. *Managing Public Expenditure: A Reference Book for Transition Countries*. Paris: Organisation for Economic Co-operation and Development.

Florio, M. 1997. "The Economic Rate of Return of Infrastructures and Regional Policy in the European Union." *Annals of Public and Cooperative Economics* 68 (1): 39–64.

———. 1999. "An International Comparison of the Financial and Economic Rate of Return of Development Projects." Department of Economics Working Paper 99.06, University of Milan.

Florio, M. and S. Vignetti. 2005. "Cost-Benefit Analysis of Infrastructure Projects in an Enlarged European Union: Returns and Incentives." *Economic Change and Restructuring* 38 (3): 179–210.

Fontaine, E. R. 1997. "Project Evaluation Training and Public Investment in Chile." *American Economic Review* 87 (2): 63–67.

Government of Uganda. 2008. *Engineering Audit of CHOGM Activities*. Report prepared for Uganda Auditor General, Kampala.

———. 2009. *Status Report on the Engineering Audit of CHOGM Work Undertaken by Ministry of Works and Transport*. Report prepared for the Uganda Auditor General, Kampala.

HM Treasury, United Kingdom. 2003. *The Green Book: Appraisal and Evaluation in Central Government*. London: TSO.

Pritchett, L. and F. de Weijer. 2010. "Fragile States: Stuck in a Capability Trap?" World Development Report Background Paper, World Bank, Washington, DC. https://openknowledge.worldbank.org/handle/10986/9109.

U.S. GAO (General Accountability Office). 2012. *Highway Projects: Some Federal and State Practices to Expedite Completion Show Promise*. Performance audit report, Washington, DC.

CHAPTER 3

Country Experiences of Public Investment Management

Introduction

The World Bank has conducted many studies of public investment management in a diverse range of countries. By adopting the systemic eight-stage diagnostic framework and considering how each stage interacts with others, the studies assess the whole public investment cycle rather than just the project cycle or some of its components.

Taken together, this set of studies provides an extensive and diverse set of experiences on how countries' PIM systems are actually functioning—in terms of institutional arrangements, inputs, processes, and outputs from the PIM system. As chapter 1 noted, the approach is based on the assumption that improvements to the features covered by the diagnostic framework are likely to be associated with better-designed and implemented projects that have greater developmental impact. Although we do not have much empirical evidence with which to test any specific connections between institutional arrangements and investment outcomes, the book maintains the following:

- The presence of eight "must-have" features optimizes PIM results. In the stylized typology represented by a two-by-two system performance matrix (introduced in chapter 2), a country's PIM performance migrates toward the top left cell (cell A, where projects are both well designed and well implemented).
- Different country groupings tend to have different patterns of weakness in the must-have features—and different patterns of results in the matrix.
- Different country groupings also differ in the feasible points of entry for strengthening the PIM system.

It is therefore worth the analytic investment in diagnosis to find out in detail how the eight must-have features look in a given country. Although challenges differ across countries, there are naturally also different approaches to strengthening PIM in different settings.

This chapter attempts to summarize and synthesize the main findings that emerge from the country case studies. The next section describes the coverage of the country cases. The "PIM System Typologies" section then identifies and describes some PIM systems, distilled from the case studies, which capture more or less distinctive patterns of PIM system functionality. The final section, "Toward a Strategy for PIM System Reform," describes general approaches to the reform of PIM systems, as well as specific country reform experiences from the case studies, and identifies stylized PIM reform typologies. It also identifies some of the main challenges in reforming PIM systems and possible entry points for external engagement.

Country Coverage

Table 3.1 presents the list of country cases drawn upon in this synthesis, categorized by region; by country level of development; and by whether the country is natural resource-dependent, aid-dependent, or a fragile state.[1]

- *Level of economic development.* The country's level of development is based on the country classification in the International Monetary Fund's (IMF) *World Economic Outlook*, which defines two major groupings: "advanced economies" and "emerging and developing economies" (IMF 2010).[2]
- *Natural resource-dependent states.* Natural resource dependence is defined as having an average share of hydrocarbon and/or mineral fiscal revenues in total fiscal revenue of at least 25 percent during a representative period.[3]
- *Aid-dependent states.* Aid dependence has been defined in qualitative terms as the presence of significant donor funding of public investment.
- *Fragile states.* This study uses the World Bank's definition of "fragile situations" to include countries with a low Country Policy and Institutional Assessment (CPIA) score or those with a United Nations or regional peacekeeping or peace-building mission during the past three years.[4]

PIM System Typologies

While table 3.1 describes countries according to their income level and aid and other characteristics, our interest is in assessing countries according to the functional characteristics of their PIM systems. The translation from income level classification to PIM system typology is not straightforward—not all advanced economies have advanced PIM systems and some emerging economies do have advanced PIM systems.

The PIM system typologies are identified as follows:

- Advanced PIM systems (Korea, Ireland, U.K., U.S.A, and Chile).
- Emerging PIM systems (China, Vietnam, Brazil, Peru).
- PIM in New and aspiring EU members (Slovak Rep., Slovenia, Latvia, Poland, Albania, Macedonia, Montenegro, Serbia).

Table 3.1 Country Case Studies of Public Investment Management Systems by Classification and Region

Country classification	Africa	East Asia and Pacific	Europe	The Americas
Advanced economies		Korea, Rep.	United Kingdom Ireland Spain Slovak Republic Slovenia	United States (state level)
Emerging and developing economies		China Vietnam	Poland Latvia Albania Macedonia, FYR Montenegro Serbia	Brazil Chile Peru
Of which				
Natural resource-dependent states	Angola Congo, Rep. Equatorial Guinea Nigeria (Lagos state)	Mongolia Timor-Leste		
Aid-dependent states	Congo, Dem. Rep. Lesotho Sierra Leone Uganda Zambia		Bosnia and Herzegovina Kosovo[a]	
Fragile states	Congo, Dem. Rep. Sierra Leone Zimbabwe[b]	Timor-Leste	Bosnia and Herzegovina Kosovo	

Note: A country's development classification is based on definitions of "advanced economies" and "emerging and developing economies" in the International Monetary Fund's *World Economic Outlook* (2010).
a. Although Kosovo has recently started to receive international assistance in the form of concessional loans following the declaration of independence in 2008, previously there were restrictions on the assistance Kosovo could receive, and public investment was largely domestically financed.
b. In Zimbabwe, the national budget has been the main source of financing for public investment, with donors providing mainly humanitarian support using parallel nongovernmental systems.

- PIM in Aid-dependent states (D.R. Congo, Lesotho, Sierra Leone, Uganda, Zambia, Bosnia, Kosovo).
- PIM in Fragile states (D.R. Congo, Sierra Leone, Zimbabwe, Timor-Leste, Bosnia, Kosovo).
- PIM in Natural resource-dependent states (Angola, Rep.Congo, Eq.Guinea, Nigeria, Mongolia, Timor-Leste).

Although there is heterogeneity within each of the typologies, countries within each type share a pattern of key PIM features. Countries with advanced PIM systems generally achieve functionality across all the must-have features. The emerging economy group displays the greatest variation in systemic capability. Middle-income countries such as Brazil, China, Vietnam, and Peru fall into a group that for our purposes is best categorized as "emerging PIM systems," with some areas of relative strength but still significant weaknesses compared with the advanced PIM systems. Because of the specific requirements of European Union (EU) membership, a number of candidate and member countries display common PIM features and are classified under a separate typology.

As is evident, there is considerable overlap between the aid-dependent, resource-dependent, and fragile states in the sample. A country belonging to two or even all three of these categories is likely to exhibit some of the features of each category. In that sense, countries that are, say, both aid-dependent and fragile may constitute a further subtypology. In the immediate postconflict period, a country is highly likely to be aid-dependent; however, a number of specific features of PIM functionality are likely to distinguish such countries from the more usual donor-dependent situations. As the time since the conflict lengthens, PIM functionality is likely to more closely resemble the aid-dependent typology. At the same time, a country that receives some external assistance but has a large domestically financed capital investment program may exhibit some features of donor dependence with respect to donor-financed projects but not necessarily for domestically financed projects.

Advanced PIM Systems

The most effective PIM systems among the case study countries are in Chile, Ireland, the Republic of Korea, and the United Kingdom.[5] While Korea, Ireland, and the United Kingdom are advanced economies (with 2012 per capita incomes ranging from $22,670 to $39,110) Chile displays very advanced PIM capability as a developing economy (with per capita income of only $14,060) suggesting that developing countries can build robust investment systems. Although there is considerable variation in the institutional arrangements, modalities, and histories across these countries, in general they exhibit all of the eight must-have features and go considerably beyond that basic standard in nearly all respects.[6] The countries with advanced PIM systems tend to exhibit the following features:

- *Investment guidance, project development, and preliminary screening.* National or sector strategy documents are specific enough, and have sufficient coherence and authority, to actually guide public investment and are used systematically to screen new projects (with at least some projects dropped at the preliminary screening stage; for example, in Chile, 5–8 percent of project proposals are rejected at initial screening). Sector strategies are fully costed and are closely integrated and consistent with medium-term budgets.

- *Formal project appraisal.* Project development follows a well-defined set of procedures, with approval required for projects to advance at specific stages. Projects are appraised using the full range of techniques as appropriate. There are comprehensive central guidelines on project appraisal, including detailed guidance on the appraisal of public-private partnerships (PPPs). In all four countries, PPPs are effectively treated as a choice of modality of public investment and considered relative to a comparator public sector project. Major efforts have been put into building capacity for project appraisal in all four countries, but especially in Chile (since the 1980s), Ireland (since joining the European Economic Community in 1973), and Korea (since the 1997 Asian financial crisis). Appraisal is centralized in Chile and Korea and decentralized in Ireland and the United Kingdom.

- *Independent review of appraisal.* This is a key feature of all four of these countries (although arrangements vary markedly). In the United Kingdom, Treasury approval is required for road projects of more than £500 million, although the level of Treasury involvement in reviewing appraisal of other transport projects varies widely depending on scale and complexity. Business cases for projects are also subject to independent review under the Gateway process.[7] In Ireland and the United Kingdom, major infrastructure projects are subject to a public hearing before the end of the appraisal stage. In Chile, project appraisal is conducted by the planning ministry rather than by the sponsoring ministry. To subject these appraisals to independent review, a separate unit was created within the planning ministry. In Korea, the Public and Private Infrastructure Investment Management Center (PIMAC) was established in 1999 in the Korea Development Institute (a semiautonomous agency under the umbrella of the Ministry of Strategy and Finance) to conduct prefeasibility studies of large projects independent of the sponsoring ministry. In practice, PIMAC conducts all appraisals for projects above a threshold.

- *Project selection and budgeting.* In general, only projects that have been subject to thorough appraisal and have been independently reviewed are selected for funding in the budget. Multiyear budget authority supports effective project implementation, and there is provision for virement between projects and carryover of unspent funds between years. In Chile, there is a pipeline of appraised and approved projects that are eligible for budget funding. In all four countries, medium-term public investment envelopes are in place.

- *Project implementation.* There is a strong focus on managing the total project costs over the life of each project. Clear roles and responsibilities are in place for project implementation; accounting systems record total and annual project costs; and there are regular reports on financial and nonfinancial progress and close monitoring by (a) a line ministry responsible for subordinate implementing agencies and/or (b) the central fiscal authority. Sound procurement systems are consistently implemented using advanced techniques for allocating risks between government and contractors (although problems still arise).

- *Project adjustment.* A distinctive feature is that specific mechanisms are in place to trigger a review of a project's continued justification if there are material changes to project costs, schedule, or expected benefits. For example, in Korea, projects are automatically subject to reappraisal if real costs rise by more than 20 percent. In Chile, when the lowest tender is 10 percent or more above the estimated price, the project is subjected to a reappraisal.

- *Facility operation.* Comprehensive and reliable asset registers are maintained and are subject to external audit. In the United Kingdom, full accrual balance sheets are in place across the central government, and the Gateway process focuses specifically on readiness for service. In Chile, there is systematic recording and checking of completed capital assets.

- *Basic completion review and evaluation.* All four countries put significant effort into ex post review. However, in Chile and Korea the executive's role is still largely confined in practice to reviewing completed assets against project plans. In Ireland and the United Kingdom, efforts are made, in addition, to selectively evaluate the impacts of investment projects on outcomes. In all four countries, investment projects are subject to audit by the supreme audit institution, including value for money audits. In Ireland and the United Kingdom, special reviews are commissioned to identify systemic factors affecting project cost or quality.

Emerging PIM Systems

In many respects the success of emerging economies such as China, Vietnam, and Brazil in catalyzing high growth begs questions about their approach to managing public investment. As shown below, China and Vietnam display some similarities and appear to have functionality in key aspects of PIM. Brazil's growth has been spurred by natural resource exports, which have enlarged its investible surplus, but displays surprising weakness across all stages of the PIM must-have functions that leaves it at high risk of inefficiency in its public investments. Given differences across these three countries we follow more of an individual narrative rather than attempt to shoe-horn them into a discussion based on the eight stages of PIM.

China over the past two decades has had investment rates (public and private) approaching 50 percent of gross domestic product (GDP) while Vietnam has averaged over 40 percent of GDP. Was high growth achieved through high rates of investment or did efficiency also play a role? Was efficiency achieved through particular management innovations that deviate from the must-have features? Or did the countries achieve some functional equivalent through specific institutional arrangements?

China and Vietnam have to be viewed in the context of major structural, financial, and policy changes over the past decades that have transformed highly centralized, planned economies into systems that now feature considerable decentralization of the responsibility for public investment. In some areas the central authorities have retained control so the system of PIM is uneven. It is therefore more difficult to assess a national PIM system which (a) represents a moving target and (b) may not be fully representative of the real nature of PIM.

Because of the common legacy of central planning, both China and Vietnam focus on some elements of the eight stages, focusing on strategic guidance derived from five year plans and sectoral and regional development plans, formal project appraisal, and project selection and budgeting. However, there are also some differences.

In China, the National Development and Reform Commission (the successor agency to the State Planning Commission) controls investment planning and approval. Whereas under the previous material planning system the focus was on physical inputs and outputs, there is more attention now to location, cost, funding source, and benefits from the project. However, high levels of investment and growth have encouraged a culture of "build it, and they will come" and economic and social benefits are not well assessed in project planning. There is no independent review of project appraisal although the MOF has more recently established an investment appraisal commission to offer a view from a budgetary perspective. While the MOF participates in the project selection process its responsibility is focused on implementing the projects for which the capital budget has been allocated by NDRC. There is, however, no systematic oversight of the implementation process with considerable discretion left to the implementing agency to manage project cost overruns without a need for review or re-appraisal. Cost overruns are not uncommon and may be due to changes in the scope of the project, as with the Beijing-Tianjin Intercity Railway which faced a 75 percent cost overrun, in large part because the original 200km/hr railway was upgraded to a 350km/hr railway. Facility operation and evaluation stages also appear to not be closely managed and ex post evaluations are not often undertaken.

China has made repeated efforts to rationalize and reform public investment which have included efforts to clarify the rationale for public investments (on the basis of national security, market failure, or social needs), to define the role for central and local governments, to establish specialized investment companies and lending agencies (China Construction Bank, China Development Bank, etc.) for fiscal lending for public projects, and to reduce administrative impediments to private investment. Guidance has also been given to strengthen project selection and ensure independent review of project appraisal and to specify construction standards. However, because most public investment has shifted to local governments, which rely less on budgetary revenues and interpret these guidelines to only apply to projects funded by the budget (itself a declining share), many aspects of good PIM are not adhered to at the local level.

In Vietnam, the process of "Doi Moi" which described the transition from a planned to a market economy coincided with both a significant increase in public investment and efforts to attract private investment. The large scale but gradual dismantling of the centrally planned system has led to enormous changes in public management systems in Vietnam and a fairly complex institutional and regulatory landscape. Sources of financing have also diversified and create particular challenges for a coherent management system. Projects are approved at various stages by the National Assembly (pre feasibility and feasibility stages of national projects), by the Prime Minister or Minister of Planning and Investments (MPI) and the State Appraisal Council, or, for projects by lower levels of government, by relevant corresponding provincial or local level councils. Whereas all public investment used to be centrally managed by MPI, over time a clearer distinction has been made between government and state-owned enterprise investments, and lower levels of government have been given greater responsibility

The Power of Public Investment Management • http://dx.doi.org/10.1596/978-1-4648-0316-1

for selecting and managing investments. By 2011 local governments became responsible for executing nearly 77 percent of the total capital budget. However, the legacy of the central command economy has not been fully dismantled. The decentralization in capital budgeting continues to co-exist with the prevalent "ask-and-give" mechanism in PIM. Such co-existence leads to the poor coordination between budget allocation and project approval, such that many local authorities approve projects with the expectation that they can obtain additional transfers from the central budget.

Vietnam is making an active effort to develop a robust approach to PIM and has introduced a number of regulations to guide this process. However, the guidance to public investment remains inadequate in key respects, and environmental screening, project preparation and appraisal, procurement, and project evaluation are not always effectively addressed. There is also a need to integrate the management of investments via PPPs under a common framework. A number of plans and strategic documents provide investment guidance but appear not to offer an adequate basis for effective prioritization of public investments. With regard to project appraisal, limited technical capacity and issues of objectivity and conflict of interest in appraisal (there is no independent review of project appraisals) weaken the effectiveness of project selection. However, donor-funded projects are subject to the appraisal criteria required by donor agencies. Budgeting for projects appears to be reasonably well managed, particularly through clarity and transparency in rules for transfers to provincial governments. But project implementation is hampered by problems in site acquisition and delays in procurement, which then require adjustment in project costs and schedules. Vietnam does have a regulation requiring the maintenance of an asset register. However, ex post evaluation of projects is not required and is only undertaken on aid-financed projects. To establish a uniform framework across all stages of PIM, Vietnam adopted a new Law on Public Investment in June 2014.

Brazil reflects a somewhat different set of PIM characteristics (generally weaker) reflecting both the history of fiscal instability and hyperinflation during 1985–94 and the subsequent period of fiscal austerity, which curbed fiscal deficits by restraining investments. These conditions eroded planning and investment capabilities in government and their effects have still not been overcome and investment management remains weak. Booming economic growth derived from Chinese demand for natural resources restored fiscal resources for public investment in 2003–10 but the investment management capacities at each of the eight stages of PIM are inadequate. The government has adopted a second-best approach, focusing efforts on specific investment portfolios, but even these efforts are less than acceptable, with emphasis on execution of projects and speed of public spending without efforts to ensure careful screening and selection of projects. In contrast to China and Vietnam, which have embarked on far reaching changes to the institutions and process of PIM, Brazil still needs to prioritize this important institutional reform agenda. The high-profile 2014 World Cup and 2016 Olympic games may offer an opportunity for Brazil to realize the critical need for strengthening PIM and spur the necessary reform initiatives.

PIM Systems in New and Prospective EU Members

It is clear from the case studies that EU membership and prospective membership have a significant impact on country PIM systems. The transport infrastructure study identified new member states of the EU (Latvia, Poland, the Slovak Republic, and Slovenia) as sharing a distinctive pattern of PIM system functionality that differed from the older member states (Ireland, Spain, and the United Kingdom). This functionality was clearly influenced by specific features of the EU's Structural and Cohesion Funds, which finance infrastructure in the poorer regions of EU member states and through which transfers on the order of 2–3 percent of GDP per year have been made to new EU members.[8] The western Balkans study also identified specific mechanisms that heavily influence the PIM systems of countries that have been invited to be candidates for EU membership or that aspire to candidate status.

Box 3.1 summarizes the distinctive features of the "EU effect" and cites some country practices from this group. To some extent, the "EU effect" resembles the influence of aid donors more generally. However, there are important differences between the mechanisms for aid delivery and those for EU funding to member states and potential member states. For instance, transfers from the Structural and Cohesion Funds are a legal right of EU membership, not discretionary development assistance on the part of the EU. Second, although a donor may temporarily require a recipient to implement specific projects to donor standards (for

---

Box 3.1 The "EU Effect": Common Features of PIM in New and Prospective EU Member States

PIM systems in states that are new members of the EU, or are prospective or aspiring members, tend to exhibit the following features:

Investment guidance, project development, and preliminary screening. The EU requires all member states and candidate countries to have a National Development Plan (NDP) in order to be eligible for Structural and Cohesion Funds and EU pre-accession funding. For member states (which must also have an NDP), the focus of national and sector strategy documents is on maximizing the country's share of projects financed by the EU's Structural and Cohesion Funds. Planning documents cover a fixed seven- to eight-year period aligned to EU budgetary cycles. There is often a lack of coherent overall national strategies applying to both EU and domestically financed investment; for example, in Latvia, the national strategy is devoted exclusively to projects financed by the EU. Albania has put considerable effort in recent years into developing an integrated strategic planning and budgeting framework that is beginning to provide a firm basis for PIM.

Formal project appraisal. EU-issued appraisal methodologies are used in sectors where EU funding is important (see, for instance, EC 2008). Appraisal for non-EU financed investment is

box continues next page

Box 3.1 The "EU Effect": Common Features of PIM in New and Prospective EU Member States
(continued)

underdeveloped except in Albania, where recent regulations defining steps in project development and appraisal guidelines have been put in place, although implementation is still weak.

Independent review of appraisal. The quality of cost-benefit analysis in the new member states
is not independently reviewed within each country. In Albania and Serbia, recent efforts have
been made to introduce an independent review function.

Project selection and budgeting. Alignment of planning periods helps to reduce uncertainty of
external funding. Medium-term fiscal frameworks are in place but in an early stage of development, and in effect the selection of investment projects is still done in the annual budget
round. Albania aside, the central fiscal agencies are not functioning as effective gatekeepers.
Integration of capital and current spending is weak, although Albania has introduced program
budgeting to attempt to address this.

Project implementation. Special project monitoring and control structures are put in place, and a
joint monitoring committee provides coordination with the EU. There is full harmonization with
relevant elements of the EU legal framework, including procurement laws, regulations, guidelines, internal audit, and reporting. Compliance with the EU's procurement framework is more in
terms of form than substance; for example, there is little evidence of the use of modern techniques of sharing risks with contractors. Internal audit is at an early stage of functionality and in
some cases (such as the Slovak Republic) is almost exclusively focused on EU-financed projects.

Project adjustment. There are no specific domestic mechanisms to trigger a review when projects are off-track.

Facility operation. Asset registers range from nonexistent (in Albania) to full coverage in theory,
but in practice, there are important weaknesses in recording new capital assets (in the former
Yugoslav Republic of Macedonia and Montenegro).

Basic completion review and evaluation. In the new member states, postproject reviews are
generally not done. The supreme audit institutions provide basic financial oversight of implementing agencies and projects but not value-for-money reviews. In the western Balkans, the
only supreme audit institution that plays any role in auditing investment projects is in Albania.

---

example, procurement standards), EU members and accession candidates (and
potential candidates that want to be taken seriously) must revise a number of
laws to full harmonization with (that is, make them identical to) relevant EU law.
This represents a more or less permanent change in the legal framework regulat-
ing PIM. It also avoids the problem of multiple donors each imposing a different
national standard for implementation of their separate projects.

On the other hand, although donors supposedly focus on public investment
requirements *within* each recipient country, the EU's Structural and Cohesion
Funds (and the Instrument for Pre-Accession Assistance [IPA][9]) focus also on
investment needs that *span* member states, such as regional and transcontinental

transport networks—reflecting the unique nature of the EU as an international grouping of states based on some shared jurisdiction, in which externalities between member states are to some extent internalized within the EU. The Structural Funds heavily influence the sectoral and subsectoral allocation of public investment toward EU (regional) priorities rather than national priorities.

The "EU effect" is a strong version of a regional effect, evident in one or two other regional integration agreements with respect to procurement. For instance, the West African Economic and Monetary Union (UEMOA) and the Economic Community of Central African States regional agreements involve harmonization of procurement laws among the member states, as further discussed in chapter 6.[10]

PIM in Aid-Dependent States

A number of PIM features and practices are common to the countries in this study that are aid-dependent: Bosnia and Herzegovina, the Democratic Republic of Congo, the Republic of Congo, Lesotho, Sierra Leone, Uganda, and Zambia. In addition, Timor-Leste was highly aid-dependent until 2005 when oil and gas revenues came on stream, and the country still exhibits some aid-dependent features.[11]

Aid dependence affects PIM across the whole investment cycle and results in a highly distinctive pattern of PIM functionality, as summarized in box 3.2.

A distinctive feature of aid-dependent states is weak appraisal capacity and reliance on donors to select and design good projects. In Sierra Leone and Uganda, for example, while basic elements of project justification are in place, very few projects are carefully appraised. Weaknesses in project appraisal are, however, of considerably less concern in a country where major donors generally conduct in-depth project appraisal. Where public investment is fully financed from domestic sources, or where aid is largely in the form of budget support, weaknesses in government capacity to appraise projects create an immediate risk that low-quality projects will be accepted into the budget and implemented. Given the scarcity of capital and of implementation capacity, the selection of a low-quality project imposes a high opportunity cost on any society: the loss of the benefits of the well-appraised project that could potentially have been implemented instead. Reducing this risk considerably is the involvement of the major multilateral donors providing or contracting for in-depth appraisal of projects they finance.

However, a good PIM system in an aid-dependent state nevertheless requires independent government review of donor-appraised projects, for a number of reasons. First, the quality of appraisal is uneven across donors as well as across projects for a given donor. Independent review of individual projects by the government is needed to ensure that full account is taken of domestic conditions and capacity constraints, local impacts, and prospective developments of which a donor may not be fully aware.

Second, there are legitimate concerns about the collective effect of multiple donors on a country's capacity to develop a robust PIM system. Quite often, governments are unable to establish a disciplined domestic process for reviewing

Box 3.2 Common Features of PIM in Aid-Dependent Countries

PIM systems in donor-dependent settings tend to exhibit the following distinctive features:

Investment guidance, project development, and preliminary screening. Government strategy documents such as Poverty Reduction Strategy Papers (PRSPs) tend to be directed toward the donors rather than covering both external and domestic investment in an integrated and coherent manner.[a] They are at a level of generality that limits the extent to which they can provide a basis for preliminary screening of projects, and they are often not supported by effective sector strategies. Successive iterations of a PRSP often address these weaknesses, although in some cases national strategy processes that were initially promising have stalled (for example, in Bosnia and Herzegovina).

Formal project appraisal. There is a reliance on donors to conduct appraisal, with a serious lack of appraisal capacity within the government, in addition to a lack of guidance on defining the project preparation process and on appraising domestically financed projects and PPPs. Donor capacity building regarding appraisal tends to be agency-specific, with little or no domestic training capacity. There is also the disappointing reality of many decades of efforts to train cadres of staff in project appraisal techniques only to have trained staff reassigned to other functions with little care to retaining and utilizing these skills by country authorities. While there are exceptions, problems of overall civil service management impact many aspects of capacity in government.

Independent review of appraisal. Reflecting reliance on donors as well as the reluctance of government to accept checks on discretionary authority, most countries lack the capacity for independent review, either of donor projects or domestically financed projects.

Project selection and budgeting. In many countries the budget is still divided into a recurrent and a development budget, with weak integration between them and substantial off-budget aid. Aid-coordinating units manage the relationship with donors, but this is often more of a process management function than a strategy or investment priority-setting function. The use of public investment programs (PIPs) remains quite common, but these can be poorly connected to fiscal policy and the budget. In practice, a PIP tends to be more of a coordination tool than a tool to manage the project portfolio strategically or to help enforce review of individual project proposals before they can be considered for budget funding. Agreement by a donor to finance a project may be tantamount to the project being included in the budget—subject to basic screening for consistency with a PRSP (which is not difficult given its generality) and the affordability of any required counterpart financing. Central financial agencies are not functioning as effective gatekeepers either for donor-funded projects or for domestically funded projects.

Project implementation. Unpredictability of donor funding (especially budget support) interrupts project implementation due to lack of alternative financing. In Lesotho, volatility and unpredictability in receipts from the Southern African Customs Union is a big challenge to budgeting (World Bank 2012a). Weak project management capacity induces donors to set up multiple Project Implementation Units (PIUs) within implementing agencies that may initially help

box continues next page

Box 3.2 Common Features of PIM in Aid-Dependent Countries (continued)

to speed implementation and compliance with fiduciary standards but also cut across and negatively affect in-line capacities and accounting and reporting systems. Some rationalization of PIUs is taking place in a number of countries such as Bosnia and Herzegovina and Sierra Leone. Procurement is undertaken by PIUs or donors to varying donor standards rather than national procurement standards, although modernization of procurement laws has recently been put in place across most countries and work is under way to strengthen procurement practices. Nevertheless, delays in procurement have a significant impact on project implementation in most countries. In Uganda, the lack of good project and contract management was noted to create the risk of payments before completion of projects. Many governments are also not aware of project expenditures directly financed by donors in many cases, limiting their ability to track and report on project costs and implementation. Timor-Leste is an exception to this rule with all donor-funded investments captured in the national budget.

Project adjustment. There is reliance on donors to supervise the project implementation process and trigger review of projects that are off-track. There is a lack of similar formalized mechanisms for domestically financed projects. Few countries consistently track the accrued cost of an investment relative to the estimated cost. Fewer have established processes to abort projects that may become economically unviable as costs escalate.

Facility operation. There are generally formal hand-over procedures upon completion of donor projects but inadequate asset registration systems and inadequate funding for operation and maintenance, in part because of weak integration of recurrent costs of donor projects into fiscal policy and budgets. In Sierra Leone, as with many other countries, the lack of asset registers contributes to systematic underfunding of maintenance and a rapid deterioration of investments. The focus is on the project cycle, not the investment cycle, reflecting the focus of donors on the project cycle.

Basic completion review and evaluation. There is reliance on donors to review and evaluate their projects. Otherwise, with one or two notable exceptions (such as Bangladesh, where over half of public investment spending is domestically financed), there is little or no systematic basic postproject review, let alone evaluation, and limited use is made of findings from donor evaluations to improve future project design and implementation.

a. A PRSP "contains an assessment of poverty and describes the macroeconomic, structural, and social policies and programs that a country will pursue over several years to promote growth and reduce poverty, as well as external financing needs and the associated sources of financing. They are prepared by governments in low-income countries through a participatory process involving domestic stakeholders and external development partners, such as the IMF and the World Bank" ("Poverty Reduction Strategy Papers [PRSPs]: A Factsheet," http://www.imf.org/external/np/exr/facts/prsp.htm).

---

and managing donor-funded projects. Projects approvals are granted under pressure from donors to suit their own commitment schedules. In the long term this undermines PIM capacity development. Some donor practices may also impose other costs: donors often do not properly assess the current and future implications of development projects for the government's recurrent budget. Donors focus up to the point of physical completion and handover of a project, whereas the government has to operate and maintain the assets to deliver public

The Power of Public Investment Management • http://dx.doi.org/10.1596/978-1-4648-0316-1

services for many years more. With government budgets themselves not effectively integrating capital and current expenditures this can impair the effective operation and maintenance of investments. There may also be interactions between projects, and between sectors and subsectors, that require some adjustment to project design, such as sequencing or phasing of implementation, which may not be adequately factored by government when confronted with individual donor-funded projects.

Third, a review of the donor's project appraisal is also desirable to help counter the clear empirical tendency toward "optimism bias" among those preparing projects—that is, the tendency for project proposals to systematically overestimate project benefits and to underestimate costs. Pressures in aid-agencies to disburse aid can also undermine the objectivity of project appraisal and should be checked by independent review. But recipient governments may be unwilling to look a gift horse in the mouth and this may sustain uneconomic projects.

Recipient governments should also be analyzing whether the overall portfolio of individual projects constitutes a well-designed program. That is, does the package of projects reflect the government's priorities, is it designed to make maximum development impact, and does it impose future burdens on the recurrent budget that are affordable? When the individual projects are aggregated across donors, the overall "program" may reveal concerns about the sectoral allocation, regional distribution, macroeconomic impacts, proliferation of small projects, overall impact on vulnerable groups, or affordability and sustainability. Although major donors are now trying to coordinate more closely at a strategic level and to align their project portfolios with the recipients' priorities, this is less true of some other donors, and there is often significant activity by nongovernmental organizations (NGOs) outside the donor coordination framework.

In addition, some donors are willing to finance development projects but do not themselves develop and appraise the projects or finance project appraisal. In these instances, a recipient government's lack of capacity to develop projects, at least to the feasibility stage, may cause the country to miss out on additional financing from these sources—as, for example, in Sierra Leone.

Finally, weaknesses in project appraisal create serious risks for the quality of domestically financed investment as well as investment financed by donors through budget support. In aid-dependent states, budget submissions for domestically financed investment from ministries, departments, and agencies (MDAs) typically lack well-specified project proposals and may arrive after the deadline for submission, leaving little time for any assessment by central finance agencies—which also typically lack in-depth capacity for review of appraisals. MDAs are often not indicating the future recurrent cost impacts of development projects on their (often separate recurrent) budgets.

PIM in Natural Resource-Dependent States

Countries rich in oil, gas, and mining resources face the fundamental challenge of translating prospective wealth beneath the ground into productive assets above the ground. Effective public investment represents a key link in realizing the potential developmental contribution of extractive industries to broad-based growth and improved social welfare. However, owing to capacity and political constraints, many of these countries consistently fall short in terms of the quantity and quality of their capital spending.[12] Consequently, "investing in the capacity to invest" could potentially yield a high developmental return (Collier 2007)—strengthening the government's capacity to build, operate, and maintain priority physical infrastructure effectively and efficiently.

Resource revenue-dependent governments face a number of generic as well as specific challenges to improving public investment:

- Revenue volatility and "boom and bust" cycles.
- Public investment through a variety of modalities (such as semiautonomous state-owned natural resource companies, establishment of sovereign wealth funds with investment mandates, or resources-for-infrastructure arrangements)[13] in addition to traditional budget financing and government construction.
- The scale of public investment in relation to the size of the economy (which creates congestion and crowding effects).
- The rapid scaling up and cutting back of capital spending that often takes place in resource-dependent settings during boom and bust cycles.

Furthermore, public investment decisions are relatively discretionary compared with decisions on current spending, which creates additional challenges from a political economy perspective in natural resource-dependent states where there is often a lack of checks and balances on executive action.

A number of PIM features and practices are common to the countries in this study that are dependent on natural resources: Angola, the Democratic Republic of Congo, the Republic of Congo, Mongolia, and Timor-Leste.[14] However, this group of countries also exhibits considerable diversity. For instance, Mongolia and Timor-Leste have only recently become resource-dependent; Mongolia is a transition economy; and Angola and Timor-Leste are postconflict societies. These factors also have specific impacts on PIM, with the result that there is considerable variation in the PIM systems across these countries. Nevertheless, some common stylized patterns can be discerned that appear to be related to resource dependence, as summarized in box 3.3.

PIM in Fragile States

Postconflict and fragile states exhibit a distinctive pattern of PIM system functionality, as summarized in box 3.4. In the immediate postconflict period, PIM analysis and decision making is focused on emergency reconstruction and is, at least to some extent, the responsibility of a parallel administration staffed by internationals (for example, in Bosnia and Herzegovina, Kosovo, and Timor-Leste). There is a difficult transition to manage from emergency to development assistance, the relinquishing of external authority and reactivation of local PIM systems, and the shift to more traditional forms of international involvement.

Box 3.3 Common Features of PIM in Natural Resource-Dependent States

PIM systems in resource-dependent states tend to exhibit the following features:

Investment guidance, project development, and preliminary screening. Government strategy documents may not apply to all public investment because of the important role that semi-autonomous, state-owned national resource companies play in financing investment. Strategy documents often do not guide actual investment decisions, which are often made in a nontransparent manner.

Formal project appraisal. There is typically a lack of capacity to conduct sound project appraisal, particularly when resource revenues and public investment spending are increasing rapidly. Abundant revenues weaken MDAs' incentives to prioritize and carefully appraise projects. The lack of checks and balances on executive power typical in these countries (except Mongolia) results in a lack of demand for project appraisal and the politicization of public investment decision making. Nonstandard modes of investment such as resources-for-infrastructure arrangements are not appraised against standard public investment.

Independent review of appraisal. There is a lack of capacity and a lack of demand from decision makers for independent review of projects prior to decision making.

Project selection and budgeting. Separate development and recurrent budgets are common, with weak integration of recurrent project costs in fiscal policy and the budget as well as low transparency of investment projects (Timor-Leste aside). The use of PIPs is common, but these can be poorly connected to fiscal policy and the budget, and they constitute a large number of projects with a lack of national or sector-specific strategies.

Project implementation. Weak implementation capacity, including procurement and project management (coupled with poor planning), results in chronic underspending of the investment budget. Except in countries where revenue stabilization funds are effective, revenue volatility can create boom and bust cycles, exert periodic short-term pressures to cut investment spending, and result in large expenditure arrears (for example, in Angola). Timor-Leste aside, multiple modes of project implementation are common, including (variously) public infrastructure investment by a national resource company, infrastructure spending by international resource companies, and resources-for-infrastructure projects.

Project adjustment. There is an absence of processes to trigger review of projects that are off-track, in part due to a dominant executive and relative lack of resource constraint but also due to weaknesses in project accounting and monitoring.

Facility operation. There are inadequate asset registration systems and inadequate funding for operations and maintenance, in part due to weak integration of recurrent project costs in fiscal policy and the budget.

Project evaluation. There is little or no systematic basic postproject review or evaluation (because of lack of demand from decision makers and lack of capacity). Mongolia, where the supreme audit institution publishes reports on its audits of investment projects, is a limited exception.

Box 3.4 Common Features of PIM in Fragile States

Although dependent on the length of time since the conflict ended, PIM systems in post-conflict and fragile states tend to exhibit the following features:

Investment guidance, project development, and preliminary screening. State capability to formulate strategic direction has typically collapsed, and a multiplicity of donors, essentially constituting a parallel administration, tries to rebuild basic infrastructure destroyed in the conflict. Donors coordinate using multidonor needs assessments and multidonor trust funds. There are also typically specific forms of poverty resulting from conflict—such as impoverished regions where conflict was concentrated—that may affect public investment planning (Dudwick and Melsson 2008). The approach to national strategy formulation is of necessity constrained by the need to rebuild social consensus shattered by the conflict, and it generally takes many years to develop coherent and authoritative national strategies that effectively guide, first, donor-financed and then, domestically financed investment. Fragmented societies can result in duplication of infrastructure, failure to capture economies of scale, and neglect of intercommunity communication links.

Formal project appraisal. There is weak capacity and almost total reliance on donors, who are financing a high proportion of all public investment. In the immediate postconflict stage, donors tend to suspend or fast-track value for money studies, in part because the focus is on replacing infrastructure that has been destroyed by war or disaster. Over time the focus shifts to rebuilding domestic appraisal capacity.

Independent review of appraisal. There is effectively no capacity for independent review.

Project selection and budgeting. A lot of aid is off-budget, and the recurrent cost impacts of donor projects are poorly integrated into the budget. There are periodic large, unplanned-for increases in demands on the current budget as donor funding winds down from the peak. Project selection may be highly politicized because public investment is used to try to "buy the peace."

Project implementation. There is a plethora of PIUs and weak procurement capacity in relation to the needs for reconstruction, but procurement reform is common (for example, in Bosnia and Herzegovina, Kosovo, and Timor-Leste). There is weak monitoring of project implementation. In Zimbabwe, the hyperinflation rendered the government financial management information system unusable, projects were often halted because of cost inflation, and the capital budget execution rate was only 25 percent in 2009.[a]

Project adjustment. There is reliance on donor systems to trigger a review when projects are off-track.

Facility operation. There is a lack of asset registers and possible failure to reestablish clear administrative responsibilities for asset ownership[b]; ineffective project hand-over arrangements; evidence of new assets not fit for purpose; and insufficient operation and maintenance funding.

Basic completion review and evaluation. There is little or no basic postproject review, and the country may even lack a functioning supreme audit institution to conduct basic compliance checks on projects.

a. With the end of the hyperinflation, the execution rate improved to 90 percent in 2010 before falling to 65 percent in 2011 (World Bank 2012b).
b. However, Zimbabwe was an exception, with basic asset registers in place in line ministries.

After the initial years following the conflict, this typology comes to resemble in some respects the typical aid-dependent typology as donors help to rebuild PIM functionality—except where the country is also resource-dependent, in which case features of that typology will also be present.

Toward a Strategy for PIM System Reform

This concluding section discusses approaches to the reform of PIM systems. The first part describes three key challenges for PIM reform. This is followed by a general discussion of the sequencing of reforms and the different broad stylized approaches to reform sequencing evident from the case studies. The third subsection then discusses the main elements of PIM reforms in individual case study countries. The "Patterns of PIM Reform" subsection identifies reform patterns and challenges by PIM system typology, while the last subsection identifies possible entry points for external engagement.

Taking Stock: The Three Key General Challenges of PIM Reform

In general, PIM reforms face three particular challenges. First, public investment tends to be highly politicized. Compared with recurrent spending, decisions on individual projects are discrete and relatively discretionary. This, together with the location-specific and long-lived nature of projects, makes public investment an attractive means for politicians to visibly and credibly claim that they have delivered benefits to particular constituents—although, in many countries, starting projects seems to take precedence over finishing them and delivering real benefits. Any consideration of PIM system reform must therefore recognize that the current pattern of investments and how the PIM system functions are likely, at least to some extent, to reflect the interests of key decision makers. It is therefore important to assess how motivated political leaders are to improve the functioning of the PIM system; where a push for reform might come from; and which elements of reform are more likely to be supported, tolerated, or vigorously opposed.

Second, public investment is an area of high corruption risk.[15] The opportunities for private financial gain can distort investment choices and project implementation decisions (as discussed in chapter 6 on procurement). Reforms are likely to upset the current distribution of illicit gains, although some reforms (such as procurement reforms) are more likely to do so than others.

Third, PIM is an extremely demanding area of public management. Even the basic "must-have" functionality requires governments to possess a reasonably long-term horizon and the discipline to apply good principles of management to each stage of the investment program.

It is important therefore to ensure that PIM system reforms are

- Incentive-compatible, meaning that advice recognizes the political incentives facing elected officials and does not counsel a politically unrealistic policy approach;

- Based on a sound understanding of, and tailored to fit, individual country trajectories, circumstances, and practices;
- Technically feasible such that the yardstick in the technical analysis is "good enough" practice, not good (or best) international practice for more developed countries; and
- Carefully designed and sequenced in recognition of implementation capacity and so that, to the extent feasible, early gains are achieved that help to build support for the reforms.[16]

How the PIM system functions, and the prospects for reform, will be conditioned in the following ways by the broader public management and public financial management (PFM) environment in which the system is nested:

- The relative power of the executive and legislative branches varies across countries and influences the ability of each branch to influence PIM.
- The formal and informal roles and influence of the ministry of finance within government also vary widely, affecting the ministry's ability to act as a gatekeeper for the quality of new projects entering the budget and its ability to prompt remedial action during project implementation.
- The culture of relationships between civil servants and elected officials influences the ability of civil servants to engage in direct discussion with political leaders on the technical merits of individual projects. The broader civil service culture (such as whether there is a disregard for compliance with the law) or a legalistic culture (that encourages formal adherence to rules at the expense of results) also affects the PIM system. (See the discussion of procurement in chapter 6.)
- The civil service remuneration system will influence the ability to attract and retain specialized skills required for PIM or the prospects for PIU reform in aid-dependent settings.
- Finally, the wider PFM system in which the PIM system is nested also influences the feasibility of PIM reforms. The general quality of budgeting, cash planning, accounting and reporting, treasury systems, the internal control environment, and internal and external audit capacity all have a major impact on the functioning of the PIM system.

Therefore, it is critical to design a strategy for PIM reform. These are the aspects to which we now turn.

Designing a Reform Strategy: Sequencing Is Critical

In thinking about PIM reforms, a useful starting point can be to conceive of the PIM system as comprising two broad subsystems: project preparation and project implementation. A simple typology of PIM system performance is shown in chapter 2 in table 2.2. The objective is to move to cell A—in which well-designed projects are well implemented. Reducing the number of poor projects selected for funding often appeals as an obvious starting point in PIM reform, but it involves a time lag before the benefits are felt while new projects move through the PIM system to service delivery. Improving project execution may generate faster benefits—although only if the projects are not poor projects that generate negative net benefits. A relevant consideration here is the size of the current stock of projects relative to the annual flow of new projects entering the PIM system. When spending on public investment is increasing rapidly, there may be large potential gains from strengthening project planning. Where new spending is low compared with spending on a large stock of already-committed projects, the larger gains may be from improved implementation.

It must be remembered, however, that PIM is a system, and there are interdependencies across the different stages of the investment cycle. Lessons from improvements in project implementation can, in principle at least, feed back into better planning of new projects:

- Closer monitoring of project implementation and completion of basic post-project reviews could potentially generate useful information on the sources of weakness in project planning. Bangladesh provides a good example of improved monitoring (World Bank 2011, 31–33).
- The gains from a one-off (or regular) basic postproject review of a portfolio of recently completed projects could be a cost-effective and rapid way of identifying needed improvements in project planning. This is part of the PIM reform strategy recommended in the case studies of Brazil and Timor-Leste.
- On the other hand, stronger capacity for project appraisal could improve project implementation by helping to identify (from among the projects that are significantly over budget or behind schedule) those that should be terminated because their expected net benefit is now negative (although actually stopping a project during implementation is acknowledged to be difficult in any country).

The key strategic issue in a PIM assessment is, in fact, to identify which components of the system are constraining performance *at the margin*. In any system, some components may be inframarginal: they are performing at a suboptimal level—relative to what is realistically achievable—but they are not affecting system performance because of more serious weaknesses elsewhere in the system. The objective should be to identify the *binding* constraints on system performance now and in the short-to-medium term. For instance, although in many countries project preparation is weak, it is also the case that in some countries key decision makers are satisfied with their current informal, nontransparent approach to project selection and there is currently no effective demand for better project appraisal.

Therefore, although a partial analysis may suggest the need to strengthen project preparation, a system-level analysis may in this instance suggest the need to focus initially elsewhere in the system (such as improving project execution or attempting to increase the demand for better appraisal).

These issues of sequencing are illustrated by different approaches across the country cases, as described below. These approaches are not all mutually exclusive and are intended to describe broad themes rather than to suggest a single focus of reform.

- *Implementation first:* The focus here is on improving chronic poor project execution rates, on the presumption that poor project planning is not the main problem, or that ex ante appraisal is limited in what it can achieve, or that project selection is highly politicized, or that the fastest gains can be made at the implementation stage of the cycle. Brazil exemplifies this approach (described in the case study as one of "more projects, less appraisal"), but it is also a feature of countries that lack demand from decision makers for better project appraisal (for example, resource-dependent states such as Angola) and of aid-dependent states where there is a reliance on donors to conduct appraisal.

- *Better planning first:* The key to better projects is seen as improved strategic planning and preliminary screening as well as higher-quality appraisal, on the basis that it is hard to improve or stop a poor project once it has been approved. Chile and Korea exemplify this approach, but it is also evident in the western Balkans. Korea in particular exemplifies the strategy of preventing low-quality projects at the prefeasibility study stage before they are launched, with a high rejection rate of 44 percent.

- *Center of excellence:* This is a strategy of building analytical capacity for project appraisal in one government center, usually the ministry of finance or the planning ministry. The center of excellence strengthens appraisal by setting clear expectations, issuing guidelines on implementing them, and reviewing the quality of projects submitted (perhaps selectively). It also helps to build capacity in MDAs through staff training. Examples include Chile, Ireland, and Korea.

- *Center of power:* Dissatisfaction with chronic underexecution of the investment budget causes leaders of government to set up a project monitoring function reporting directly to them. Examples include the intensive monitoring under the Chief of Staff Office in the President's Office in Brazil, the Strategic Policy Unit in the Office of the President in Sierra Leone, and the National Development Agency under the Prime Minister's Office in Timor-Leste. Project appraisal and selection may also be centralized. For example, high-level political committees have been established in some of the Balkan countries (Kosovo, the former Yugoslav Republic of Macedonia, and Serbia) to give more direction to public investment, while in Vietnam the prime minister occasionally sets up a temporary appraisal council to appraise a specific project.

- *Decentralization:* Responsibilities for PIM have been decentralized to a significant degree in Bolivia, China, Peru, and Vietnam. In Bolivia, decentralization has occurred in the context of a rapid scaling up of spending on public investment, financed by rapid growth in natural resource revenues.

- *Legal change first:* One strategy is to change the law to introduce new requirements and then work on implementing them (for example, the World Bank's recommended approach in Sierra Leone to strengthen project appraisal) rather than working to improve system functioning and amending the legal framework in parallel (as pursued in procurement reform in Belize).

- *Contracting out:* This is a strategy of selectively contracting for the services of nongovernment suppliers in project appraisal or project management to supplement capacity but sometimes also to introduce an element of independence and credibility. The case study countries offer numerous examples. For example, Timor-Leste is appointing an independent procurement company to execute procurement of large contracts. From outside these case study countries, Algeria provides an example of large-scale contracting out of the project appraisal function to an international consulting firm.[17]

- *Bypass the system:* Some public investment modalities effectively bypass the whole mainstream PIM system. These include PPPs and resources-for-infrastructure contracts. The motivation may be to seek efficiency gains from private sector involvement or to create some contestability for a chronically weak PIM system. On the other hand, the objective may be to escape the usual scrutiny, shift spending off-budget, or take advantage of corruption opportunities. This "bypass" strategy seems to be growing rapidly, with PPPs being implemented or investigated in virtually all the study countries— despite the common lack of a policy or management framework—and resources-for-infrastructure deals increasingly being used in resource-dependent states (typified by the Democratic Republic of Congo).

- *Transparency:* Transparency is less a sequencing issue than a cross-cutting theme, but a number of the country cases reveal that increasing transparency was an important element of reforms. For instance, in Chile the PIP is available to the public online, and the public can query the website on the full list of current and past projects. In Ireland and the United Kingdom, many projects must go through a public hearing before approval. In Timor-Leste, there is a high degree of transparency around flows of oil and gas revenues into the Petroleum Fund as well as the method of calculation of annual withdrawals from the fund to finance public spending, with quite detailed information on investment projects in the annual budget. NGOs are actively monitoring the appraisal and implementation of selected projects. In Brazil, 75 percent of procurement contracts by value are let by electronic tendering, and civil society concern over unfinished projects led to the establishment of a specialized unit in the supreme audit institution to audit projects. In Vietnam, local communities participate in discussions on prioritization, implementation supervision, and postcompletion operation of smaller-scale projects.

Finally, transparency is likely to be an important element of improved PIM in many countries, especially in resource-dependent states where there is typically a lack of checks and balances on the executive branch. The pursuit of transparency, however, gives rise to the following considerations:

- It is important to define the information to be disclosed with specificity and to take a broad approach to transparency that incorporates clarity of roles, assurances of integrity, active oversight by the legislature, and opportunities for public participation in monitoring public investment. Greater PIM-specific transparency could include elements from the Construction Sector Transparency initiative (CoST), which is developing measures of project information, bidding statistics, and time and cost overruns.[18] It could also include better integration of donor-financed activities in the annual budget documents and accounting and fiscal reports of countries receiving development assistance.

- It is also necessary to pursue transparency at all stages of the investment cycle if rent seeking and corruption are not simply to shift elsewhere in the cycle.

- Requiring a government to take concrete steps up front—such as instituting regular publication of ex ante and ex post information on public investment, establishing independent institutions, or empowering civil society monitoring— might in some countries be an indication of a government's commitment to PIM system reform. However, there will be other states where future reneging on such obligations will be foreseen to entail minimal domestic political cost and where such initiatives cannot therefore function as credible commitments.

PIM Reforms in the Country Cases

The different focus of reforms is illustrated by the distinctive reform elements across the country cases, as summarized in table 3.2. The China and Korea studies provided relatively more detail on reform dynamics over time.

In Korea, the 1997 Asian financial crisis prompted reforms to address the fundamental causes of the recession, which, in the public and fiscal sectors, entailed a more market-oriented approach and managerial strategies to increase efficiency and transparency. To strengthen PIM, the government organized a cross-ministerial task force to develop an action plan. The task force was jointly headed by the Ministry of Planning and Budget (formed in 1999 by the merger of the Board of Planning and Budget and the Office of National Budget) and the Ministry of Construction and Transport. In July 1999 the task force issued a Comprehensive Plan to Enhance Efficiency of Public Investment. A key element of this plan was the strengthening of project appraisal due to distrust of the quality of feasibility studies being prepared by line ministries. The Ministry of Strategy and Finance (MOSF) initially attempted to take over responsibility for feasibility studies, but the line ministries resisted. The compromise was to

Table 3.2 Main PIM Reform Elements by Country

Country	Distinctive elements of PIM reform
Albania	• Coherent, realistic, and authoritative national strategy, supported by sector strategies, linked to the budget • PIM integrated into performance-based, medium-term budget planning system • Structured decision-making process with well-defined roles and responsibilities linked to the budget process at the appropriate points of coincidence • Strengthening of appraisal, including defining steps in project preparation • Ministry of Finance playing a more active gatekeeping role
Brazil	• Succession of high-level political initiatives to institutionalize regular and routine monitoring and active intervention to speed up implementation of portfolio of high-priority projects
Chile	• Effective preliminary screening of projects for strategic alignment • Long period of broad capacity building in project appraisal across government • Comprehensive framework for PPPs • Mechanisms to trigger a review of projects' continued justification during implementation
China	• 1979–83: Withdrawal of government from full support to investment throughout the economy • 1983–2003: Series of incremental steps to decentralize control and create funding sources (state banks) to replace budget funding of investment • 2004: Clearer definition of the scope of government and private investment, and distinction between central and subnational governments; mechanisms to attract private investment; strengthening of project appraisal and implementation; and emergence of local investment corporations
Ireland	• Post EU-accession in 1973, development of comprehensive national and sector strategies • Medium-term investment envelopes by MDAs • Strengthening of Department of Finance for both project appraisal and monitoring of implementation • Capacity building across government in appraisal • Use of independent institutions, transparency, and external contracting • Selective impact evaluation
Korea, Rep.	• Total Project Cost Management (TPCM) system introduced in 1994 • Planning and budget ministries merged in 1999 • In 1999, cross-ministerial task force designs action plan to strengthen PIM • Preliminary feasibility study introduced, conducted by new unit in the Korea Development Institute, a semiautonomous institution • TPCM system strengthened by addition of Reassessment Study of Feasibility mechanism • Ministry of Land Transport introduces ex post performance evaluation system • In 2006, TPCM further strengthened by addition of Reassessment of Demand, and legal framework for PIM strengthened in National Finance Act
Timor-Leste	Advanced level of transparency introduced with respect to • The relationship between the Petroleum Fund and the annual budget • No off-budget public investment (for example, by a national oil company or resources-for-infrastructure projects) • Most donor-funded projects in which the government is a partner shown in the budget
Uganda	• Over the past decade introduced national and sector plans; Medium-Term Expenditure Framework; consistency between development and current budgets; Integrated Financial Management Information System and internal control and internal audit
United Kingdom	Continual strengthening of an already advanced system through • More operationally effective sector strategies • Medium-term investment envelopes by MDAs • Introduction of voluntary Gateway review process, managed by new independent entity within Treasury • Comprehensive framework for PPPs • Selective impact evaluation

Note: EU = European Union; MDAs = ministries, departments, and agencies; PIM = public investment management; PPP = public-private partnership.

introduce a new system of preliminary feasibility studies under the control of MOSF but conducted by the Korea Development Institute, a semiautonomous entity. The MOSF played a leading role in strengthening appraisal and evaluation, the Total Project Cost Management (TPCM) system, and the medium-term expenditure framework (MTEF).

The TPCM system was introduced in 1994, and MOSF has since been revising the "Guidelines for Total Project Cost Management" on an annual basis. TPCM includes all costs accrued over the life of the project, regardless of the source of funding, and the system applies to a series of defined stages, namely project conception; the prefeasibility study and feasibility study; the draft design phase; the blueprint design phase; the contracting phase; and the construction phase. There is also a Reassessment Study of Feasibility intended to prevent unnecessary cost increases by focusing a decision on whether or not to continue a project, and in 2006 a Reassessment of Demand was introduced to verify that the demand forecasts for a project's outputs remain valid.

The China case study also provides a relatively detailed account of the reform process since the late 1970s, identifying five sometimes overlapping reform strands:

- Reducing the role of government in financing and controlling investment.
- Clarifying the boundary between public and private spheres.
- Boosting government financial support to fill gaps in investment that markets cannot or will not address.
- Strengthening mechanisms for ensuring efficiency in the use of public resources.
- Creating enabling conditions for private investment.

China also illustrates that countries can go through different phases or stages of reform (as summarized in table 3.2). A highly distinctive feature of the Chinese reforms has been the emergence within the past 10 years of local investment corporations (LICs) at the municipal level, in the context of large-scale decentralization of PIM financing and authority. LICs are hybrid financial organizations that mix public (fiscal) and private (finance) funding to engage in both public and private profit-making investment in urbanization.

From the above, it is clear that PIM system reform may be best approached by identifying a small number of fairly substantive changes that address the most binding constraints to system performance, rather than attempting many changes across all parts of the PIM system at the same time.

Patterns of PIM Reform
Returning to the previously discussed PIM system typologies, this subsection attempts to draw out common patterns in country reform experience.

Approaches to Reform in Advanced PIM Systems
There has been a trend across these four countries (Chile, Ireland, Korea, and the United Kingdom) toward strengthening appraisal by establishing clear expectations of what is expected of new project proposals, building capacity across

government in the techniques of project appraisal, and implementing institutional reforms to strengthen the independent review of appraisal. Appraisal techniques have broadened and deepened over time, with increased attention to proposed project management arrangements, risk management strategies, and procurement strategies.[19]

At the same time, however, attention has been paid to other key components of the PIM cycle, such as defining clear stages in the project cycle and establishing decision points before projects can proceed to the next stage; strategic alignment and preliminary screening; fully costed sector strategies integrated with MTEFs; multiannual budgeting and authority to spend; accounting and reporting to enable a focus on managing the total costs of projects over their life; and putting sound legal, policy, and management frameworks in place to regulate PPPs.

It also seems apparent from these four countries that evaluation is perhaps the last step in the cycle to receive sustained attention. Basic postproject review has been in place in all four countries for some time, but impact evaluation is still at a relatively early stage even in Chile and Korea despite the length of time that PIM reforms have been under way and the extent of progress achieved in those two countries.

Approaches to PIM Reform in Middle-Income Countries
Middle-income countries represent a wide variety of PIM reform experiences. China has moved since the late 1970s from full government support for investment throughout the economy to a more circumscribed role for public investment and encouragement of private investment. This shift has included a series of steps to replace government budget funding with financing by newly created state banks. At the same time, China has decentralized both financing and authority for public investment to subnational governments.

Vietnam has also embarked on decentralization of PIM to subnational governments and has modernized much of its legislation relating to public investment, introducing a new procurement law in 2005, regulations on project appraisal and monitoring and evaluation, culminating in the enactment of a dedicated Law on Public Investment in 2014. Significant efforts have gone into procurement reform, including publication of a procurement bulletin and setting up a procurement information gateway.

Brazil has also put considerable effort into procurement reform, including the use of electronic tendering. In addition, it has invested top-level political commitment into speeding the implementation of a large portfolio of priority projects.

Approaches to PIM Reform in Aid-Dependent Settings
PIM reforms in the aid-dependent states tend to focus on strengthening project implementation through the following:

- *Procurement reform.* This effort includes modernizing procurement laws, establishing new procurement authorities, training procurement officers, and strengthening internal and external audits.[20]

- *High-level political impetus to monitor progress in implementing individual projects.* This tends to start with an initiative to set up new parallel systems under top-level political direction because of dissatisfaction with current monitoring arrangements and to focus on execution of the annual budget (rather than total project cost and nonfinancial indicators of progress).

- *Rationalizing and reducing the number of PIUs.* In some countries, decisions have been made, in conjunction with donors, not to establish new PIUs; not to allocate any new projects to existing PIUs; to combine or rationalize existing PIUs within a single institution or sector, and sometimes across donors; to attempt to report project spending implemented by PIUs through the national treasury system; to transfer PIU staff to in-line planning departments; or to terminate PIUs and mainstream the functions (although this is problematic given the much higher salaries PIU staff are typically paid relative to regular civil servants carrying out the same functions in in-line positions).

In addition, some aid-dependent countries have put effort into improving the quality of national strategic plans or PRSPs. There is also a trend toward integrating responsibilities for public investment planning and budgeting inside the ministry of finance (for example, in most of the western Balkan countries and Sierra Leone). The PIP as a tool has been sidelined with the development of medium-term fiscal frameworks in many of these countries, and in one case (Albania) the PIP has been terminated. In other cases, however, the PIP remains an important tool (as in Uganda) or one that is being reintroduced (as in Sierra Leone).

Approaches to PIM Reform in Fragile Settings
In these situations, donors are dominant in the early postconflict years, and the focus of effort is on rebuilding a consensus around national priorities and developing strategies for public investment (for example, PRSPs in Sierra Leone and Timor-Leste); establishing mechanisms within the government to coordinate donor financing (all countries); and procurement reform. In those fragile states that are natural resource-dependent, attention then tends to turn to speeding up project implementation through closer monitoring of projects (such as in Angola and Timor-Leste).

Approaches to PIM Reform in New and Aspiring EU Members
In these countries, effort has been put into a number of different parts of the project cycle, such as an emphasis on national strategy documents, the application of cost-benefit analysis, procurement reform, and internal and external audits. However, there is a clear tendency for all of these efforts to be focused on projects implemented with EU funding and for domestically financed investment to lag considerably behind.

The Power of Public Investment Management • http://dx.doi.org/10.1596/978-1-4648-0316-1

Among the six western Balkan countries, priority has been given to strengthening project planning through improved strategic guidance, a more medium-term orientation to investment planning, definition of steps and decision points in project preparation, and better appraisal. Although procurement reform has also been implemented in all six countries, in general the rationale was that it is difficult to improve implementation and evaluation of projects that have not been well designed in the first place.

PIM System Reform Priorities and Possible Entry Points

Table 3.3 points to some general priorities for PIM system reform across the different PIM system typologies. These priorities are derived from the patterns of

Table 3.3 Main PIM Reform Priorities by Country Typology

Advanced PIM systems	• Total quality and cost management over the complete PIM investment cycle • Efficient allocation of risk between government and contractors • Rigorous appraisal of PPPs against standard modes • Strengthening impact evaluation
Aid-dependent settings	• Preliminary screening of projects against comprehensive, authoritative, and costed national and sector strategies • Building capacity for project preparation and appraisal • Consistency between development and recurrent budgets • Strengthening budget gatekeeping • Better insulation of investment spending from donor funding volatility • More effective project accounting, reporting, and monitoring • Strengthening implementation of procurement • Rationalizing and mainstreaming PIUs • Basic postproject review, effective compliance audits of projects by supreme audit institution, and more effective asset management and service delivery
Resource-dependent settings	• Comprehensive national and sector strategies applied across all public investment modalities • Building demand and capacity for project appraisal • Consistency between development and recurrent budgets • Strengthening budget gatekeeping • Better insulation of investment spending from revenue volatility • Sound frameworks for appraisal of nonstandard modes of investment • Strengthening implementation of procurement • Basic postproject review, effective compliance audits of projects by supreme audit institution, and more effective asset management and service delivery • Transparency of public investment across PIM cycle
Postconflict and fragile settings	• Reestablishing national consensus over public investment priorities • Donor coordination • Building capacity for basic project appraisal • Consistency between development and recurrent budgets • Basic project accounting, reporting, and monitoring • Procurement capacity • Basic postproject review • Transparency of public investment across PIM cycle • Managing the transition from emergency to development assistance
EU-accession settings	• National and sector strategies that reflect both domestic and EU financing • More effective appraisal and independent review of non-EU funded projects • More effective oversight of implementation of non-EU funded projects • More cost-effective procurement

current system functionality synthesized from the case studies, together with an assessment of priority areas at the margin for strengthening PIM system functionality.

Not surprisingly, there are overlaps between the different typologies, reflecting both some of the common technical challenges and the fact that the typologies themselves are not mutually exclusive. It goes without saying that these general considerations should always be accompanied and driven by detailed country-specific analysis.

Notes

1. Table 3.1 shows the list of cases on which this chapter is based. Most of them are single country studies but there are two state level studies (the United States and Nigeria), and there are three country group studies: (a) PIM in transport infrastructure for European Union member states including Ireland, Latvia, Poland, the Slovak Republic, Slovenia, Spain, and the United Kingdom; (b) PIM in the western Balkans including Albania, Bosnia and Herzegovina, Kosovo, the former Yugoslav Republic of Macedonia, Montenegro, and Serbia; and (c) a PIM in Latin America, a cross-country study for 25 Latin American countries. Most of the studies are specifically based on applying the framework in Rajaram et al. (2010), in some cases augmented in specific dimensions. The remaining studies, which mostly predated the development of that framework, used an approach to assess the functionality of PIM systems that is consistent with, and in many respects overlaps with, the Rajaram et al. (2010) framework. The country cases are available on request.

2. The *World Economic Outlook* indicates that this classification "is not based on strict criteria, economic or otherwise, and it has evolved over time. The objective is to facilitate analysis by providing a reasonably objective method for organizing data" (IMF 2010, 147).

3. Although the IMF defines natural resource dependence as either fiscal dependence or an average share of hydrocarbon and/or mineral export proceeds in total export proceeds of at least 25 percent (IMF 2007), for the purposes of this study fiscal dependence would seem to be the relevant indicator in terms of the direct impact on PIM.

4. The World Bank defines a country as a fragile state if it is a low-income country or territory, International Development Association (IDA) eligible, with a CPIA score of 3.2 or below. (The IDA is the part of the World Bank that helps the world's poorest countries through loans and grants for programs that boost economic growth, reduce inequalities, and improve people's living conditions [see http://www .worldbank.org/ida/].) The CPIA is used to assess the quality of country policies and institutions.

5. In addition, the U.S. study is at the subnational level and so has not been compared directly with the other national-level studies. Based on this study, it is clear there is a high, albeit variable, level of functionality at the state level in the United States.

6. It is noteworthy that there is only partial overlap between this group of countries with advanced PIM systems and the advanced economies in the dataset as defined by the IMF. Chile is classified by the IMF as an emerging and developing economy (albeit one that was admitted to membership of the Organisation for Economic

Co-operation and Development [OECD] in 2010), but it has for some time been regarded as having an outstanding PIM system. On the other hand, the Slovak Republic, Slovenia, and Spain are classified as advanced economies, but the case studies (admittedly of transport infrastructure only) find their PIM systems to have some important weaknesses.

7. The Gateway review process is a series of short, focused, independent peer reviews at key stages of a project or program. The reviews highlight risks and issues that, if not addressed, would threaten successful delivery. The Gateway process has been operating in the United Kingdom since 2001.

8. Although the older member states are also eligible for EU funds—and some, like Greece, Ireland, Portugal, and Spain, benefited heavily from these resources—the transfers are now smaller relative to the states' domestic investment spending, and their impact is more marginal. For instance, in Ireland, earlier concerns that MDAs conducted cost-benefit analysis only to comply with EU requirements led to creation of a unit in the Department of Finance to monitor compliance with DoF requirements. This perhaps reflects Ireland's transition to being an old member state. Compliance with EU requirements is also now a concern in Bulgaria, where the Ministry of Finance has been attempting to harmonize approaches so that EU-funded and domestically funded projects are subject to the same analytical requirements.

9. The IPA is a harmonized instrument intended to mirror the Structural and Cohesion Funds and by its use prepare candidates and potential candidates for membership, when the transfers involved will be significantly greater and a legal right of EU membership.

10. Outside the case studies in this volume and at a lower level of cooperation, the Collaborative Africa Budget Reform Initiative (CABRI) has initiated an infrastructure dialogue in response to common challenges in the region of ensuring value for money in public infrastructure projects, including difficulties in appraising projects and low execution rates. The initiative has developed case studies and papers on functional PIM issues. For more information, see http://cabri-sbo.org/en/programmes/infrastructuredialogue.

11. In addition, as noted in table 3.1, although Kosovo has recently started to receive international assistance following the declaration of independence in 2008, previously there were restrictions on the assistance Kosovo could receive, and public investment was largely domestically financed.

12. See Kaiser (2012) for further discussion of the political economy of public investment in resource-rich settings.

13. In a resources-for-infrastructure arrangement, a government contracts with a foreign entity or entities both to extract a nonrenewable natural resource and to construct public infrastructure financed from the proceeds of the natural resources extracted. Instead of entering the host government's financial management systems, the revenues from natural resource extraction accrue to the extracting company and are used to directly finance the construction of infrastructure.

14. Chile, Sierra Leone, and Vietnam are also defined by the IMF as resource-dependent states, but they are not considered further in this section. Neither Chile nor Sierra Leone was dependent on natural resources for fiscal revenues in the 2000–05 period, and the impact of natural resource revenue volatility is not discussed in the three case studies (although the impact of aid volatility in Sierra Leone is).

15. In Transparency International's 2011 Bribe Payers Survey, public works contracts and construction was the sector ranked most likely, out of 19 sectors, to engage in bribery of public officials or political parties or of other firms. Of relevance to resource-dependent states, the oil and gas sector and the mining sector ranked fourth and fifth, respectively (Transparency International 2011, 14–22).

16. The Lesotho PIM study used the term "lock-in reforms" that catalyze or make other actions fall into place and that enhance overall PIM system efficiency (World Bank 2012a).

17. See the Lesotho country study for a discussion of the benefits and costs of outsourcing the appraisal function in a low-capacity environment compared with relying on appraisal within the government (World Bank 2012a).

18. For more information about the Construction Sector Transparency Initiative (CoST), see www.constructiontransparency.org.

19. This effort has included increased attention to measurement methods for difficult-to-monetize costs and benefits (such as environmental); strengthening ex post evaluation; and design and use of multicriteria analysis to aid decision making.

20. These are the four standard recommendations in the Country Procurement Assessment Reports, further discussed in chapter 6.

Bibliography

Brumby, J. and T. Velloso. 2010. "Public Investment Management in Brazil." Country Study, World Bank, Washington DC.

Collier, P. 2007. *The Bottom Billion: Why the Poorest Countries Are Failing and What Can Be Done About It.* Oxford,U.K.: Oxford University Press.

Doan, Q., T. Le, and D. Nguyen. 2013. "Vietnam: PIM in a New Market Economy." Country Study, World Bank, Washington, DC.

Dudwick, N. and A. Melsson. 2008. "A Stocktaking of PRSPs in Fragile States." PREM Notes 127 (November 2008), Poverty Reduction and Economic Management Network, World Bank, Washington, DC.

EC (European Commission). 2008. "Guide to Cost Benefit Analysis of Investment Projects: Structural Funds, Cohesion Fund and Instrument for Pre-Accession." Directorate-General for Regional Policy, EC, Brussels.

Frank, J. 2013. "Public Investment Management in Latin America and the Caribbean: Institutions under Evolution." Country Study, World Bank, Washington, DC.

Frank, J. and G. Guerra-Garcia. 2013. "Peru Revamps Its Public Investment System." Country Study, World Bank, Washington, DC.

Groom, S. 2013. "Western Balkans: PIM in 6 EU Accession Aspirants." Country Study, World Bank, Washington, DC.

Habib, R. and M. Petrie. 2013. "Timor-Leste: PIM since Independence." Country Study, World Bank, Washington, DC.

Hasnain, Z. 2013. "Mongolia: The Politics of Public Investments." Country Study, World Bank, Washington, DC.

IMF (International Monetary Fund). 2007. *Guide on Resource Revenue Transparency.* Washington, DC: Fiscal Affairs Department, IMF.

IMF (International Monetary Fund). 2010. World Economic Outlook database. Washington, DC: IMF.

Kaiser, K. 2012. "Investing Resource Wealth: The Political Economy of Public Infrastructure Provision." In *Rents to Riches? The Political Economy of Natural Resource-Led Development*, ed. N. Barma, K. Kaiser, T. Minh, T. Minh Le, and L. Viñuela, 165–216. Washington, DC: World Bank.

Kim, J-H. 2013. "Public Investment in Korea." Country Study, World Bank, Washington, DC.

Le T., G. Raballand, and P. Palale. 2013. "Zambia: Reforming a Broken PIM System." Country Study, World Bank, Washington DC.

Petersen, J. and H. Vu. 2013. "Infrastructure Investments by State Governments in the United States: Grading the Decision-Making Process." Country Study, World Bank, Washington, DC.

Rajaram, A., T. Le, N. Biletska, and J. Brumby. 2010. "A Diagnostic Framework for Assessing Public Investment Management." Policy Research Working Paper 5397, World Bank, Washington, DC.

Transparency International. 2011. *Bribe Payers Index 2011*. Berlin: Transparency International. http://bpi.transparency.org/bpi2011/results/.

Treichel, V. 2013. "Lagos State, Nigeria: PIM Investment in Infrastructure for a Modern Megacity." Country Study, World Bank, Washington, DC.

Wong, C. 2013. "China: PIM under Reform and Decentralization." Country Study, World Bank, Washington, DC.

World Bank. 2010. *World Economic Outlook 2010*. Statistical Appendix. Washington, DC: IMF.

———. 2011. *The Quality of Public Investment Management in Bangladesh*. Draft report, accessible under "Public Investment Management Review 2011" (accessed March 3, 2013), http://www.spemp.com/documents.php?Page=Documents.

———. 2012a. *Lesotho: Public Investment Management Efficiency Review*. Report 65694-LS, Washington, DC.

———. 2012b. *Public Investment Management Efficiency Review: Zimbabwe*. Report 69610-ZW, Washington, DC.

Yusuf, F., D. Addison, and M. Petrie. 2013. "Sierra Leone: PIM in a Post-Conflict Economy." Country Study, World Bank, Washington, DC.

CHAPTER 4

Approaches to Better Project Appraisal

Introduction: The Importance of Effective Project Appraisal

This chapter focuses on the proper roles of project appraisal in public investment management (PIM). Effective appraisal can support appropriate choices of outputs and designs and reduce the risk of excessive costs of construction and operation. As a result, it can also lower the chances of failure to complete or efficiently deliver services. Rigorous project identification and selection systems act as screening mechanisms to prevent inappropriate and inefficient projects from getting into the project cycle and gaining political support and momentum that can make them difficult to stop at later stages. Project appraisal therefore is a key tool to enhance wealth creation through designing, selecting, and implementing public sector projects with positive net benefits to an economy.

Project appraisal can achieve this by

- *Screening out* "white elephant" *projects* that have large draws on the capital and current budgets without providing any significant benefits;
- *Designing projects and programs*[1] in terms of technology, scale, timing, organization, ownership, financial arrangements, and so forth to maximize net economic benefits;
- *Ensuring proper costing and financing of the investment phase* of a project to allow completion within time and financial budgets;
- *Ensuring that self-financing projects are financially viable and that non-self-financing projects will have adequate budget support* over their operational lives so that the benefits of the expected service delivery can be realized;
- *Ensuring that the risks of a project are diversified or allocated* to those parties that can absorb them at lowest cost or have the control and incentives to ensure that the risks are minimized; and
- *Ensuring equitable distribution of the gains and losses* from a project, namely, that (a) private partners get a reasonable return with incentives to perform and bear risks without capturing any unintended large share of the surplus; (b) any

low-income groups targeted by poverty alleviation projects capture most of the benefits; and (c) any groups suffering major costs as a result of the project, such as through resettlement or environmental damage, are adequately compensated.

But realities are often different. Studies of infrastructure projects internationally show major problems with cost and time overruns and benefit overestimations (such as overestimating future road and rail traffic). Too often, capital projects are approved and are implemented despite having very low or even negative economic rates of return. Powerful political interests are able to circumvent an approval process or hide the project in the budget where there is a weak and nontransparent appraisal and approval system.

To address these challenges, this chapter underscores the need to treat appraisal in a systemic manner as it affects all stages of the project cycle.

With this background and motivation, the chapter is structured as follows: The next section describes the different methodological steps involved in appraisal. "Institutional Arrangements for Project Appraisal" highlights the organizational aspects of appraisal. "Challenges in Project Appraisal" discusses the main challenges while also identifying and diagnosing a range of common failures in project appraisal. Finally, "Actions for Improved Project Appraisal" provides suggestions for strengthening appraisal.

Methodological Aspects of Project Appraisal

Stages of Appraisal

Stage 1: Prefeasibility

Prefeasibility is the analysis of the proposed investment based on existing data to justify whether the proposal has sufficient merit for a full-fledged feasibility study. It is the key stage for (a) screening out clear losers and white elephants before major design costs are incurred or political commitments made; (b) considering the major design elements in a project (technology, scale, timing, location, organization, ownership, and so on); and (c) identifying where the major uncertainties in the available information lie in order to target subsequent information gathering.

At the prefeasibility stage, a basic approval should be required by joint committees with representatives from the sector agency involved plus finance and economic planning agencies. *Approval based on prefeasibility appraisal* serves two purposes: First, it should screen out all grossly negative projects. Second, it should direct the design and information-gathering efforts to areas that may improve the expected benefits of the project or clarify or mitigate potential costs or risks.[2]

Stage 2: Feasibility

The feasibility study is the detailed analysis of projects that survive the first stage of screening. Added surveys, studies, testing, and so forth should be conducted to reduce the uncertainty in key factors determining the viability of the project.

A second basic approval should occur at the feasibility stage. *Approval after feasibility appraisal* moves projects forward for financing and inclusion in the budget. This approval should select out the projects with the highest net present value (NPV) to the economy that can be financed. Further approvals may be required if final detailed blueprints are still required or if the project enters some competitive bidding process with private contractors.

Stage 3: Detailed Blueprint

The detailed design of the project includes the engineering specifications and construction designs as well as plans for procurement and implementation. These become the basis for final budgets and contracting of the construction and operation of the project.

At each stage, the economic and financial appraisal criteria are reestimated.

Appraisal Stages in Practice

Modern appraisal systems typically distinguish these successive stages with realistic time frames and assignment of responsibility to institutions. In practice, however, such stages are not always clear-cut. The distinction between a prefeasibility study and a final detailed design that can be procured and implemented is clear, but the cutoff points between the interim stages are not that distinct, as in the following examples:

- When considerable information already exists for a project in a sector from prior analysis and experience, a prefeasibility study may look much like a feasibility study.
- Infrastructure-intensive projects dominated by large upfront construction phases often require a relatively detailed construction design to come out with a reasonable estimate of the construction time and cost in a feasibility study.

The key issue is to have an initial screening at the prefeasibility phase to avoid unnecessary costs of designing and appraising an unattractive project and to prevent political momentum from building up behind such a project. As already noted, evidence-based identification of excess demand as the core approach to identifying projects also plays a critical role in screening out bad projects.

Components or Modules of Appraisal

- *Demand or market analysis* is key to estimating the economic impacts, benefits, and financial revenues. It is the key driver of project selection.
- *The technical or engineering module* is the basis of technology and scale selection, planning the construction phase, and costing the construction and operations.
- *Organization, ownership, human resources, and financing* brings in questions of the appropriate organizational home of the project (government, public authority, nongovernmental organization, or private sector); the allocations of risks and incentives to make the project most efficient; labor requirements and availability; and the financing options.

- *Financial analysis* (including internalized risks and environmental costs) is key to assessing the financial viability and default risks as well as, in the case of public sector projects, the demands on future government budget revenues.
- *Economic analysis (including external risks and environmental costs)* determines the net benefits generated by the project to all stakeholders in the economy. It is the key determinant of the economic wealth creation (or destruction) expected from a project.
- *Distributional analysis* disaggregates the net economic benefit to reveal the net benefits or costs expected by all key stakeholders: service beneficiaries, government and other project financiers or sponsors, competing businesses, suppliers of inputs, and workers and populations displaced or affected by the project.

The manuals listed in box 4.1 elaborate on these components. These manuals all use the so-called Harberger or "weighted average" methodology for the economic analysis of a project or program (Harberger 1971, 1972).

A number of different methodologies were developed in the 1960s and early 1970s, but since the early 1990s, the Harberger approach has largely been accepted and followed outside Europe. Box 4.2 lists the various approaches and major references to them and discusses the similarities and differences between them.

If all the methods are applied with consistent adjustments, they should come to similar conclusions in the selection of investment projects. The Harberger approach turns out to be more practical in that it measures all the costs and benefits in units of the domestic currency so that the values of the costs and benefits correspond to the actual losses and gains of the stakeholders (including the taxes received and subsidies paid by the government), and the values in the economic analysis are also consistent with the values in the financial analysis.[3]

Box 4.3 contains a listing of guidelines for project appraisal issued by governments in a selection of advanced economies.

Box 4.1 Selected Project Appraisal Manuals

1. "Cost-Benefit Analysis for Investment Decisions" (Jenkins, Kuo, and Harberger 2011).[a]
2. *Project Appraisal Manual and Guidelines.* Volume 5 of the *Reform Project Compendium with Toolkit: A User's Guide to State Fiscal Management Reform* (USAID 2008).[b]
3. *Economic Analysis of Investment Operations: Analytical Tools and Practical Applications* (Belli et al. 2001).
4. *Handbook on Economic Analysis of Investment Operations* (Belli 1996).

a. Earlier versions of this manual predate 1985.
b. This manual was originally prepared by Graham Glenday, G. P. Shukla, and J. Tham as the *Project Appraisal Manual and Guidelines* for Governments of States of Jharkhand, Karnataka, and Uttarakhand, India, under the USAID Reform Project (January 2007).

Box 4.2 Cost-Benefit Methods for Economic Analysis of Investment Decisions

The United Nations Industrial Development Organization (UNIDO) Guidelines method values all costs and benefits in terms of changes in consumption values and uses a discount rate appropriate to valuing the social time preference for consumption (Dasgupta, Marglin, and Sen 1972; Squire and Van der Tak 1975). Importantly, this means that all investment has to be valued in terms of its forgone consumption values—typically significantly larger by a factor that could be more than double the investment. This approach also arose out of a central planning framework for government decision making that postulates that decision makers decide key economic parameters (such as the discount rate) rather than these being determined by and estimated from markets.

The Little-Mirrlees method values costs and benefits in terms of border or world prices in foreign exchange units (Little and Mirrlees 1969, 1974). Using world prices to anchor the values in a project had some attraction at the time, given the highly distorted nature of most economies. Although this is an attractive approach to dealing with the value of traded goods, it then requires that all nontraded goods and labor be converted to their foreign exchange equivalent and that all distortions be expressed in foreign exchange units. This method advocated the use of a discount rate based on the return on forgone investment.

The Harberger approach values economic costs and benefits in terms of the "weighted average" of the values of the demand and supply prices of the market responses to the project and measures values in domestic currency (Harberger 1971, 1972). Accordingly, changes in income cause changes in consumption and savings and investment so that the discount rate is a weighted average of the supply and demand prices of capital (typically significantly higher than a discount rate for consumption alone). All externalities of stakeholders, including taxes and subsidies, are measured in domestic prices. Similarly, the financial analysis of the project is measured in consistent units with the economic analysis. These practical and useful features of the Harberger method have led to its wide adoption in project appraisal internationally. Distributional analysis is also a component of this approach to disaggregate the gains and losses to all parties affected by a project and to identify potential basic needs externalities where a project supplies basic needs to the poor.

Following the publication of these various methodologies, significant controversy arose over the appropriate approach to economic analysis of projects. In 1977, Sjaastad and Wisecarver published a seminal article showing that the consumption-based approach (UNIDO guidelines) and the weighted average approach (Harberger) would give the same results if the appropriate adjustments were made to the consumption opportunity cost of investment under the UNIDO guidelines that recognized the market responses to the investment project. The issue then remained as to which approach was the most practical and useful. By the early 1990s, most project appraisal outside of Europe followed the Harberger approach.

Box 4.3 Project Appraisal Guidelines in Advanced Economies

The following are some examples of guidelines for project appraisal or cost-benefit analysis issued by governments in advanced economies:

1. *Handbook on Benefit-Cost Analysis* (Australian Government 2006).
2. "Canadian Cost-Benefit Analysis Guide" (Government of Canada 2007).
3. "Guidance on the Methodology for Carrying Out Cost-Benefit Analysis" (EC 2006).
4. "Guide to Cost-Benefit Analysis of Investment Projects" (EC 2008).
5. "Cost Benefit Analysis Primer" (Government of New Zealand 2005).
6. *The Green Book: Appraisal and Evaluation in Central Government* (HM Treasury, United Kingdom 2003).
7. "Guidelines and Discount Rates for Benefit-Cost Analysis of Federal Programs" (U.S. OMB 1992).
8. "Guidelines for the Appraisal and Management of Capital and Expenditure Proposals in the Public Sector" (Government of Ireland 2005).

Basic Decision Criteria in Project Appraisal

The net benefits of investments are judged in terms of NPVs and internal rates of return (IRRs) from financial and economic perspectives. In making comparisons between mutually exclusive projects or optimizing the net benefits from a project design, the NPV is the appropriate criterion. Core issues in the application of both NPV and IRR criteria are the explicit and consistent treatment of inflation and risk in the development of cash flows and the estimation of discount rates.

For all public sector investment decisions, the determination of the NPV from an economic perspective is the bottom-line criterion. In practice, this criterion needs to be considered in conjunction with any significant externalities, costs of risks, or distributional considerations that may not have been captured in the values entered into the economic costs and benefits of the project.[4]

The major outputs out of feasibility analysis should be the design and selection of projects that raise the NPV through decisions on (a) location, scale, timing, technology, product design, and other aspects of the project; (b) organization, ownership, and financing of the project; (c) the distribution of gains and losses such as compensation of losers through suffering social and environmental costs; and (d) the allocation of risks to stakeholders that can bear them at the lowest cost or that have the capability and incentives to control or reduce the risks.

In cases where the benefits are difficult to value, cost-benefit analysis (CBA) is typically reduced to CEA. CEA is used to measure the cost per unit of service or, less frequently, outcome of a program. For example, in the case of a vaccination program, CEA can be used to estimate the costs per vaccination delivered over some planning period as well as the cost per added quality-adjusted life years gained. CEA is clearly a critical tool in budget decisions as well as key to setting contract or regulated prices to cover the costs of a private contractor or regulated supplier.

Implications of Different Project Types for CBA and Criteria

CBA gets applied to two basic categories of project or program: (a) self-financing or commercial projects or programs, and (b) non-self-financing or budget-supported projects or programs:

- *For self-financing or commercial projects* (which would include regulated price sectors and concession arrangements for private participation in the supply of utilities and infrastructure, aside from commercial private projects supported by international financial institutions [IFIs] or development agencies), the determination of financial viability is critical. It is also key to estimating the bids that private firms are expected to make to participate in a public-private partnership or supply a service at a regulated price.

- *For non-self-financing projects*, financial viability or sustainability is an issue of determining the feasibility of future budget support to the operation and maintenance of such projects. This determination requires an identification of the future surplus revenues to support the project. Without such a determination, the future service delivery and corresponding economic net benefits are at risk. This is critical to avoid building health facilities without health professionals and medicines or schools without teachers and books.

Some public sector projects are primarily designed to deliver basic services to the poor. In such cases the determination of the net benefit expected to accrue to the poor is critical, particularly if the NPV to the project is negative even after crediting it with some basic needs externality.[5] Such a determination allows a transparent estimate of net cost to the economy of transferring the benefits to the target group, which can then be compared with other modes of transferring the same benefits to them.

Role of Appraisal in Public and Private Investments

Governments use a range of organizational and financial arrangements to deliver public sector projects and programs. These include traditional government-owned and -operated projects; government-owned corporations; public-private partnerships or concessions with special private corporations; and privately owned and operated but publicly regulated projects.

At the same time, a variety of arrangements are used for financing the asset purchases and ultimately paying for the project. Financing ranges from government equity and debt to private equity and debt (with or without government guarantees). The ultimate funding of a project can range from full reliance on general public funds (largely tax revenues) to increasing reliance on user charges. Even in the extreme case of commercially structured projects, public funds may be involved through tax incentives or subsidies. Although a range of factors enter into these choices of project arrangements, often the search for modalities that improve the efficiency and performance of the project are core considerations. These arrangements also affect some critical considerations in project appraisal.

The Power of Public Investment Management • http://dx.doi.org/10.1596/978-1-4648-0316-1

Four key changes occur in the appraisal of otherwise similar projects:

- *Financial appraisal.* For publicly funded projects, financial appraisal focuses on the adequacy of budget revenues to cover the operating, maintenance, and debt service costs to ensure service delivery. For self-financing projects that rely on user charges, financial appraisal focuses on the financial viability of the project, whether the project is implemented through a regulated corporation or concession with a corporation.
- *External cost of public funds.* To the extent that a project draws upon public funds to cover its costs, the economic appraisal has to recognize the external costs of raising added public funds, namely the combined economic efficiency, administrative, and compliance costs of an added unit of revenue.
- *Costs of market risk.* To the extent that the revenues of a project are derived from user charges, the sponsors of the project face the costs of systematic or market risk. This risk may be shared with consumers or taxpayers by some pricing agreement for the delivered services.
- *Productivity or cost-effectiveness.* The different arrangements result in different incentives for improved project efficiency through reduced construction and operating costs or enhanced quantity or quality of services.

Box 4.4 provides some further fundamental contrast between the public and private sectors in project decision making.

Level of Effort and Modalities of Project Appraisal in Practice

Project appraisal is itself an investment project. Large, complex projects can require major investment in human and financial resources to design and arrange all the technical, organizational, contractual, and other features of a project and to improve the NPV of investment decisions (including preventing negative-NPV projects). The level of effort can relate to collecting more accurate data; conducting tests or studies to improve estimates of outcomes; increasing the sophistication and detail of the analysis or the number of options considered; and seeking the optimal location, scale, timing, and so on of a project.

The issues in considering the appropriate investment in project appraisal include the following:

- Does an increased level of effort in appraisal lead to an increase in the expected NPV for all types and sizes of project?
- What is the project appraisal capacity in the public sector or available to the government?
- Does the cost of the appraisal exceed the NPV of the project?

How the tasks required to identify, design, and appraise projects are organized and managed depends significantly on the organization of the government and its agencies. Such impact on these tasks is covered in the next section, "Institutional Arrangements for Project Appraisal."

Box 4.4 Public and Private Sector Differences in Decision Making

Private Sector

In the private sector, some information is available about the prevalence of capital budgeting decision-making techniques. For example, a 2002 survey of U.S. corporations showed that some three-quarters used NPV of cash flow techniques and that the prevalence of use rose significantly by firm size and had risen since earlier surveys (Graham and Harvey 2002). This may be taken to suggest that more successful private corporations use better investment decision-making tools.

In the private sector, there is a clear link between the NPV of investments and the bottom-line net worth of a corporation; hence, not surprisingly, shareholders' interests are served through the selection of profitable projects.

Further, there is a direct link between the market demand for firms' products and their NPV estimates for investments in the delivery of these products—all costs ultimately have to be paid out of project revenues.

Public Sector

Outside of the self-financing projects in the public sector (typically regulated utilities or user-fee-financed infrastructure such as toll roads or port facilities, often implemented with private participation), the public sector lacks two key links:

- In the public sector, there is a weak link between public demand for a service and the perfor-mance and net economic success of public projects and programs.
- The taxpayer, as the ultimate bearer of all public sector costs, has only weak and indirect mechanisms of voting and voice for expressing demand for services and for net economic gains to be earned by public projects and programs.

As a way of controlling the costs of appraisal, threshold setting has become the most popular approach to project appraisal in both developing and developed countries. In this appraisal approach, projects above a defined threshold should be subjected to rigorous appraisal and normally approved by a central agency. Box 4.5 presents the classification of projects subject to different methods of appraisal in Ireland. Threshold-based appraisal is considered a cost-effective way to avoid clogging the appraisal system, particularly where there is limited appraisal capacity, and to help raise the demand for appraisal at the central agencies.

Although applying size thresholds to the required depth of appraisal aims to use scarce analytical resources efficiently, some qualifiers to the threshold approach are well recognized:

- Programs may be formed out of many small or repeated investments (such as schools, health facilities, and road segments) such that the overall program may be large and above the appraisal limit whereas each individual project may be below the limit. Fragmentation of programs should not be used as

---

Box 4.5 Formal Project Appraisal in Ireland

The Irish Department of Finance has developed "Guidelines for the Appraisal and Management of Capital and Expenditure Proposals in the Public Sector" (Government of Ireland 2005). The guidelines specify the commensurate methods for appraisal depending largely on scales of proposed projects. In particular, it classifies five different groups of project proposals subject to different appraisal methodologies:

- A simple assessment should be carried out for minor projects with an estimated cost below €0.5 million, such as projects involving minor refurbishment works and fit-outs.
- Projects costing between €0.5 million and €5 million should be subject to a single appraisal incorporating elements of a preliminary and detailed appraisal.
- A multicriteria analysis should be carried out at minimum for projects of between €5 million and €30 million.
- A full-fledged CBA should be carried out on projects of over €30 million.
- A CBA is also applicable to innovative projects costing above €5 million that (a) involve complex or specialized issues or untried technology; (b) involve issues that have not been previously investigated in-depth; (c) are regarded as pilot projects on which larger programs may be modeled; or (d) would generate additional substantial ongoing operating or maintenance costs.

Source: Government of Ireland 2005.

---

a way of avoiding the application of project appraisal in the design and selection of the program.
- Repetition of similar investments should lower the costs of conducting subsequent project appraisals in two respects:
  - Detailed spreadsheets from an earlier appraisal can be reused with changes in the parameters for the new project.
  - Detailed analysis of a particular project (such as a school, hospital, road segment, or water system) reveals key parameters driving the NPV, given the cost structures in a country, such that these can be used to screen investments without necessarily doing a case-by-case appraisal of all projects. For example, cutoff demand levels can be established for the number of children in a district required to support a school of a particular size and type, the population size and density required to support a health or water facility, or the road traffic required to support the upgrading of a road segment.

Even though the threshold approach helps to significantly limit the number of full-fledged CBAs or CEAs to be conducted, full appraisal may still be infeasible, technically or politically, in low-income developing countries. In developing countries that fail to rely on the CBA due to both insufficient capacity and political will, some other approaches are being suggested such as benchmarking sector assets or service delivery capacity on some similar successful middle-income country (see, for example, Oxcarre 2010).[6] In general, the choice of project appraisal methodologies largely depends on both institutional capacity and demand for quality appraisal.

In aid-recipient countries, typically there exists a dual system of appraisal: (a) the government or domestic appraisal system applicable to government-financed public investments, and (b) the donor's system applicable to donor-financed projects. The World Bank, in particular, has used rigorous CBA since the early 1970s and is appraising its funded projects under the 1994 policy guidance titled "Economic Evaluation of Investment Operations." This guidance specifies that economic analysis is to be conducted for every investment project and that CEA is to be applied instead of CBA when the project is expected to generate benefits that cannot be measured in monetary terms (World Bank 1994).[7]

How the tasks required to identify, design, and appraise projects are organized and managed depends significantly on the organization of government and its agencies. Such impact on these tasks is covered in the next section, "Institutional Arrangements for Project Appraisal."

Special Approvals Critical to Feasibility of Project Completion

Aside from the possible requirement to conduct a general environmental impact assessment, projects may also need the following:

- Land access or allocation.
- Specific environmental approvals such as rights to clear forests or damage land as well as approvals about reforestation and land reclamation.
- Arrangements to offset major social externalities such as loss of property rights by indigenous people, resettlement costs, or job displacement.

In many countries and sectors, special approvals are critical to the realization of a project. It is imperative that these be sequenced in the appraisal and approval process to prevent major appraisal and real capital expenditures from being undertaken where subsequent delays or failures to obtain critical approvals result in major deferrals in completion or even abandonment of incomplete projects.

Institutional Arrangements for Project Appraisal

Core Public Sector Organization

In many governments, the ministries of finance and economic planning play key roles in project appraisal and capital budgeting. The scope and intensity of involvement can vary from a high degree of control and involvement in project planning and appraisal to one of coordination and oversight depending upon the degree of decentralization and performance budgeting and management being employed by a government.

In a government using traditional central planning approaches, the central economic agency tends to be highly active and dominant in project appraisal, particularly in cases where a dual budgeting system is followed, with the planning agency having a strong degree of control over the development or plan budget. Functional or service-delivery ministries are largely restricted to a project implementation and operational role, particularly if a government still has a public works department that undertakes or manages most of the construction phase of infrastructure projects.

Levels of Decentralization: Privatization, Corporatization, Concessions, and Regulation

At the other extreme, a government may decentralize much of the sector planning to the functional ministries or specialized agencies (such as a road or water authority), and the implementation or operation may involve a high level of private participation. Governments employ a range of different degrees and types of decentralization of investment and operational responsibilities:

- Privatization with regulation.[8]
- Private participation with a time-limited concession to build and operate public capital.[9]
- Private participation in the construction of a facility that is leased and operated for the government and revenue-financed through a contracted series of rental or availability payments to the private partner.[10]
- Contracting out of specific services such as construction, management, operation, or maintenance to a private contractor.
- Corporatizing a specific set of government functions.[11]

Subnational governments are assigned responsibility for certain functions or services to be financed out of some combination of their own source revenues and transfers of funds from a higher level of government. Subnational governments have varying degrees of freedom in capital budgeting prescribed by law or as conditions of the transfer of funds for their use.

All types of decentralization are typically designed to improve transparency and accountability for a specific set of service delivery functions to enhance the efficiency of performance. Typically decentralization also implies delegating a greater degree of responsibility for detailed planning and appraisal to the agency responsible for delivering the service. This should also imply that the agency has greater responsibility for collecting information about demand for and delivery of services as well as for planning, designing, and appraising projects to deliver services to meet current and expected excess demand. The information generated by the responsible agency about its plans and operations should be available to central agencies to ensure quality control, to monitor performance against targets, and to advise in the coordination of budget allocations across sectors over time.

A key empirical question is whether the greater degree of decentralization that many governments are employing in all aspects of their operations has led to improved use of project appraisal techniques and improved investment performance. Decentralization is expected to demand and allow greater transparency and accountability in service delivery in the responsible agency. The expectation, therefore, is that well-implemented decentralization strategies would lead to demand-driven performance improvements.

But decentralization is a double-edged knife. In PIM decentralization, subordination in the appraisal process can generate conflicts of interest and compromise the quality and validity of appraisal unless clear top-down priorities and guidelines are maintained. It is commonly observed (and reflected in country cases developed for this volume) that capacity cannot be of use in this context when appraisal is merely to support the ex ante selection of projects or programs by a sector or subnational agency.

Outsourcing of Project Appraisal
The actual conduct of project appraisal is often outsourced to private consulting businesses specializing in this work. This is in addition to contracting out project construction, the management of large construction projects, and specific functions in the operation of a project (maintenance, billing and collections, and so on)—practices that all have long histories.

Over recent decades, private participation has involved the private sector in both building and operating public infrastructure in exchange for a combination of fees charged to service users and grants or rental payments from the government. In all cases of contracting out to the private sector, greater efficiency is sought. Whether this is achieved, however, depends on the nature of the accountability and incentives in the contract and the quality of the contract oversight. In these cases, the private sector, of necessity, has to undertake its own appraisal of a project. In the procurement and contracting process, the government should get access to and review the project appraisal conducted by the private partner against its expectations for the project.

Outsourcing project appraisal to the private sector requires the following:

- Clear guidelines on the methodology have to be available to all parties. The private sector can be expected to minimize costs and satisfice; hence, the minimum standards for the conduct of appraisal have to be clear. In addition, the appraisal should always be constructed and transferred to the government in the form of spreadsheet models that the contracting agency can use for subsequent testing of assumptions and alternatives.
- The government officials overseeing the contract should gain a full understanding of the project appraisal and be able to modify the appraisal to test alternatives; to defend the results of the appraisal to budget decision makers; and to use the appraisal to conduct further steps of budgeting, procurement, implementation, and monitoring.

Donor-Agency, International, and Other Financial Institutions
Financial institutions providing major sources of debt financing to projects (whether public or private) with limited recourse or guarantees will either need

access to the project appraisal conducted by the sponsor or need to conduct their own project appraisal to determine the risks of default and, if necessary, place conditions on aspects of the project to mitigate their risks. This practice is common in regulated or self-financing sectors such as electricity, ports, toll roads, urban water, and transportation.

Official donor agencies, national development banks, and IFIs often expand the appraisal to also consider the economic and distributional consequences of a project. They appraise these aspects of a project and consider them in approving the provision of financing.

A key issue is the consistency and coordination of appraisal methodologies and content between governments, donor agencies, and IFIs. In many low-income developing countries—particularly where the donor agency or IFI may supply upward of 80 percent of the project financing—the government tends to rely on and not question the appraisal methodology and results, even though local people are the beneficiaries of project services and the loan and operating costs will ultimately need to be paid out of future government revenues. As with the use of contracted services to conduct project appraisal, if the government has access to the spreadsheet appraisal models developed by donor agencies or IFIs, it should have the capacity to understand and test these models and their assumptions as a key element in the design, approval, and budgeting of the project.

Challenges in Project Appraisal

A number of problems in project selection and implementation result from poor project appraisal, defeating its core objectives—primarily to stop bad projects and to help good projects be selected.

"White Elephant" Projects

These are high-capital-cost projects with grossly negative social rates of return. Such projects should be screened out at or before the prefeasibility stage. Otherwise, powerful political interests can circumvent an approval process or hide the project in the budget where there is a weak appraisal and approval system.

Three types of white elephant projects can be identified:

- *Excess-capacity infrastructure,* such as a road or airport with little or no traffic demand. Operation and maintenance (O&M) still has to be funded. These projects can arise through a combination of investment payoffs to a small number of powerful beneficiaries, typically local politicians or contractors.

- *Capital investment that is completed but for which little or no O&M funding is available* over its operating life such that minimal services are delivered relative to its potential capacity. Examples are hospitals or schools without adequate professional staff and supplies. These situations can arise where

(a) donor agencies fund the capital investment, but completely inadequate budget provision is made for the O&M, or (b) corrupt motivations exist to provide short-term contract and job benefits without negative consequences for the lack of long-term service delivery. Dual budgeting with a high degree of separation of capital budget decision making from current budget decision making makes underfunded O&M more likely. If recurrent funding is not part of the approval process, it may even be omitted from the appraisal.

- *Capital investment that is never completed and is abandoned,* such as incomplete bridges, houses, buildings, and so forth. Typically, these projects are motivated by corrupt access to contract funds where there is no effective oversight and accountability in the administration of contracts or subsequent use of the capital assets. They also arise where there is a change in political regime, and the new regime abandons long-gestation projects started by the old regime, or the current regime is powerful enough to publicly abandon projects only built for corrupt payoffs.

These project abandonment problems can be limited by (a) a strong appraisal and approval process; (b) the involvement of external financial institutions with a stake in the performance of the project; and (c) the use of variable length authorization and appropriation of funding. If the funding is fully authorized and appropriated up front in legislation, then the initiation of the investment project requires explicit commitment, and attractive projects are more likely to get approval. In addition, the abandonment or reversal of the project requires explicit legislative action and not merely a failure to appropriate or spend budgeted funds.

Delayed Construction or Too Many Overbudgeted Projects

Studies of infrastructure projects internationally show major problems with cost and time overruns and benefit overestimations (such as overestimating future road and rail traffic). The Construction Sector Transparency Initiative (CoST) spearheads an international effort to achieve greater transparency and accountability in public sector construction.[12] Results based on the United Kingdom and seven developing economies show significant problems of cost and time overruns. Another study of 256 major infrastructure projects in 20 countries showed significant biases and variance in estimation of costs and benefits, with average cost overruns of around 44.7 percent for rail, 33.8 percent for bridges and tunnels, and 20.4 percent for roads (Flyvbjerg 2007). These and other problems arise from a range of technical and institutional factors.

Construction phases of projects are longer than planned because of

- Poor design and planning, poor selection of contractor, procurement delays, or poor contract completion incentives or oversight; and
- Failure to get prior approvals or arrange special approvals for land, mineral rights, environmental damage, or social resettlements.

The Power of Public Investment Management • http://dx.doi.org/10.1596/978-1-4648-0316-1

Moreover, weak capital budgeting selection and approval processes lead to overloaded capital budgets that spread funding across too many projects, such that each underfunded project takes longer than planned. This situation arises from political pressures to have projects included in a budget as well as deliberate understatement of total capital costs or revealing only the initial-year costs but not the remaining total costs. As a result, project benefits are delayed and often overall costs rise, thereby reducing the final net benefits of the projects.

Poor Performance in the Operational Phase
Poor service delivery from a project (despite a successfully completed construction phase) can arise from the following:

- Poor technical design.
- Poor performance incentives, targets, monitoring, or oversight.
- A lack of budgeted funds to provide for O&M, which can arise from dual or short-term budgeting or a bias toward capital investment by donor agencies despite inadequate recurrent revenues.

The poor project appraisal, in turn, reflects a number of institutional and technical issues in a specific country's political and economic context: lack of statistical data and reliable forecasting models; lack of centrally established, uniform guidelines; lack of capacity; and lack of demand for high-quality project appraisal.

Lack of Excess-Demand Data and Forecasting Models
The lack of service delivery demand and supply data is often related to weak or no performance budgeting and management by service delivery ministries or agencies. Alternatively, a lack of demand for service delivery information at the center leads to weak or absent service delivery monitoring units within line ministries or agencies. Ideally, a demand modeling and forecasting capacity, either in central or in sector agencies, should also exist to assess future gaps in service delivery.

This lack of current or future service delivery information has serious consequences:

- There is lack of technical capacity to identify service gaps and the impact or benefits of expanded services.
- This, in turn, limits the ability to identify priorities and plans for both current and strategic budgets.
- It also limits the ability to conduct either CEA or CBA in the appraisal of projects and programs that depend critically on the estimates of demand for the project or program services.
- There is more random and idiosyncratic project selection.

In the extreme, "parachute projects" can circumvent the appraisal system because of a lack of objective information on service supply and demand to identify potential projects. This can undermine public sector economic performance if these projects are large and provide services with low demand—a major new road that attracts little traffic, for example.

Lack of Guidelines or Conflicting Guidelines

Failure by central agencies of government to issue project appraisal guidelines means that there is no effective or consistent external scrutiny of the project selection process and even no need to conduct good-quality appraisal. The more decentralized the operations of a government become, the more evident the problem, given that line ministries, regulators, public authorities, aid agencies, financial institutions, private partners, private contractors, and others are all involved in designing and appraising projects. All ministries and agencies should be following the same fundamental methodology incorporating consistent appraisal parameters to get consistent and comparable results.

The training of staff and consultants to conduct project appraisal depends upon the methods being explicitly stated and widely available. Availability of guidelines should also be supplemented with training, as needed.

Lack of Capacity

Three types of missing technical capacity negatively affect the sound application of project appraisal in capital budgeting:

- Capacity to collect and forecast demand for public services, particularly in sectors where services are provided as public goods without charge. (See also the "Lack of Excess-Demand Data and Forecasting Models" subsection above.)
- Capacity to conduct project appraisal, including the estimation of economic prices and costs of key resources such as capital, foreign exchange, and labor. A high-level technical unit in the central economic planning agency should be responsible for providing or overseeing economic methods and estimates.
- Capacity by decision makers to use project appraisal in project design, selection, and budgeting.

Lack of Demand for High-Quality Project Appraisal

Politicians and bureaucrats at all levels of government have a range of objectives in the pursuit of investment spending. In addition, public investment spending should be viewed, ultimately, both as a channel to potentially create productive assets and as a vehicle for distributing rents for political purposes. Given the prevailing political economy of a specific country, careful attention needs to be given to potentially increasing the demand side for better public investment in general and for project appraisal in particular (Barma, Kaiser, and Le 2011). It is worth noting that capacity building without successfully creating demand for high-quality project appraisal, currently or within the medium term, is by itself a wasteful investment.

If decision makers are not accountable to the legislature, taxpayers, voters, or civil society, then low-quality projects can enter the budget because there is no explicit opportunity cost of displacing high-quality projects evident to the legis-lature or public. Political decision makers resort to, or are allowed to use, input-oriented budgeting (budgeting for jobs, contracts, licenses, and so on) rather than output-oriented budgeting (budgeting to enhance service delivery) if there is a lack of performance information and evaluation and if there is a lack of transpar-ency and accountability in the project design, appraisal, approval, and budgeting process.

Lack of transparency in budgeting arises where the public investment plan is not published and project appraisal documents are not available for professional review and ideally for public information. This also limits the capacity of the legislature, either as a whole or through sector-specific over-sight committees, to hold the ministries and agencies accountable. If the legislature has limited access to budgeting information, then the taxpayers, voters, and civil society in general are equally limited and cannot effectively pressure their political representatives to ensure good project selection and implementation.

An added dimension to the lack of demand can also arise from decision mak-ers' lack of capacity to know how to use good project appraisal results in selecting and budgeting projects. Again, the incentive to gain this capacity is also driven by the demands of political accountability.

Actions for Improved Project Appraisal

There are important interdependencies, overlaps, feedbacks, and synergies between the stages of the project and budget cycles (as shown in figure 4.1) so that improvement in any one stage (such as project appraisal) depends upon and affects performance of other stages: the system is greater than the sum of its parts. These considerations are important in considering how to improve project appraisal and the overall PIM system. The interdependen-cies between the cycles and PIM stages affect considerations of sequencing and whether multiple interventions are needed to achieve the desired synergies.

The history of budget reforms internationally also shows that budget reform is a slow and continuous process. This slow pace of improvement arises in any slow-moving cycle in which overall good performance requires a full cycle of good performance at all stages to be completed. It also arises because getting feedback from a later stage such as ex post project evaluation to educate the conduct of ex ante design, costing, and appraisal requires more than one cycle to be completed. This is aside from the delays caused by the time it takes to train staff and to change organizations and operating procedures for good capital budgeting.

In recommending actions below to improve the role of capital budgeting in a government from "poor" to "good enough" practice (given the resource and capacity constraints of a government at a point in time), issues of sequencing, interdependencies, and synergies are kept in mind.

Figure 4.1 Interdependencies, Overlaps, Feedbacks, and Synergies of Budget and Project Cycles

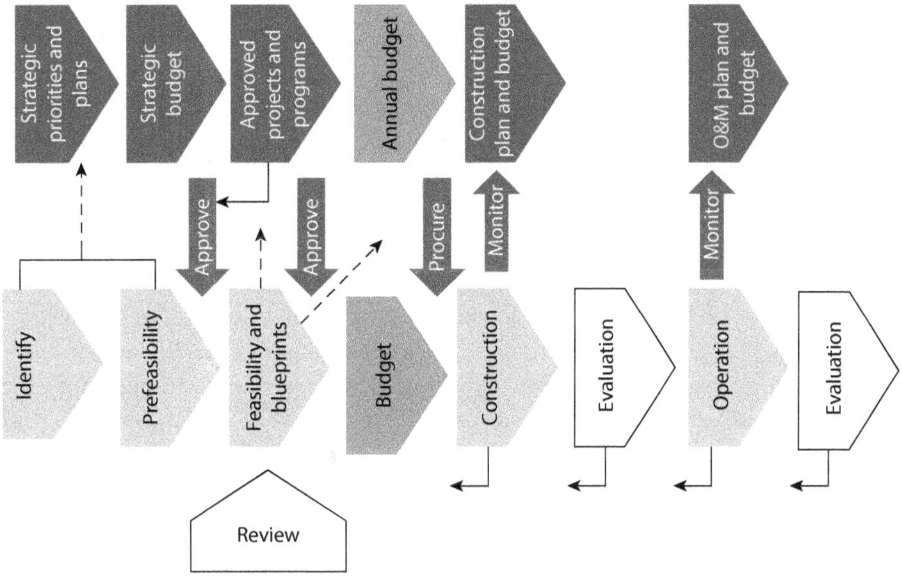

Note: O&M = operation and maintenance.

Some rough prioritization is also considered in the recommendations below, starting from the most important. There are three key areas for improvement: (a) creating demand for improved project appraisal; (b) strengthening key stages of the project cycle; and (c) reforming the budget system to support project appraisal and capital budgeting.

Strong Demand for Project Appraisal by Key Decision Makers

Whether good project appraisal is conducted depends critically on whether key politicians and officials (particularly in the ministries of finance and economic planning) demand it before any project is approved and budgeted. The fine points of sophisticated appraisal techniques embedded in full-fledged CBA or CEA are often trumped by crude vested interests.

The only reasonable constraint on biased interference is some institutionally robust arrangement of project evaluation and approval as part of a broader approach to budget formulation and management. Transparency of (a) the appraisal process integrated into the budgeting process, and (b) the respective findings (or independent review) can be important checks and balances on politically motivated project selection. Depending on the governance context of a country, such arrangements may involve the creation of some authority with a gatekeeper mandate to stop bad projects.

In the context of decentralized project appraisal, central agencies may have aligned interests in raising their role in PIM, which cuts across different stages of PIM. Moreover, during implementation, regular monitoring of projects and some relatively simple measure of project completion and operation would help discipline the incentives for ministries and departments to treat the capital budget as an entitlement that must be maximized without reference to the actual creation of physical assets and their eventual effective operation and maintenance.

No process is foolproof, and in an overly challenging governance environment, such robust restraint may not be politically feasible or may be likely to be compromised in some way. In many other situations, however, it could prove effective to at least mitigate the risk of gross abuse of the capital budget.

Strengthening Capital Budgeting to Yield Positive Synergies

Improve service delivery and demand information. This information is critical to identifying the excess demand for services to inform the prioritization of projects for strategic budgeting and to estimate the impacts and net benefits in conducting project appraisal. This effort should also include the building of sector demand forecasting models and the related training of officials. Generally, the promotion of performance budgeting and management in a more decentralized organization of government operations should help to enhance the availability of service supply and demand information.

Strengthen the capacity to conduct project appraisal. It is important to recognize that project appraisal training becomes effective only if the officers trained can work in a budget system that demands and supports the use of project appraisal as a tool to identify, design, and select projects. Budget decision makers should also be capable of using and demanding the decision-making information that project appraisal methods can potentially supply. Capacity building needs to viewed and conducted in the broad context of building the capacity of both people and the budget system, including how the latter integrates into the legislative side of budget formulation and oversight.

Publish guidelines on the conduct of project appraisal. The adoption and publication of project appraisal guidelines is key to gaining consistent standards for conducting project appraisals. Special guidelines may exist for (a) the appraisal of public-private partnerships and investments in price-regulated sectors; (b) the conduct of ex post project evaluations; and (c) special sectors, such as health services. These guidelines need to be part of an overall set of budget guidelines that would cover all stages of the capital and overall budget system. A government needs to require use of project appraisal guidelines by all parties including government agencies, consultants, and donor agencies. It also needs to specify the formats of reports and spreadsheets used in the project appraisal so that these can be transferred to the reviewing, approving, or budgeting agency or unit for their use.

Establish a review process for project appraisal. A professional unit in an external organization should act as a peer review group for the units conducting project appraisal on a selective or random basis. A peer review unit should be in the central ministries to review work in the line ministries and agencies, but there should also be a unit outside of government in a university or research organization that can provide quality control on the conduct of project appraisal.

Note that this peer review is in addition to the accountability mechanisms that should be fostered to encourage political decision makers to select good projects based on good-quality designs and appraisals. Box 4.6 presents two different practices in Belarus and Ireland. The Gateway review process for programs and projects in the United Kingdom is another example of independent peer review. The case study of the Republic of Korea describes the role of the Public and Private Infrastructure Investment Management Center (PIMAC) in the Korea Development Institute in reviewing and conducting preliminary feasibility studies of projects developed by line ministries for the Ministry of Strategy and Finance before they are approved for detailed feasibility studies and blueprint designs.

Strengthen project implementation monitoring. The monitoring of the construction and implementation phases of projects is critical to ensure efficient project implementation and sufficient funding of the planned project, but it also feeds back information to the project design and appraisal stages on the unit costs, sources of delay, and other aspects that will educate the design and appraisal of new projects.

Strengthen project evaluation. Ex post evaluation of projects upon completion of construction phases and after a period of operations is the ultimate audit of project performance and the quality of the ex ante appraisal. This evaluation

---

Box 4.6 Independent Review of Appraisal in Belarus and Ireland

Belarus

The State Appraisal Agency (SAA) was established with a mandate to appraise all public investment projects. It charges a fee of 5–10 percent of project preparation costs to the implementing agency. The agency consists of about 70 senior experts on construction and other capital investment. In most cases, the agency provides its appraisal result within 30 days. With sufficient resources available from fees charged to the proposal-submitting agencies, the SAA has managed to recruit highly qualified technical professionals and has provided extensive training to ensure appraisal quality. The agency claims that about $300 million was saved by its review in 2006.

Ireland

The Department of Finance requires that line departments involve external review in their appraisal. Agencies are allowed to carry out their CBA in-house, but they have to commission outside experts to review the results of their appraisals. For example, the Department of Transport now engages professional companies to carry out audits of compliance with the Department of Finance guidelines and audits of progress in project implementation. The projects to be audited are selected by the department's Investment Monitoring Group. The auditors engaged are required to submit detailed reports of all audits carried out, setting out their findings and making recommendations where appropriate.

Sources: Cho 2008; Ferris 2009.

---

educates future project identification, design, and appraisal in the most complete fashion. Ideally, it should be conducted by a separate or independent group with strong capacity in project appraisal.

Budget System Reforms to Support Project Appraisal and Capital Budgeting

Some of the key budget system reforms that facilitate the increased demand for quality project appraisal and capital budgeting include the following:

Improved transparency in the capital budget. At a minimum, a public investment plan needs to be included with annual budgets. The plan should give enough detail of budgeted projects and their costs to allow review by a legislature, taxpayers, voters, and civil society. Ideally, summary or complete project appraisals could be made available on a website. Transparency of the decision-making process enhances the accountability of the decision makers.

Strict adherence to project approval rules. Rules need to be made concerning which types and sizes of projects need to go through more- or less-thorough project appraisal. The appraisal methods should be laid out in guidelines. The rules should pay special attention to (a) the projects requiring special approvals, especially dealing with land acquisition, environmental impacts, and social disruptions; and (b) the arrangements for funding the O&M of projects and the long-term sources of such funds. The approvals required need to be specified and the procedures followed.

Performance budgeting. Implementing performance budgeting and management processes in service delivery ministries and agencies should enhance service-delivery information flows. These practices benefit the prioritization of projects and programs and their costing and appraisals. They also strengthen the accountability of managers in designing, appraising, selecting, and implementing projects and programs in these ministries and agencies.

Variable length authorization and appropriations for major projects. The introduction of variable length authorizations and appropriations into budgets has the benefit of focusing attention at the start of a project on its scope and scale such that (a) decisions to initiate the project are taken with due diligence; and (b) once the project has been initiated, it receives the planned flows of funds to assist its timely completion and operation. They should also be used in the context of any budget support required for long-term concessions or leases.

Medium-term or strategic budgets. The implementation of medium-term or strategic budgets helps to put a focus on the longer-term funding requirements of projects. It also demands a pipeline of projects and programs with increased information about their economic impacts, benefits, and costs in order to develop the priorities for a strategic development or capital budget. The transparency of this process tends to enhance the accountability pressures for better project design, appraisal, and selection.

Integrated budgets. Where dual budgets are used with the development budget under a separate agency, reforms need to be implemented to coordinate the approval of projects and programs with the ministry of finance to ensure the long-term financial viability of public projects. In addition, any long-term funding commitments for projects, concessions, leases, and so forth should be included in the ministry of finance budget. Over time, the development or planning agency should be integrated into the ministry of finance—particularly where a greater degree of decentralization of service delivery is being used in the government—as a first step toward full integration of the development and recurrent budgets.

Notes

1. "Program" in the context of public investment refers to a program of similar or related investments such as may occur with expanding the investment in education, health facilities, or training programs rather than one isolated, possibly large, infrastructure investment project.

2. The more systematic the sector project identification process is in a government, the fewer bad projects should actually enter the prefeasibility stage where formal budget approvals start.

3. For a summary of theory and international practice of estimating discount rates for project appraisal, see Zhuang et al. (2007). For a more in-depth treatment of discount rates, see Burgess and Jenkins (2010).

4. Where costs or benefits are excluded, the NPV gives the room available to absorb the omitted cost if it is positive or the price of the omitted benefit if it is negative. For example, in a project designed to benefit a poor target group, if the NPV is negative and the project goes ahead, this becomes a measure of the economic cost of transferring the benefit and can be compared with the amount of benefit received by the poor.

5. Basic needs externality is an estimate of what other members of a society are willing to pay to increase the consumption level by a low-income group of some basic-need commodity or merit good (food, water, shelter, and so on). This is an efficiency gain rather than the application of a distributional weight.

6. OxCarre (2010, 5–6) recommends that low-income countries, especially those with the potential for rapid transformation financed by natural resource wealth, establish their own view of the future structure of the public capital stock based on some credible models from successful middle-income countries. From there, countries would establish benchmarks for "important unknowns" such as energy demand; road, rail, and air traffic; and enrollment in tertiary education—ultimately establishing the guiding principles for public investment selection. In this type of arrangement, CBA can be used to complement the information from international benchmarking, guiding project choices within each sector or investment category.

7. The World Bank's Independent Evaluation Group has recently evaluated the use of CBA in Bank-funded investment operations. It finds that the use of CBA has declined in the Bank and raises a number of concerns about the rigor of appraisal (World Bank 2010).

8. Sectors such as electricity and telecommunications have been decentralized to the degree that capital investment decisions are fully privatized but the market is regulated to deal with the natural monopoly issues. These arrangements are referred to as Build Own Operate.

9. Each concession has to be contracted and negotiated with private partners and overseen by some regulator. Typically, such concessions are self-financing through charges

on the public for the use of service such as in the case of a toll road or sea or airport facility. Where the concession is not fully self-financing, some viability gap funding is provided. These arrangements are referred to as Build Own Operate Transfer.

10. This arrangement tends to occur with the provision of buildings for various purposes: offices, schools, health facilities, or residences for a health or educational facility. These arrangements are referred to as Build Lease Transfer.

11. A corporate entity or authority is established to serve a specific set of functions such as revenue collection, national statistics, central banking, road construction or maintenance, water supply, or air or seaport services. The corporation could be financed fully by budget revenues or these could be supplemented by charges for its services. The corporation would have a legislated degree of autonomy in its decision making (including capital budgeting), but it would be subject to performance targets and oversight from its parent ministry.

12. For methods and results of CoST, see http://www.constructiontransparency.org/.

Bibliography

Australian Government. 2006. *Handbook on Benefit-Cost Analysis*. Canberra: Department of Finance and Administration.

Barma, Naazneen, Kai Kaiser, and Tuan Minh Le. 2011. *Rents to Riches? The Political Economy of Natural Resource-Led Development*. Washington, DC: World Bank.

Belli, Pedro. 1996. *Handbook on Economic Analysis of Investment Operations*. Washington, DC: World Bank.

Belli, Pedro, Jock R. Anderson, Howard N. Barnum, John A. Dixon, and Jee-Peng Tan. 2001. *Economic Analysis of Investment Operations: Analytical Tools and Practical Applications*. WBI (World Bank Institute) Development Series. Washington, DC: World Bank.

Burgess, David F., and Glenn P. Jenkins, eds. 2010. *Discount Rates for the Evaluation of Public Private Partnerships*. Kingston, ON: McGill Queen's University Press.

Cho, Junghun. 2008. "Public Investment in Belarus: A Case Study Applying the Framework for Reviewing Public Investment Efficiency." Unpublished manuscript, World Bank, Washington, DC.

Dasgupta, Partha, Stephen Marglin, and Amarrya K. Sen. 1972. *Guidelines for Project Evaluation*. New York: United Nations Industrial Development Organization.

EC (European Commission). 2006. "Guidance on the Methodology for Carrying Out Cost-Benefit Analysis." Working Document 4, Directorate-General for Regional Policy, EC, Brussels.

———. 2008. *Guide to Cost-Benefit Analysis of Investment Projects*. Final report, Directorate-General for Regional Policy, Brussels.

Ferris, Thomas. 2009. "Public Investment Management in Ireland." Unpublished manuscript, World Bank, Washington, DC.

Flyvbjerg, Bent. 2007. "Policy and Planning for Large-Infrastructure Projects: Problems, Causes, Cures". *Environment and Planning B: Planning and Design* 34: 578–97.

Government of Canada. 2007. "Canadian Cost-Benefit Analysis Guide." Catalogue BT58-5/2007, Treasury Board of Canada Secretariat, Ottawa.

Government of Ireland. 2005. "Guidelines for the Appraisal and Management of Capital and Expenditure Proposals in the Public Sector." Department of Finance, Dublin. http://www.finance.gov.ie/documents/publications/other/capappguide05.pdf.

Government of New Zealand. 2005. "Cost Benefit Analysis Primer." New Zealand Treasury, Wellington. http://www.treasury.govt.nz/publications/guidance/planning/costbenefitanalysis/primer.

Graham, John R., and Campell R Harvey. 2002. "How Do CFOs Make Capital Budgeting and Capital Structure Decisions?" *Journal of Applied Corporate Finance* 15 (1): 8–53.

Harberger, Arnold C. 1971. "Three Basic Postulates for Applied Welfare Economics." *Journal of Economic Literature* 9 (3): 785–97. Reprinted in A.C. Harberger, *Taxation and Welfare*, Little Brown, 1974.

———. 1972. *Project Evaluation: Collected Papers*. New York: MacMillan.

HM Treasury, United Kingdom. 2003. *The Green Book: Appraisal and Evaluation in Central Government*. London: HMSO.

Jenkins, Glenn P., Chun-Yan, Kuo, and Arnold C. Harberger. 2011. "Cost-Benefit Analysis for Investment Decisions." Development Discussion Paper 2011-08, JDI Executive Programs, Queen's University, Kingston, Canada.

Little, I. M. David, and James A. Mirrlees 1969. *Manual of Industrial Project Analysis in Developing Countries*. Development Centre Studies. Paris: Organisation for Economic Co-operation and Development.

———. 1974. *Project Appraisal and Planning*. London: Heinemann.

OxCarre (Oxford Centre for the Analysis of Resource Rich Economies). 2010. "Natural Resource Charter, Precept 9: Efficiency and Equity of Public Spending. Technical Guide." OxCarre, Deparament of Economics, University of Oxford. http://naturalresourcecharter.org/sites/default/files/Precept%209.pdf.

Rajaram, Anand, Tuan Minh Le, Nataliya Biletska, and Jim Brumby. 2010. "A Diagnostic Framework for Assessing Public Investment Management." Policy Research Working Paper 5397, World Bank, Washington, DC.

Sjaastad, Larry A., and Daniel Wisecarver. 1977. "The Social Cost of Public Funds." *Journal of Political Economy* 85 (3): 513–47.

Squire, Lyn, and Herman G. van der Tak. 1975. *Economic Analysis of Projects*. Baltimore, MD: John Hopkins University Press for The World Bank.

USAID (U.S. Agency for International Development). 2008. *Project Appraisal Manual and Guidelines*. Volume 5 of the *Reform Project Compendium with Toolkit: A User's Guide to State Fiscal Management Reform*. Washington, DC: USAID.

U.S. OMB (U.S. Office of Management and Budget). 1992. "Guidelines and Discount Rates for Benefit-Cost Analysis of Federal Programs." Circular A-94, OMB, Washington, DC. http://www.whitehouse.gov/omb/circulars_a094/.

World Bank. 1994. "Economic Evaluation of Investment Operations." Operational Policy (OP) 10.04, World Bank, Washington, DC.

———. 2010. "Cost-Benefit Analysis in World Bank Projects." Fast Track Brief, Independent Evaluation Group (IEG), World Bank, Washington, DC.

Zhuang, Juzhong, Zhihong Liang, Tun Lin, and Franklin De Guzman . 2007. "Theory and Practice in the Choice of Social Discount Rate for Cost-Benefit Analysis: A Survey." ERD Working Paper 94, Asian Development Bank, Manila.

CHAPTER 5

Public Investment Management under Uncertainty

Introduction

Mainstream analysis of public investment management is geared toward immediate implementation of projects. Performance measures are often couched in terms of speed of implementation. In fact, cost and time overruns are crucial factors for efficiency in resource use and effectiveness of investment programs. Highlighted by a score of examples in country cases, projects need to be implemented as quickly as possible to avoid the physical deterioration implied in stop-and-go construction—and, above all, to minimize the opportunity cost for the use of resources for other socially beneficial investments.

All these well-founded principles are based on the assumption of certainty—in, among others, the availability of funding, the technical capacity and possibility to actually construct and implement projects, and also the climatic conditions. All eight steps of PIM in the Rajaram et al. (2010) framework assume a reasonable degree of certainty.

But how is PIM affected under uncertainty and risk? In an economically more globalized world, uncertainty is an important ingredient, particularly with regard to finance and availability of resources. Another important factor is climate change. Although its effects are already a reality and have direct and visible impacts around the globe, the specific scope and level of effects are still uncertain: the intensity, timing, geographic coverage, and frequency of extreme events in the future are currently still highly speculative, especially regarding outcomes at the local level.

This chapter uses the example of climate change to illustrate how the process of public investment is affected, and how it would need to be structured, to factor in the phenomenon of uncertainty. Given the uncertainties associated with key variables such as temperature and rainfall as well as the interactions between them, it is more than likely that their future effect will be underestimated or overestimated at various stages over the next century. Under scenarios of uncertain speed in events associated with climate change, countries may engage in premature or excessive adaptation; they may procrastinate unduly or adapt inadequately; or they may engage in maladaptation regarding the quality and nature of the specific measures that can be taken. Climate change is therefore a valid example to illustrate aspects of uncertainty in the project cycle.

It is not the purpose of this chapter to inform the reader about the phenomenon of climate change or any specific adaptation measures—although to the extent that weather patterns are already changing, it would be negligent of governments to avoid considering what policies and measures may be required to adapt to the new conditions. Climate change serves as a relevant example that already has significant impact on many of the investments in countries and, as a cross-sectoral issue, is particularly well suited to highlight the challenges of project management under uncertainty. Countries around the world are already spending substantial amounts of resources related to climate change: they are likely to spend between $70 billion and $100 billion (in 2005 prices) annually to the middle of the 21st century (World Bank 2010a). As will be discussed further below, uncertainty deriving from climate change affects all sectors, whether they involve roads, bridges, health, or education, among others. Without delving deeper into sector-specific arrangements, the lessons of this analysis are, however, relevant for all types of uncertainty, whether economic, fiscal, or political.

The chapter is structured as follows:

- "Understanding the Phenomenon of Risk and Uncertainty" discusses four possibilities of risk and uncertainty derived from the "knowns" and "unknowns."
- "Popular Risk Assessment Methods" discusses several risk assessment methods and their advantages as well as shortcomings. Importantly, it proposes how cost-benefit analysis can be structured to incorporate uncertainties into the economic appraisal.
- "Examples of Real Options" provides approaches that exploit the opportunity to delay full implementation of an adaptation measure until better information becomes available. These examples are intended to stimulate further thought about possibilities rather than being definitive guides to action.
- "Public Investment Management under Uncertainty" summarizes the fundamental changes in the project cycle related to uncertainty.
- "Final Considerations" summarizes the recommendations of the chapter.

Understanding the Phenomenon of Risk and Uncertainty

Uncertainty is itself hard to define. Knight ([1921] 2009, 9, 121) distinguishes between risk and uncertainty. Risk involves events whose outcome is identifiable, and the probability distribution underlying them is known. Uncertainty, on the other hand, refers to situations where the outcomes are also known, but the probability model is "unmeasurable" and unknown.

In the case of climate change, we have little or no experience of likely outcomes. It is possible to form guesstimates of some possibilities, such as the effect of increased temperatures, but entirely unforeseen events may also occur.

Because they are unpredictable, it is not possible to even identify such events, let alone attach probabilities to them, so they are wrapped in uncertainty. For this reason, the classical Knightian definition of uncertainty is inadequate.

One approach to thinking more broadly about uncertainty is to draw on a schema such as the one presented in table 5.1. The categorization of risk and uncertainty shown is only illustrative and should not be taken to represent a definitive taxonomy.

Quadrant I: "Known Unknowns"

This situation is analogous to Knightian uncertainty. The event and its consequences are generally understood, but there is little or no knowledge of the probability of occurrence. Technical specialists generally have some idea of possible effects that can be categorized as "known unknowns." Because they are not fully certain, potential events in this category can be regarded as representing "uncertainty" for all practical purposes.

It is usually possible to adopt contingency measures of some sort to deal with major issues and problems that might reasonably be expected to occur in this category of Knightian uncertainty. However, there is a risk that any planning or instituted measures can be excessive, premature, inadequate, misdirected, or implemented too late. Because any miscalculation can result in undue cost, a methodology is required that can reduce such fiscal risks (see the "real options" section below).

An example of a "known unknown" might be the following:

• Scientific evidence exists connecting higher sea temperatures to cyclones, but there is uncertainty as to the magnitude of any increase in frequency of future cyclones (see, for example, IPCC 2012, 160).

Quadrant II: "Known Knowns"

Where a reasonable degree of knowledge exists about the likelihood and consequences of events, the incidence of costs and benefits is also likely to be reasonably well identified. The situation is akin to Knightian "risk." In such cases, it is

Table 5.1 A Synoptic Perspective of Climate-Change Risk and Uncertainty

	Known consequence or probability	Unknown consequence or probability
Known event	II. "Known knowns" (For example, increased local temperatures for longer periods will affect crop cycles.)	I. "Known unknowns" (For example, rising ocean temperatures may increase the intensity of cyclones, but the frequency of occurrence is not known.)
Unknown event	III. "Unknown knowns" (For example, an indigenous person knows of a rare pest that will thrive in a warmer climate but has not told the responsible authorities about it.)	IV. "Unknown unknowns" ([ex post only] For example, sewer pipes have been corroded due to reduced water flow in adaptation to drought.)

possible to employ conventional discounted cash flow techniques when undertaking economic appraisals of projects that include some allowance for climate-
change effects.

Examples of "known knowns" might include the following:

- Local crop cycles will change with increased temperatures.
- Such changes have already been observed in various locations (for example,
  Shi et al. 2006; Yang et al. 2007), with farmers being able to plant crops earlier,
  fruiting periods lasting longer, and so on.

Quadrant III: "Unknown Knowns"

Other scenarios shown in table 5.1 are less certain. There might be awareness
and knowledge in some individuals, but not in others, as in these examples:

- This category is probably closest to Taleb's (2007) example of social opacity
  where Europeans were not aware of the existence of black swans until several
  hundred years ago, but indigenous Australians and probably Malay, Chinese
  (Menzies 2002), and other traders knew of them.[1]
- Officials or technical specialists may be generally unaware that a rare pest
  will emerge and thrive in a warmer climate, but an isolated farmer or an
  indigenous person may know from experience that a serious problem is likely
  to occur.

Quadrant IV: "Unknown Unknowns"

By definition, the category of "unknown unknowns" represents total ex ante
ignorance, being revealed only after an event has occurred. For practical
purposes, the "unknown unknowns" category is taken to mean events that
would not normally be actively perceived, even by those who might have been
expected to know.[2]

Examples of "unknown unknowns" might include the following:

- The outbreaks of the human immunodeficiency virus and acquired immune
  deficiency syndrome (HIV/AIDS) in the late 1960s and the virulent ebola
  virus in 1976 appear to have been unexpected and largely unpredictable. They
  could therefore be considered to be examples of "unknown unknowns." On
  the other hand, it is at least arguable that pandemics are not a new phenomenon, even if they take different or new forms.[3]
- In agriculture, an "unknown unknown" could be the sudden devastation of
  European vineyards in the mid-19th century by the grape phylloxera aphid,
  although it might also be argued that human experience of introduced pests
  make this more of an "unknown known."
- A better example of an "unknown unknown" is the sudden emergence in 1986
  in the United Kingdom of mad cow disease (bovine spongiform encephalopa-
  thy, or BSE), apparently due to prion proteins in animal by-product feed given
  to cattle.

Popular Risk Assessment Methods

Incorporating risk into public investment is challenging. A first step is to select a risk assessment method that allows analysts to structure adequate responses.

It bears noting that events in quadrant III ("unknown knowns") of table 5.1, and especially quadrant IV ("unknown unknowns"), are revealed or become generally known only after the fact. (The example of Melbourne's sewers is particularly insightful [see box 5.1].) Hence standard techniques for dealing with significant uncertainty are not suitable. In turn, conventional cost-benefit analysis can be used to evaluate "known knowns" (quadrant II), while "real options" can be applied to augment conventional cost-benefit analysis to account for the uncertainties of quadrant I ("known unknowns").

Unsurprisingly, there is little consensus on how the issue of uncertainty should be addressed for the appraisal of public investments. However, three major techniques have become popular: (a) multicriteria analysis, (b) cost-effectiveness analysis, and (c) cost-benefit analysis.

Multicriteria Analysis

Multicriteria analysis can take various forms and names, but the underlying methodology used invariably resembles the simplified approach illustrated in table 5.2. It is used to aggregate the contributions of a selected set of attributes or criteria to the achievement of an overall objective or project.[4]

Box 5.1 Dealing with an "Unknown Unknown" in Public Investment: The Example of Melbourne's Sewers

Melbourne's sewers were designed with specific gradients to operate at a certain flow rate. Although the design engineers may have been aware of some risk at the time, there does not seem to have been any general anticipation of the possibility that water saving campaigns due to a prolonged drought or climate change would have the unintended consequence of reducing flow rates below minimal "self-cleaning" transmission velocities. The unforeseen outcome of greater deposition of biological matter has been an "increased ... risk of sewer corrosion [from hydrogen sulphide gas buildup] and odours due to more concentrated and warmer sewage" (Melbourne Water 2011).

The possibility of greater deposition may well have been appreciated by design engineers who assumed a certain flow rate. However, it is less likely that they would also have considered the further possibility of corrosion from the production of hydrogen sulphide gas due to more concentrated and warmer sewage. The outcome of corrosion could therefore be classified as an "unknown unknown" that bears some relationship to climatic conditions.

Table 5.2 A Simplified Multicriteria Analysis: Hypothetical Dike Building Project

Attribute (criterion)	Units	Impact	Score (−4 to +4)	Weight (%)	Weighted score
Additional rice crop each year	Kilograms	13,000	2	10	20
Easier planning of production	—	—	4	40	160
Reduction in people drowned	Number	4	3	10	30
Employment	Jobs	23	3	20	60
Cost of project	$	89 million	−4	20	−80
Total				100	190

Note: — = not applicable.

The first step in a multicriteria analysis is the selection by an analyst or policy maker of a range of attributes or impacts considered to be relevant to the issue at hand. In table 5.2, the hypothetical analyst has chosen to represent the construction of a flood-proof dike. Increased production, easier planning by the local authorities, reduced drownings, and increased employment prospects are seen as the main benefits. Where the cost of the project is included, the scoring scale generally needs to include a negative quantity.

In the next step, each of the selected attributes is given a score (usually on the basis of an ordinal Likert scale[5]), generally by the analyst or a focus group.[6] The analyst or focus group then assigns weights to each of the impacts to reflect their relative importance within the analysis.[7] The weighted scores are aggregated to provide a single figure that decision makers use to assess the desirability of proceeding with the project.

In other words, multicriteria analysis begins by taking cardinal values (the physical, numerical, or financial units in which impacts have been specified); recasting them within an ordinal scoring system; and then multiplying by an interval scale (the weights).

But there are several shortcomings with this proceeding:

- Because any number of other impacts might have been equally reasonably considered to be relevant, this stage of the analysis is clearly subjective, irrespective of the analyst's intent or desire to be objective. There is no theoretical basis to guide the choice of criteria.[8]
- Another problem is that of overlapping criteria, resulting in double-counting. This contrasts with cost-benefit analysis, where the analyst is required to address all relevant impacts from the perspective (the "standing") of society as a whole, and double-counting is specifically eschewed.
- Apart from the arbitrary and atheoretical nature of selecting attributes and assigning scores and weights, the process is fundamentally flawed mathematically. In essence, it aggregates incommensurable quantities such as kilograms of rice and lives saved from drowning through the artifice of

attaching scores and weights. It is little different from attempting "to add apples and oranges" (Dobes and Bennett 2009). Equally important, the result is not replicable. Different analysts can validly produce widely diverging results and conclusions.

It is sometimes suggested by proponents of multicriteria analysis that the approach is nevertheless valuable because it can play a useful role in helping people think through the objectives that they are trying to achieve and the relative importance of different objectives. It is also relatively easy to use. Nevertheless, the very nature of the approach means that there is a considerable (and unjustifiable) risk of bias that allows bureaucrats, politicians, or other stakeholders to advocate their own special interests.

Cost-Effectiveness Analysis

Cost-effectiveness analysis is often used in everyday life, and it is easily presented to and understood by policy makers. A measure of technical efficiency, it expresses a result in terms of the cost of achieving a specific objective: for example, the number of lives saved for the cost of a dike. At its most simple, it can reveal projects that generate the "biggest bang for the buck." Although generally used only for a single output or effect, cost-effectiveness analysis can be extended to multiple outputs and inputs through data envelopment analysis or stochastic frontier analysis (see, for example, Coelli et al. 2005) and related techniques.

However, the very lack of a common numeraire to represent "adaptation" means that comparisons can be made only between projects of a very similar nature. It is not possible to compare a dike project with a water project, for example, if the comparison made is between number of lives saved per dollar and kilograms of additional rice grown per dollar.[9]

Cost-effectiveness analysis also cannot be used to assess which projects will generate the largest benefits for society as a whole. It is therefore of only limited use as a policy decision tool for comparing different adaptation projects and programs.

Another limitation that may have important political economy implications is the potentially contradictory results that can arise when comparing cost-effectiveness ratios for projects of different size. Boardman et al. (2006) provides several examples.

Cost-Benefit Analysis
Explaining the Method

Assuming certainty, a conventional cost-benefit analysis is illustrated in figure 5.1 as the construction of a dike in 2012 to prevent flooding. Arrows above the horizontal timeline represent the values of projected benefits; those below represent costs. It is standard to show costs and benefits as accruing at the end of each year. Figure 5.1 assumes certainty, or at least a very high level of confidence, about the value of future benefits and costs. Future values of costs and benefits are

Figure 5.1 Conventional Cost-Benefit Analysis under Conditions of Certainty: Hypothetical Dike Building Project

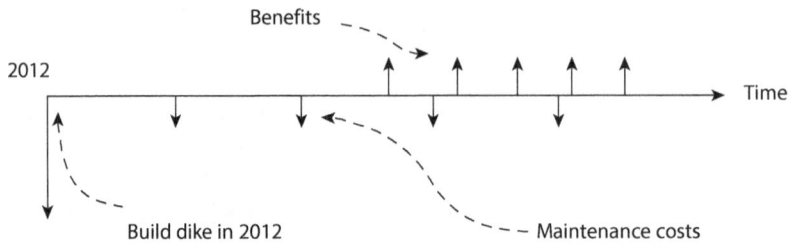

Note: Arrows above the timeline represent projected benefits; arrows below the timeline, projected costs. Future values of costs and benefits are discounted back to the present (here, 2012) to obtain the net present value of the project.

normally discounted back to the present—in this case, the year 2012—to obtain the net present value of the project.

The textbook decision criterion for conventional cost-benefit analysis is invariably given as net present value needing to be greater than zero, implying that the present value of social benefits must exceed that of social costs. However, even negative net present values may turn out to be positive once option values (see "real options" below) are added to the conventional result. In practice, decision makers also need to take into account budget constraints and the net present values of alternative projects.

Despite a number of shortcomings discussed below, cost-benefit analysis[10] remains the only rigorous analytical tool available in terms of assessing issues such as the relative merits of different adaptation projects and strategies (box 5.2). In particular, it affords policy makers an unambiguous decision tool by requiring that the present value of benefits to society as a whole exceed the present value of social costs incurred. In other words, of all the analytical tools available, it alone permits the comparison of adaptation measures, not only with each other but also with alternatives that are not as closely associated with climate-change effects.[11]

Nevertheless, cost-benefit analysis requires considerable care on the part of the analyst for the following reasons:

- As with consideration of any other potential investment of community resources, estimates of costs alone are not enough to decide whether the investment is socially worthwhile. Because costs are generally estimated in terms of financial damage or replacement cost, they are a conceptually inadequate indicator of the benefits that might be gained from implementing appropriate adaptation measures. For example, a flooded river may destroy household mementos such as photographs, or it may even result in illness or loss of life. The true economic cost needs to be measured in the household's willingness to pay to avoid all the effects of flooding, or its willingness to pay to accept them, in order to capture intangible economic values as well as tangible costs.

Box 5.2 What Is Really Measured in Cost-Benefit Analysis?

Benefits in a cost-benefit analysis are more correctly measured as willingness to pay to avoid damage or willingness to accept compensation for the damage. (Hensher, Rose, and Greene 2005 and Bateman et al. 2002 provide detailed explanations of the "stated preference" methods involved.) A householder may be willing to pay much more than simply the avoided damage to furniture in a flood, for example, because the household also places a (negative) value on the general inconvenience caused by the flood or the loss of family mementos. In this case, using only a "damage avoided" measure would underestimate the benefits of fewer floods. Appraisal of adaptation policies and projects will provide more credible results if the conceptually correct measure of benefit is used.

Some studies of adaptation actions (for example, Agrawala and Fankhauser 2008, 23, table 1.1) present results in terms of "cost-benefit" analysis that are more accurately characterized as "cost-cost" studies because they compare the cost of implementing an adaptation measure with the cost of avoided damage due to climate-change effects. Although there is sometimes no alternative to using the "damage costs avoided" approach, it can only be a rough proxy for benefits.[a]

a. Estimation of benefits on the basis of "willingness to pay" to avoid floods of varying heights would ideally be carried out using a stated preference technique such as contingent valuation (Boardman et al. 2006, chapter 14; Bateman et al. 2002) or, preferably, choice modeling (Hensher, Rose, and Greene 2005).

- If policy advice is to be rigorous, any appraisal of investment needs to go beyond considering the costs of a single, specific measure; all feasible alternatives need to be evaluated. In some cases, it may be more rational to change pricing policy than to undertake direct investment: rather than building a new dam to ensure sufficient irrigation water, for example, it may be socially more desirable to change pricing arrangements for water.

- Cost-benefit analysis can be a challenge for economies with limited analytical resources. However, even "back of the envelope" analysis can provide a useful indication of whether an adaptation measure is likely to improve the well-being of society as a whole. Moreover, simplified and standardized approaches can be taken.[12]

- An important conceptual drawback of cost-benefit analysis is that it assumes that people value additional costs and benefits equally (that is, the marginal utility of money is equal for everyone). This assumption is obviously unrealistic in societies where income differentials are significantly large. Distributional weights are sometimes used to adjust the results of the analysis, but resorting to weights can also produce arbitrary and subjective results.

Nevertheless, cost-benefit analysis offers a major analytical advantage in that it is able to accommodate the uncertainty that is the hallmark of climate change.

Adapting Cost-Benefit Analysis for Uncertainty

Cost-benefit analysis offers three broad avenues for incorporating climate-change uncertainties into the economic appraisal of adaptation policies and projects:

- *Expected values:* estimation of expected values by drawing on "known" probabilities of costs and benefits.
- *Monte Carlo method:* randomization of variables that determine costs and benefits, using the Monte Carlo method.
- *Real options:* incorporation of the additional value that may be gained from (a) delaying full implementation of a project until more complete information about future costs or benefits becomes available or (b) abandoning it at some stage.

Expected Values. It is common practice in cost-benefit analysis to allow for Knightian risk (where event probabilities are known) by estimating the "expected value" of a project or policy alternative. A relatively simple procedure, it requires only the determination of probabilities of achieving benefits, or incurring costs, of specific value. For further detail on this method, see annex 5A.

Monte Carlo Simulation. In cost-benefit analysis, the Monte Carlo technique is often used to conduct a sensitivity analysis of the results where some variables may have a strong influence on the result (for example, population growth, the discount rate, prices, and so forth). The technique involves a large amount of random sampling of combinations of values from the probability distributions of each of the selected variables, to generate a single probability distribution of net present values. The mean (the expected value), or a specific range, of the composite distribution can be used as an estimate of net benefit.

The end result of a cost-benefit analysis that uses Monte Carlo methods to simulate costs and benefits on a probabilistic basis is that the net present value is expressed as a distribution of possible values rather than as a single value as in conventional cost-benefit analysis. For further detail on this method, see annex 5B.

Real Options. Conventional cost-benefit analysis can be extended to take account of uncertainty about future costs and benefits through the analysis of real options. Real options are analogous to financial options, relying on the opportunity to delay full implementation of an adaptation measure until better information becomes available to enable resolution of uncertainty about climatic impacts. The flexibility afforded by the possibility of delaying full implementation is valuable and may increase the net present value of the measure. The decision criterion in a project that embeds an option is that the net present value of the project, *plus* the option value, should exceed zero.

Note that the creation or embedding of an option in a project may mean that it is justifiable on cost-benefit grounds, even if the net present value of the project itself (that is, without an option) is less than zero. Put another way, an adaptation project such as building a dike that does not commit all of its investment resources immediately is likely to be more socially beneficial in the face of uncertainty about climate change than one where all the funds are fully expended on the project at the outset.

The real-options approach is especially attractive from a fiscal perspective because it is likely to avoid large calls on the current budget for projects that may prove to be unnecessary or that are premature in the face of uncertainty. Some lower level of prudential expenditure that is adequate to protect people or infrastructure in the near future can be undertaken, leaving decisions for greater expenditure to the medium- and longer-term future if it becomes clear that it is required.

For further detail on the real-options approach, see annex 5C.

Examples of Real Options

The examples of real options that are outlined in this section are intended to illustrate possible approaches for dealing with uncertainty. However, they are only intended to stimulate further thought about possibilities rather than being definitive guides to action. A range of other examples can be found in Dobes (2008, 2010, 2012).

Prior gathering of technical information and its analysis in consultation with both experts and stakeholders who are directly affected is essential. Local conditions ultimately determine the feasibility and viability of a project based on real options.

Interim Solutions

It is sometimes considered that long-lived infrastructure projects being built in the present need to factor in future climate change. For example, bridges or roads may need to be built higher, to ensure that they are not flooded. However, such "climate proofing" is likely to be expensive and may not be warranted if the cost of delays to transport is minor and can be internalized by local users. Photo 5.1 shows a submersible bridge built in 1890–91 that is impassable during fluvial flooding.

Although there is an opportunity cost of not being able to cross the river during the relatively short-lived floods, a higher, more expensive bridge would presumably not outweigh the benefits to be gained by users until traffic levels warranted it. In one sense, the submersible bridge represents a real option because it is a relatively cheap, interim solution and can be replaced, if warranted, by a higher bridge in the future once the effect of climate change in the area becomes apparent. The cost of the additional lateral strength in the lower, submersible version is the option premium. Alternatively, a drier-than-expected climate may mean that no further investment in a higher bridge will be necessary.

Photo 5.1 Submersible Bridge on the Herbert River, Gairloch, Queensland

Source: © The State of Queensland (Department of Environment and Heritage Protection). Reproduced, with permission; further permission required for reuse.

Anticipating Future Investments

The suspension bridge connecting Lisbon, Portugal, to the southern bank of the Tagus River also provides an example of an embedded real option. Constructed in 1966, the structure was reinforced at the time of construction to allow for the future addition of a second deck (carried out in 1999 with little disruption to traffic) to carry railroad traffic, if required (Gesner and Jardim 1998).

The same approach can be applied to areas where climate change is expected to require higher bridges in the future. A real option on a bridge subject to frequent flooding in the future might be to build a relatively cheap, low bridge (perhaps like the submersible version) but with stronger foundations so that an additional level can be added above it one day, if required.

Module Approach

Seawalls are popularly associated with protection against cyclones as well as storm surge resulting from a combination of rising sea levels and storms. Unless the strength and intensity of cyclones and storm surges in a particular area already warrant building a seawall of a specific height, a possible real option is to delay full construction—perhaps building only a solid foundation or just allocating land for this purpose. The foundation can be used temporarily for sandbags until it becomes clear that a permanent wall is required. If storm surges intensify over time, the wall can be built progressively higher.

Multipurpose Projects

A particularly interesting and creative real option has been embedded in the Stormwater Management and Road Tunnel (SMART) that runs under the financial district in Kuala Lumpur, Malaysia, to relieve traffic congestion. The tunnel has three levels: two for road traffic and a lower level for carrying flash floods from the Klang River under the city and out to the Kerayong River (see figure 5.2).[13] During major storms, cars are excluded from the two traffic lanes and special gates are opened to allow stormwater to flow through the upper levels of the tunnel. Traffic can enter again within about 48 hours of closure.

An option premium would have been paid in extra design and construction cost as well as surface congestion costs during closure. But the cost of the multipurpose tunnel is presumably less than a traffic-only tunnel combined with a duplicate tunnel dedicated solely to channelling intermittent floodwaters.

Anticipating Destruction but Allowing for Quick Reconstruction

An alternative to seawalls or reliance on bioshields was practiced by the Taino people on the coast of northern Cuba until several centuries ago. Taino houses

Figure 5.2 Stormwater Management and Road Tunnel, Kuala Lumpur

Source: © Mott MacDonald. Reproduced, with permission, from Mott MacDonald; further permission required for reuse.

were built on solid stilts and platforms, but the thatched walls and roofs were flimsy. During hurricanes, inhabitants sought shelter in nearby caves but could rebuild quickly afterward because the strong platforms remained unaffected and construction of the walls and roof was relatively simple and quick (Brahic 2009).

In effect, the strong platform, combined with proximity of the villages to caves, created a real option that was socially cheaper than building houses that were totally hurricane-proof. A modern analog is the construction in the Maldives of community shelters built on stilts to provide shelter during storms, high tides, and tsunamis as an alternative to building all dwellings to a "climate-proof" standard (Vince 2009).

Public Investment Management under Uncertainty

This section discusses the main challenges regarding uncertainty that correspond to the eight steps of the Rajaram et al. (2010) framework. Based on the considerations above, the purpose of this exercise is to underscore some of the challenges for managing public investment. Although not an exhaustive list covering all possible aspects, its main purpose is to initiate a reflection on this critical topic.

Step 1: Investment Guidance, Project Development, and Preliminary Screening

Improved future planning is essential to incorporate uncertainties related to climate change. However, planners—and also decision makers—may be excessively risk-averse and overadapt, or they may be unduly optimistic about the future and underadapt (see box 5.3 and the summary in table 5.3). There is also a risk that ministries responsible for adaptation will treat it as a "single issue," divorced from other social needs, so that excessive or premature adaptation measures divert scarce resources from other social needs such as investment in schools and hospitals.

Traditional planning would need to be complemented with increased research.[14] Research can often provide insights to inform decisions to delay implementing a project—which, as underscored further below, is often an essential approach to factoring in uncertainty until more information becomes available. Local knowledge can be important in this regard.

Step 2: Formal Project Appraisal

Because events are not known beforehand in the case of "unknown knowns" and "unknown unknowns," it is not possible to take them into account using conventional appraisal techniques. As has been highlighted above, some appraisal techniques are particularly unsuited to evaluating overall benefits to the community.

This has important political economy implications. Multicriteria analysis relies on considerable subjectivity. The very nature of the approach means

Box 5.3 The Challenge of Dealing with Climate-Change Risk at the Planning Stage

In particular, adoption of disaster management approaches based on worst-case scenarios can result in unduly excessive use of resources. Building a 10-meter-high seawall along the entire coast of China in the near future would be an extreme example of overreaction to expected changes in weather patterns. Although such "gold-plating" would ensure almost total certainty in eliminating the risk of damage from storm surges and flooding of coastal areas, the expense involved would be disproportionate to the risk. The resources used to build such a wall would undoubtedly generate higher benefits if applied to other social programs.

One means of avoiding gold-plating is to consider at the outset a comprehensive list of alternative projects, even if some are later discarded as being unviable. For example, an alternative to building a dike immediately in a coastal area may be to plant mangroves to reduce the force of storm surges and hence inundation. Bayas et al. (2011), Tanaka (2009), and Dahdouh-Guebas et al. (2005) report on some of the results of planting coastal vegetation.

Undue procrastination, too, can waste resources and human life. Failure to take timely or appropriate action can result not only in property damage but also in unnecessary death and injury to local populations. Economic growth and social well-being will be reduced below levels that they otherwise would have achieved. Unexpectedly high floods and intense forest fires in recent years provide some insight into the possible consequences of more intense rainfall patterns or hotter temperatures, even though it is not clear that they have to date been caused by man-made climate change.

Table 5.3 Adaptation Responses and Effects under Two Climate-Change Risk Scenarios

	Climate change faster than expected	Climate change slower than expected
Premature or excessive adaptation	Depending on the speed of climate change, benefits may exceed costs or vice versa.	Costs may exceed benefits if excessive adaptation measures are implemented.
Undue procrastination or inadequate adaptation	Costs may exceed benefits if property is damaged or humans suffer.	Effect is unclear.
Maladaptation (quality and nature of adaptation measure)	Effect is unclear, but maladaptation is, by definition, costly in itself.	Effect is unclear, but maladaptation is, by definition, costly in itself.

that there is a considerable risk of bias that allows bureaucrats, politicians, or other stakeholders to advocate their own special interests. Cost-effectiveness analysis provides a more objective appraisal technique but is generally limited to a single variable such as lives saved. Only cost-benefit analysis, with or without real options, provides a rigorous means of appraising all the factors relevant to a community's well-being, although it too suffers from conceptual drawbacks.

Whichever approach is adopted, creative, feasible alternative approaches to adaptation measures are more likely to be identified if comprehensive consultation takes place at a very early stage, before the design phase begins. Although the most desirable approach is likely to differ among countries and projects, the following are criteria that can be used to assign responsibilities:

- It should be acknowledged that adaptation to climate change will be primarily local in nature and that the principle of subsidiarity in decision making should be applied. In some cases, individuals will be best placed to make decisions. In other cases, regional or local governments should be in charge rather than central governments.
- Central agencies would better ensure that funds are not frittered away over time or used to gold-plate projects. Also, they have some natural advantage in exercising oversight to ensure consistency between projects, proper consideration of alternatives, and later availability of funds.
- On the other hand, line agencies are better placed to monitor the effects of climate change and the need to either implement or continue delaying full project implementation.

But local action, which is underscored above as an appropriate means, does not prevent risk or failure. In addition to the risk of over- or underinvestment in adaptation, even in cases of proper consultation and local planning there is always the risk of maladaptation through the application of inappropriate technology or unsuitable actions. An example is illustrated below in photo 5.2, where a Samoan village with a nascent tourist trade constructed a rock wall to protect its dwellings but thereby discouraged tourists who could no longer easily access the beach. This case illustrates the dilemma that may face other communities seeking to adapt to climate change.

On the other hand, caution is urged in terms of so-called mainstreaming. Where mainstreaming encourages "climate-proofing" or gold-plating, especially for long-lived assets such as bridges, there is considerable risk that climate change may not eventuate in the way initially envisaged or to the perceived extent. The adaptation component of the investment is likely to be too high, although it might equally turn out to be too low or just right.

Step 3: Independent Review of Appraisal

Nonconventional, nontechnical input from local inhabitants would need to be balanced and contrasted through independent review. Close consultation with engineers and technical specialists about alternatives is often an obvious factor. The experience of other countries with similar conditions can also be instructive. This will necessarily involve greater up-front time and cost, but it is more likely to result in the identification of more, and possibly better, alternatives that can be put to decision makers.

Photo 5.2 Climate-Change Adaptation Dilemma in a Samoan village

Source: ©Andrew Ash, CSIRO. Reproduced, with permission from Andrew Ash; further permission required for reuse.

Step 4: Project Selection and Budgeting

Most government line agencies rely on renewed funding every year or so. Central finance agencies often support funding bids on the basis of program delivery in the previous year, with delivery usually assessed in terms of the proportion of program funds that have been expended. If a line agency does not fully expend its program funding, it risks being seen as inadequate to the task.

It is therefore more likely than not that line agencies will spend or overspend their "adaptation budgets," especially if there is political pressure to "do something" about disasters or other concerns that are popularly attributed to climate change.

Another important aspect concerns possible delays in expenditures, related to the fact that it might be wise to postpone investments until more information becomes available—a central idea of the real-options approach discussed further below. If projects are implemented sequentially, the fiscal impact can be shifted into the future rather than being incurred immediately.

In contrast to conventional project management, therefore, the adaptive aspect has three important budgetary implications:

- Budgetary processes in most countries are designed to fit projects that are implemented in full from the outset, with fixed periods within which the expenditure is to occur. Because the exercise of a real option may take many years, it is not clear how funds are to be earmarked. At best, governments can put aside funds for unspecified contingencies as a form of self-insurance. Maintaining significant reserves in case a set of real options needs to be implemented in the future runs the risk of considerable opportunity cost (regret) in terms of reduced expenditure in other socially desirable areas.

- The value of any reserves or other allocation of funds for future use to exercise a real option will need to be maintained in real terms to ensure their effectiveness.[15]
- Adaptation projects that follow a real-options approach will need to provide for monitoring resources into the future—an additional project cost that is part of the "option premium."

Not all countries are likely to have the levels of institutional robustness, transparency, and fiscal management capacity to address these three implications noted above.

Step 5: Project Implementation

Real options are not simply a formulaic approach to evaluating investment. It is equally important to foster creativity in the sequential implementation of projects and to consider a wide range of potential alternative approaches.

Particularly challenging is the capacity of countries to assume and accept sunk costs related to investments. It may be appropriate at some stage to abandon further implementation of a project. Real options embedded in measures to adapt to climate change, for example, are valuable because they permit abandonment at any stage before full expenditure has been incurred. From this perspective, however, it may be desirable to involve central agencies in overseeing projects involving real options to ensure that the responsible line agency does not unnecessarily prolong or extend in scope a project that is no longer viable or warranted.

Step 6: Project Adjustment

A critical factor in the implementation of the real-options approach is that continual monitoring of underlying conditions and periodic reanalysis are required. Real options are inherently adaptive in nature—one of the key reasons why they are suited to addressing uncertainty in climate change. Projects should be flexible to allow sequential adaptation in the future through expansion, or abandonment, if required.

Use of a real-options approach will require countries to have processes in place that allow—and even encourage—implementing agencies to adjust the pace and nature of implementation. The Republic of Korea, which applies thresholds for cost and time overruns, could further develop and adapt its processes to factor in risk and uncertainty, but its experience represents a well-suited starting point to think systematically about project adjustments.

It is also clear that, during step 6 in the PIM framework, some projects will be misconceived and some will need to be abandoned, meaning that at least some budgetary resources will be wasted. This is to be expected because all projects

---

Box 5.4 The Dilemma of Residual Risk

Monitoring of sea-level rise, increased storm-surge intensity, and similar effects is required to ensure that the next stage of the project (such as increasing the height of the wall) is implemented before unexpectedly high inundation causes untoward damage. By the same token, it must be recognized that extreme or unpredictable events (including "unknown unknowns") can also occur such that even close monitoring may not prevent damage to property or lives.[a] Implementation of real options in projects cannot, in itself, eliminate risk.

a. As more information becomes available, particularly where new extremes manifest themselves, revision of the underlying analysis will be required. For example, the parameters of the extreme value distribution used in figure 5B.1 to determine annual exceedance probabilities may need to be reestimated. An alternative is to allow for a safety factor in the analysis: see, for example, Linquiti and Vonortas (2012).

---

carry some degree of risk (see box 5.4). But applying the real-options approach would imply that the wastage will be less than if many projects had been fully implemented at the outset and later abandoned as white elephants because early expectations about climate-change effects had not materialized.

Step 7: Facility Operation

Flexible project management implies that handover of responsibility for assets is periodically done according to gradual progress in construction. Flexible project management also implies provision for future operation and maintenance of the created assets, taking into account the need for potential adjustments over time as well as for adequate budget funding of service delivery agencies to operate and maintain these assets.

It would also be increasingly important to verify the extent to which real-option facilities would require postcompletion adaptation or ancillary investment before the assets can be used.

In addition, asset registers would need to be updated more frequently than for standard investments. The same holds for compiling balance sheets, on which the value of assets increased through new fixed capital expenditure would be maintained. Active monitoring of service delivery is an equally critical element to ensure that the new assets serve their intended purpose over their useful life.

Step 8: Completion Review and Evaluation

Ex post reviews would need to be done periodically and take into account evolving conditions for service delivery. The main challenge is that under a real-options approach, regular reviews should not be limited to solutions identified at the outset of a particular project or program. It is possible that new real options will emerge over time, or initial thinking may be overtaken by unforeseen events or unintended consequences. For example, a seawall may no longer be an effective solution because the beach has eroded underneath it, so new alternative measures involving migration to higher ground may need to be examined instead.

Final Considerations

Uncertainty will fundamentally challenge the management of investments. Further thought is needed to analyze all the possible effects and adjustments required. But it is clear already that capacity building—by educating businesses, government, and individuals regarding the need for flexibility (including the embedding of real options) in investment decisions—is an essential first step. An effective approach to embedding real options in adaptation measures will require capacity building in areas such as cost-benefit analysis, meaningful and effective methods for consultation with stakeholders, monitoring of relevant climatic variables, and other areas. Cultural change needs to accompany these new technical approaches.

Identification of relevant real options for adaptation projects requires a degree of creative thinking, but local knowledge is essential. It is possible to identify potential real options for many possible projects that incorporate an element of adaptation to climate change. Indeed, it is likely that the task will be made easier by the sharing of experience and knowledge among different localities and regions of the world.

Annex 5A: Estimation of Expected Values

The sum of the probability weighted set of n contingencies is the expected value of the net benefit [E(NB)] as in the following equation:

$$E[NB] = p_1(B_1 - C_1) + \dots + p_i(B_i - C_i) + \dots + p_n(B_n - C_n) \qquad (1)$$

In terms of the cost-benefit analysis previously illustrated in figure 5.1, the arrows above (benefits) or below (costs) the timeline would be adjusted by their associated probabilities. Where certainty exists, the arrow would remain unchanged because $p_1 = 1$: for example, the initial construction cost in 2012 (the present) could be assumed to be known with a high degree of confidence so the arrow would remain unchanged. Arrows could be shown as diminishing in length over time if projections of costs and benefits are determined with a lower degree of certainty. The decision criterion is analogous to that of conventional cost-benefit analysis: expected net present value greater than zero.

An alternative approach to estimating expected net present values is by means of tree diagrams (dendograms). Boardman et al. (2006, chapter 7) provide an introduction to the methodology and recommend Raiffa (1969) for a more detailed exposition. However, a key disadvantage of such diagrams is that they can quickly expand to fill the page if more than two choices (branches) are used or if the analysis extends over multiple years. An alternative is to use a spreadsheet, but this too can involve complex constructions.

Expected values, with or without decision trees, are potentially useful for appraising adaptation projects where risk is known with some certainty.

Knowledge of the probabilities that are used to calculate expected values implies a degree of confidence about the future effects of climate change. The expected value technique is therefore suited to the "known knowns" situation in quadrant II of table 5.1 of this chapter. However, its potential as an appraisal technique is limited in situations of uncertainty about outcomes, such as those in quadrants I, III, and IV.

Annex 5B: Monte Carlo Simulation

The Monte Carlo technique could potentially also be used to evaluate adaptation projects and policies where there is uncertainty about the variables involved (as in quadrants I and III of table 5.1). An example might be the estimation of future benefits of avoiding floods by constructing a dike (as shown in figure 5.1).

Most countries have sufficient historical data to generate models based on extreme value distributions. Figure 5B.1 illustrates a hypothetical extreme value distribution (for example, the Gumbel) for flood-inducing rainfall under current (2013) circumstances: only the "fat tail" of the distribution is shown because minor flooding is assumed to be internalized by the local population. It plots the annual exceedance probability (AEP) for various flood heights. For example, a 5 percent AEP (1-in-20-year flood) may currently be associated with flood heights of about 1 meter. Floods that occur once in 100 years (AEP = 1 percent) are obviously less frequent, but the area is shown in the example as potentially reaching heights of around 4 meters.

The probability distribution for 2013 can be "augmented" to take into account climate change over the coming century by shifting it to the right based on predictions obtained from physical climate models. For example, the current 1-in-20-year flood may be expected by the year 2100 to be typically 4 meters high, a level previously experienced only once in 100 years. This approach is suggested by Repetto and Easton (2009) for hurricane losses as well as by IBRD and World Bank (2010, section III.1).

The "augmented" distributions in figure 5B.1 imply deterministic certainty regarding the extent of future climate change. In reality, physical climate models will provide different, often contradictory, results. Further, climate models may assume significantly different scenarios about greenhouse gas emissions (so-called Representative Concentration Pathways [Moss et al. 2010]). A more realistic approach is therefore to employ a series of distributions for each year or period under examination. This is illustrated in figure 5B.2 where a series of extreme value distributions has been generated using different climate models for each year under examination (but only the distributions for one year are shown in figure 5B.2).

A reasonably simple Monte Carlo analysis could be undertaken by drawing values at random from each of the following variables and combining them to form a single distribution of net present value:

Figure 5B.1 Annual Exceedance Probabilities for Rainfall and Floods, 2013–2100

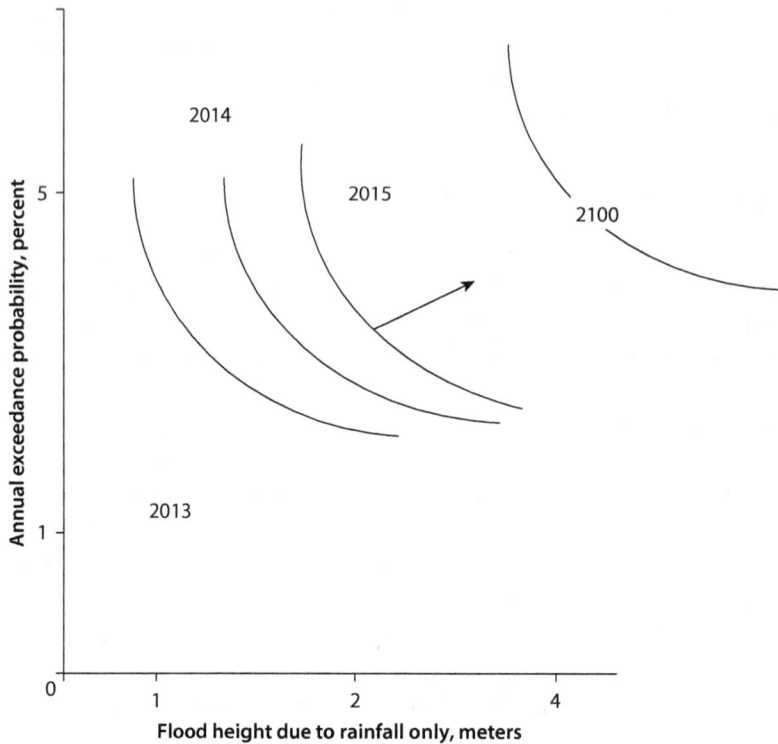

- A set of different types of climate models.
- Selection of climate scenarios (IPCC 2000).
- Annual exceedance probability (between 0 and 0.05 in the example above) for flood height.
- A year between 2013 and 2100 (to determine the "augmentation" factor).

The complexity of the model could be extended by allowing other factors (such as willingness to pay to avoid floods, the discount rate, and cost of construction of the dike) to also vary randomly.

A similar approach was used in cost-benefit work commissioned by the Australian Government (2010) for the cost of coastal inundation.

The end result of a cost-benefit analysis that uses Monte Carlo methods to simulate costs and benefits on a probabilistic basis is that the net present value is expressed as a distribution of possible values rather than as a single value as in conventional cost-benefit analysis. However, the decision criterion is similar: if the bulk of the distribution lies in the positive range, it is more likely than not that the project is socially worthwhile.

Figure 5B.2 Uncertainty in Climate Modeling in a Range of Distributions for a Given Year under Study (2013–2100)

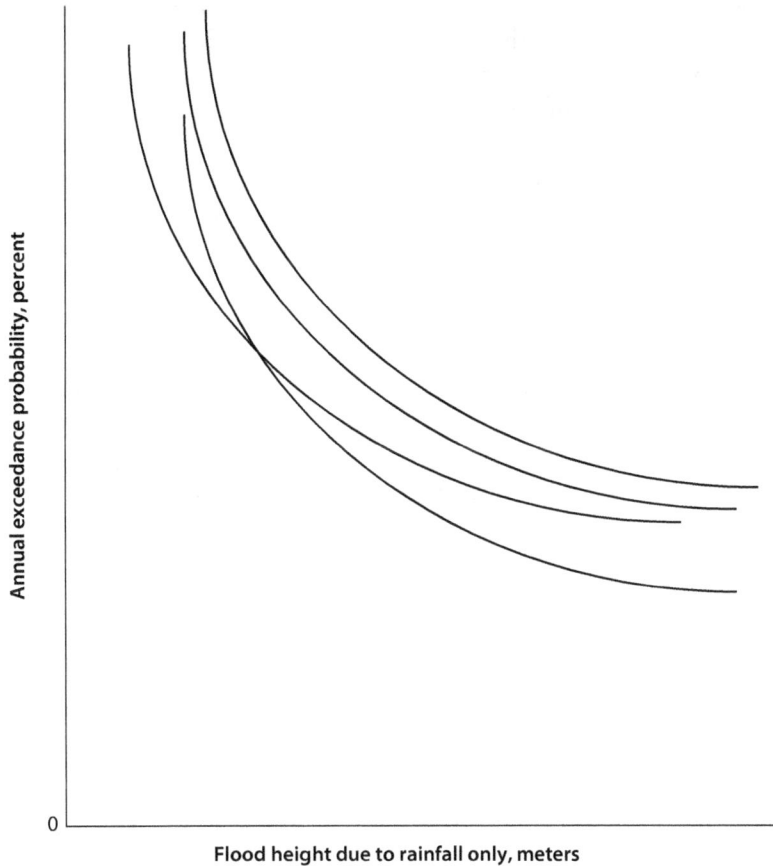

Note: The set of distributions is based on an ensemble of different climate models and scenarios for any one year between 2013 and 2100. There is no basis for preferring any one distribution over another. By implication, each is an equally probable representation of the future climate in each year.

Annex 5C: Real Options

The real-options approach can be illustrated by drawing on an approach used strategically by businesses. A business seeking to open a manufacturing plant in another country, for example, faces many uncertainties: wages may rise as the target country enjoys increased economic growth; local consumers may not accept the new product; or export infrastructure may become congested over time, causing costly shipping delays. In such cases, a business may decide to build only a pilot plant, keeping open the option of future expansion as more information becomes available and residual uncertainties are resolved.

The existence of an option to expand or abandon a project is likely to be valuable because it offers flexibility of future action but without having to fully incur the higher cost of a large-scale plant up front. An option in this case offers the opportunity to expand the investment project if the pilot plant proves successful or to abandon it if the pilot fails, but there is no obligation to expand or abandon. In other words, the risk is asymmetrical because the option will only be exercised if it increases the value of the project or minimizes cost by cutting short an unprofitable venture. However, there is invariably a cost (the "option premium") incurred in the creation of the opportunity to exercise flexibility.

The concept of a real[16] option in the context of adaptation to uncertain climate change is illustrated in figure 5C.1. Panel b shows an alternative to immediate construction of a dike: only preparatory work is undertaken (such as acquisition and preparation of land) as an interim step that creates the option (but no obligation) of construction in the future. Panel a replicates the conventional cost-benefit analysis previously presented in figure 5.1: in effect, the calculation of the net present value in panel a establishes the value of the underlying asset if the option is exercised immediately, so there is no residual option value.[17] It therefore provides a point of comparison with panel b, where the option is only exercised at some future date.

The difference in net present value between panels a and b is the "option value" that reflects the value of strategic flexibility in the face of uncertainty, and the cost of acquiring and preparing the land is the "premium" that must be paid to make available the opportunity to exercise future investment flexibility. The greater the degree of uncertainty and the longer the period during which

Figure 5C.1 Cost-Benefit Analysis of Building a Dike: Immediate vs. Deferred Construction

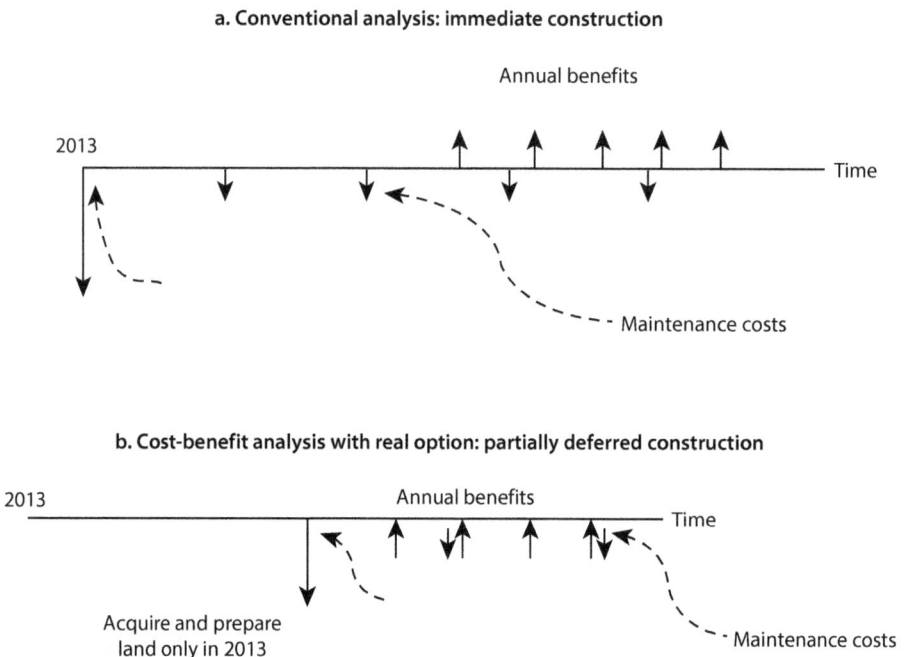

a. Conventional analysis: immediate construction

b. Cost-benefit analysis with real option: partially deferred construction

Note: Arrows above the timeline represent projected benefits; arrows below the timeline, projected costs. Future values of costs and benefits are discounted back to the present (2013) to obtain the net present value of the project.

the option can be exercised, the greater the value of the flexibility afforded by the option.

The decision criterion in a project that embeds an option is that the net present value of the project, *plus* the option value, should exceed zero. Note that the creation or embedding of an option in a project may mean that it is justifiable on cost-benefit grounds, even if the net present value of the project itself (that is, without an option) is less than zero. Put another way, an adaptation project such as building a dike that does not commit all of its investment resources immediately is likely to be more socially beneficial in the face of uncertainty about climate change than one where all the funds are expended on the project at the outset. Some of the more accessible literature on identifying and valuing real options includes Brealey, Myers, and Allen (2006, chapter 22); Boardman et al. (2006, chapters 7–8); *Economist* (1999); Luehrmann (1998a, 1998b); Neufville, Scholtes, and Wang (2006); Kester (1984); Borison (2005); and Dixit and Pindyck (1994).

Notes

1. There is a philosophical issue here in terms of the frame of reference. The problem is akin to asking whether a tree falling in a forest makes a noise if no one is there to hear it fall. If we treat, say, the 15th-century world as composed of two distinct and unconnected parts—Europe and Australasia—then European ignorance of black swans could be categorized as an "unknown unknown." However, if we consider both regions as sufficiently connected (for example, via the Silk Road and various trade routes by sea), then black swans would have been more of an "unknown known" to a European and a "known known" in Australasia. Indeed, it is possible that tales of black swans did reach Europe but were disbelieved because of cognitive experience there, but substantive evidence would be required before drawing this conclusion.

2. The Knightian definition of uncertainty does not appear to encompass this perspective of total uncertainty, and it is probably better thought of as mapping onto quadrant I, with Knightian "risk" corresponding to quadrant II.

3. Bubonic plague, typhus, rabies, periodic waves of influenza, malaria, cholera, and so on have occurred to varying degrees in the past, so it is arguable that modern pandemics such as severe acute respiratory syndrome (SARS), Hendra virus, various forms of encephalitis, Avian flu, and others fall more naturally into the "unknown knowns" or "unknown unknowns" categories.

4. World Bank (2009) presents a study using multicriteria analysis to set priorities for adaptation decisions for Mexico, Peru, and Uruguay. Although it has not commonly been used to analyze adaptation issues, multicriteria analysis has been used in relation to environmental problems more broadly. Eakin and Bojórquez-Tapia (2008) apply it to categorize household vulnerability in rural Mexico.

5. Likert scales are commonly used in questionnaires to measure attitudes or preferences of respondents. They are generally used to represent choices between five alternatives (such as "strongly disagree," "disagree," "neither agree nor disagree," "agree," and "strongly agree"), although the range can be extended or compressed (for example, to 7- or 10- or 3- or 4-point scales).

6. In table 5.2, a score of 2 has been given to additional rice production—half the score given to easier planning of production by the local authorities. A farmer

may well have reversed the scores. Again, there is no clear theoretical basis to provide guidance, although various methods have been devised to increase the sophistication of the procedure. Ultimately, however, the scores remain subjective, no matter who determines them or to what degree of mathematical sophistication.

7. In table 5.2, production-oriented aspects (rice and planning) have been given an importance that totals half the index. Cost can only influence the index to the extent of 20 percent. The weights are again subjective and can involve a considerable degree of arbitrariness.

8. An ecologist or an official from the Ministry for Environment would most likely have chosen a quite different set of criteria. Orlove (2009), for example, reports a "striking divergence" between indigenous herders in highland Peru and nongovernmental organizations regarding time horizons and the scope of projects.

9. Boardman et al. (2006, chapter 17) review other issues that limit the usefulness of cost-effectiveness analysis. Assessing the effect of climate change on the cost-effectiveness of nutrient management in a eutrophic lake, Gren (2010), for example, presents separate results for target reductions of nutrients (nitrogen and phosphorous) and water quality (minimum sight depth).

10. Boardman et al. (2006) provide a comprehensive exposition of the technique, as does Mishan (1988) in his classic work.

11. Although cost-benefit analysis has been little used to date for adaptation analysis, there are some good examples of its utility, and the number of contributions to the literature is growing. Thang and Bennett (2007) find that a lack of information on environmental protection values, especially nonmarket values, has contributed to wetland degradation in the Mekong River Delta. The World Bank (2010a) analysis suggests that irrigation projects planned for Bolivia are robust to future climate change. Nguyen's (2006) cost-benefit analysis notably questions whether the increasing reliance on dikes in the Mekong delta is socially optimal (see Howes and Dobes 2010, box 5.2, for a summary).

12. World Bank (2010b) provides a toolkit for community-based cost-benefit analysis of adaptation projects in the energy sector, which has been successfully piloted in Albania and Uzbekistan. Alternatively, governments could fund a set of generic "willingness to pay" studies that would produce approximate "plug-in values" that could be used to analyze multiple projects across the country. The Environmental Valuation Reference Inventory that is maintained by Canada and is partially funded by the Australian Government and other governments is an example of a database of such "plug-in" values (see http://www.environment.nsw.gov.au/publications/evri .htm).

13. For more information about SMART, see http://smarttunnel.com.my/.

14. Crops affected by lower rainfall or higher temperature may require gradual replacement with more drought- or temperature-tolerant species. If the pace of climate change is not too rapid, it will be possible to undertake research into available species in analog conditions or countries or even to engage in genetic engineering before implementing major agricultural changes.

15. On the other hand, economic growth ensuing as part of the implementation of adaptation projects could ensure that sufficient resources are available in the future to pay for sequential implementation of real-option adaptation projects. Maintenance of adaptation reserves would therefore not be as necessary. However,

subsidies may be required to enable compensation of those who lose from the reform process.

16. "Real" denotes "physical" assets. The concept and evaluation methodology for real options is analogous to (financial) options on financial assets such as shares.

17. Note, too, that immediate and full investment is also envisaged by the strong version of the "precautionary principle" that is often advocated by techno-scientific groups on the assumption of avoiding possible disasters.

Bibliography

Agrawala, S. and S. Fankhauser. 2008. *Economic Aspects of Adaptation to Climate Change: Costs, Benefits and Policy Instruments*. Paris: Organisation for Economic Co-operation and Development.

Australian Government. 2010. *Coastal Inundation at Narrabeen Lagoon: Optimising Adaptation Investment*. Report prepared for the Department of Climate Change and Energy Efficiency by AECOM, Commonwealth of Australia, Canberra (accessed July 25, 2010), http://www.climatechange.gov.au/~/media/publications/adaptation /coastal-flooding-narrabeen-lagoon.ashx.

Bateman, I. J., I. T. Carson, B. Day, M. Hanemann, N. Hanley, H. Tannis, M. Jones-Lee, B. Loomes, S. Mourato, E. Ozdemiroglu, D. W. Pearce, R. Sugden, and J. Swanson. 2002. *Economic Valuation with Stated Preference Techniques: A Manual*. Cheltenham, U.K.: Edward Elgar.

Bayas, J. C. L., C. Marohn, G. Dercon, S. Dewi, H. P. Piepho, L. Joshi, M. van Noordwijk, and G. Cadisch. 2011. "Influence of Coastal Vegetation on the 2004 Tsunami Wave Impact in West Aceh." *Proceedings of the National Academy of Science* 108 (46): 18612–17.

Boardman, A. E., D. H. Greenberg, A. R. Vining, and D. L. Weimer. 2006. *Cost-Benefit Analysis: Concepts and Practice*. 3rd ed. Upper Saddle River, NJ: Pearson Prentice Hall.

Borison, A. 2005. "Real Options Analysis: Where Are the Emperor's Clothes?" *Journal of Applied Corporate Finance* 17 (2): 17–31.

Brahic, C. 2009. "Saved by Stilts and Caves." *New Scientist* 2009 (2709):40–41.

Brealey, R. A., S. C. Myers, and F. Allen. 2006. *Principles of Corporate Finance*. 8th ed. New York: McGraw-Hill Irwin.

Coelli, T. J., D. S. P. Rao, C. J. O'Donnell, and G. Battese. 2005. *An Introduction to Efficiency and Productivity Analysis*. 2nd ed. New York: Springer.

Dahdouh-Guebas, F., L. P. Jayatissa, D. di Nitto, J. O. Bosire, D. Lo Seen, and N. Koedam. 2005. "How Effective Were Mangroves as a Defence against the Recent Tsunami?" *Current Biology* 15 (12): R443–47.

Dixit, A. K. and R. S. Pindyck. 1994. *Investment under Uncertainty*. Princeton, NJ: Princeton University Press.

Dobes, L. 2008. "Getting Real about Adapting to Climate Change: Using 'Real Options' to Address the Uncertainties." *Agenda* 15 (3): 55–69.

———. 2010. "Notes on Applying 'Real Options' to Climate Change Adaptation Measures, with Examples from Vietnam." Working Paper 7.10, Centre for Climate Economics and Policy, Crawford School of Economics and Government, Australian National University, Canberra.

————. 2012. "Sir Sidney Kidman: Australia's Cattle King as Pioneer of Adaptation to Climatic Uncertainty." *The Rangeland Journal* 34 (1): 1–15.

Dobes, L. and J. Bennett. 2009. "Multi-Criteria Analysis: 'Good Enough' for Government Work?" *Agenda* 16 (3): 7–29.

Eakin, H., and L. A. Bojórquez-Tapia. 2008. "Insights into the Composition of Household Vulnerability from Multicriteria Decision Analysis." *Global Environmental Change* 18 (1): 112–27.

Economist. 1999. "Keeping All Options Open." *Economist*, August 14.

Gesner, G. A. and J. Jardim. 1998. "Bridge within a Bridge." *Civil Engineering* 68 (10): 44–47.

Gren, I-M. 2010. "Climate Change and the Water Framework Directive: Cost Effectiveness in the Swedish Malar Region." *Climatic Change* 100 (3–4):463–84.

Hensher, D. A., J. M. Rose, and W. H. Greene. 2005. *Applied Choice Analysis: A Primer.* Cambridge, U.K.: Cambridge University Press.

Howes, S. and L. Dobes. 2010. "Fiscal Aspects of Adaptation to Climate Change." In *Climate Change and Fiscal Policy: A Report for APEC.* Report 56563-EAP, World Bank, Washington, DC.

IBRD (International Bank for Reconstruction and Development) and World Bank. 2010. "Economic Evaluation of Climate Change Adaptation Projects: Approaches for the Agricultural Sector and Beyond." IBRD and World Bank, Washington, DC.

IPCC (Intergovernmental Panel on Climate Change). 2000. *Special Report on Emissions Scenarios.* A special report of IPCC Working Group III. Geneva: IPCC.

————. 2012. *Managing the Risks of Extreme Events and Disasters to Advance Climate Change Adaptation.* A special report of IPCC Working Groups I and II. New York: Cambridge University Press.

Kester, W. C. 1984. "Today's Options for Tomorrow's Growth." *Harvard Business Review* 62 (2): 153–60.

Knight, F. H. (1921) 2009. *Risk, Uncertainty and Profit.* Boston, MA: Hart, Schaffner & Marx; Houghton Mifflin Co. Reprint, Orlando, FL: Signalman Publishing.

Linquiti, P. and N. Vonortas. 2012. "The Value of Flexibility in Adapting to Climate Change: A Real Options Analysis of Investments in Coastal Defense." *Climate Change Economics* 3 (2): 1250008-1–1250008-33. doi: 10.1142/S201000781250008X.

Luehrmann, T. A. 1998a. "Investment Opportunities as Real Options: Getting Started on the Numbers." *Harvard Business Review* 76 (4): 51–67.

————. 1998b. "Strategy as a Portfolio of Real Options." *Harvard Business Review* 76 (5): 89–99.

Melbourne Water. 2011. "Adapting to Climate Change. The Sewerage System." Web page, Melbourne Water, Melbourne, Australia (accessed December 3, 2011), http://www.melbournewater.com.au/content/sustainability/climate_change/adapting _to_climate_change/the_sewerage_system.asp.

Menzies, G. 2002. *1421: The Year China Discovered the World.* London: Bantam Books.

Mishan, E. J. 1988. *Cost-Benefit Analysis: An Informal Introduction.* 4th ed. London: Unwin Hyman.

Moss, R. H., J. A. Edmonds, K. Hibberd, M. R. Manning, S. K. Rose, D. P. van Vuuren, T. R. Carter, S. Meoir, M. Kainuma, T. Kram, G. A. Meehl, J. F. B. Mitchell, N. Nakicenovic, K. Riahi, S. J. Smith, R. J. Stouffer, A. M. Thomon, J. P. Weyant, and

T. J. Wilbanks. 2010. "The Next Generation of Scenarios for Climate Change Research and Assessment." *Nature* 463 (7282): 747–56.

Neufville, R., S. Scholtes, and T. Wang. 2006. "Real Options by Spreadsheet: Parking Garage Case Example." *Journal of Infrastructure Systems* (American Society of Civil Engineers) 12 (3): 107–11.

Nguyen, V. K. 2006. "An Economic Evaluation of Dike Construction Alternatives in Vietnam's Mekong Delta: A Case Study in An Giang Province." Master's degree thesis, Crawford School of Economics and Government, Australian National University, Canberra.

Orlove, B. 2009. "The Past, the Present, and Some Possible Futures of Adaptation." In *Adapting to Climate Change: Thresholds, Values, Governance*, ed. by W. N. Adger, I. Lorenzoni, and K. O'Brien, 131–63. Cambridge, U.K.: Cambridge University Press.

Raiffa, H. 1969. *Decision Analysis: Introductory Lectures on Choices under Uncertainty*. Reading, MA: Addison-Wesley.

Rajaram, A., T. Le, N. Biletska, and J. Brumby. 2010. "A Diagnostic Framework for Assessing Public Investment Management." Policy Research Working Paper 5397, World Bank, Washington, DC.

Repetto, R. and R. Easton. 2009. "Climate Change and Damage from Extreme Weather Events." Working Paper 207, Political Economy Research Institute, University of Massachusetts, Amherst.

Shi, Y., Y. Shen, E. Kang, D. Li, Y. Ding, G. Zhang, and R. Hu. 2006. "Recent and Future Climate Change in Northwest China." *Climatic Change* 80 (3–4): 379–93.

Taleb, N. C. 2007. *The Black Swan: The Impact of the Highly Improbable*. New York: Random House.

Tanaka, N. 2009. "Vegetation Bioshields for Tsunami Mitigation: Review of Effectiveness, Limitations, Construction, and Sustainable Management." *Landscape and Ecological Engineering* 5 (1): 71–79.

Thang, N. D. and J. Bennett. 2007. "Estimating Wetland Biodiversity Values: A Choice Modeling Application in Vietnam's Mekong River Delta." Economics and Environment Network Working Paper EEN0704, Australian National University, Canberra.

Vince, G. 2009. "Paradise Lost?" *New Scientist* 202 (2707): 37–38.

World Bank. 2009. *Building Response Strategies to Climate Change in Agricultural Systems in Latin America*. Washington, DC. http://siteresources.worldbank.org /EXTLACREGTOPRURDEV/Resources/503766-1225476272295/PDF_Agriculture _Climate_change.pdf.

———. 2010a. *The Economics of Adaptation to Climate Change: A Synthesis Report*. Final consultation draft, Washington, DC. http://siteresources.worldbank.org/EXTCC /Resources/EACC_FinalSynthesisReport0803_2010.pdf.

———. 2010b. "Hands-On Energy Adaptation Toolkit." Energy Sector Management Assistance Program (ESMAP), World Bank, Washington, DC. http://esmap.org /esmap/node/312. See also http://climate-l.org/2010/08/26/world-bank-presents -hands-on-energy-adaptation-toolkit/?referrer=climate-l.org-daily-feed.

Yang, X., E. Lin, S. Ma, H. Ju, L. Guo, W. Xiong, Y. Li, and Y. Xu. 2007. "Adaptation of Agriculture to Warming in Northeast China." *Climatic Change* 84 (1): 45–58.

CHAPTER 6

Procurement and Public Investment Management

Introduction

Procurement is a major aspect of every government's business process and has profound economic impact. The size of total government procurement (consumption and investment expenditure) was estimated to be about 12 percent of gross domestic product (GDP) for Organisation for Economic Co-operation and Development (OECD) countries in 2008 (OECD 2011). The corresponding figure for developing countries is typically higher. The volume of investment procurement alone is estimated to be 75–80 percent of total government procurement (Veiga Malta et al. 2011). Inefficiency in the procurement system can thus have significant effects both macroeconomically and on the cost-benefit rationale for investment decisions. Both results could adversely affect the economic welfare of citizens. Yet few economic texts pay much attention to this critical aspect of the public investment process.

Government procurement has diversified in nature, size, and complexity, particularly over the past two decades as technological change has revolutionized both the industry and service sectors and correspondingly changed the nature of government purchases. Thirty years back, the bulk of procurement included straightforward and simple goods (such as office supplies, fuel, parts, basic health supplies and medicines, and books); relatively standard civil works (such as bridges, water treatment plants, and roads); and plant-related equipment (such as generators, transformers, and water pumps). These days, governments face more complex procurement requirements such as multipart technological systems; integrated business solutions involving information technology hardware and software; concession contracts; and public-private partnerships to build, operate, and maintain major infrastructure systems.

Correspondingly, governments have access to more-advanced procurement methods and tools such as electronic procurement to take advantage of better supply strategies.[1] Presently in any country, there is likely to be a blend of simple and complex procurement, with the predominance of one or the other depending on the level of economic development, the size and structure of the economy, and the nature of the investment plans. The implications of this evolution are far-reaching for procurement systems. There is a need for much better project and procurement planning, better budgeting, nimble and adaptable regulations, control systems more focused on results and risk detection and mitigation, increased technical capacity, and better-educated procurement and project managers and professionals able to manage complex processes in pursuit of value for money. While even high-capacity governments are hard-pressed to keep up with these demands, the challenges for countries with lower capabilities are even more difficult.

One way to describe the evolution of procurement graphically is provided in figure 6.1. Administration of procurement of the nature described in the lower-left quadrant of the figure predominantly involved compliance with legal and administrative rules and procedures to achieve a competitive process and value for money. The implicit assumption is that strict compliance with well-designed rules would result in optimum results. On the other hand, procurement of the nature described in the upper-right quadrant, which is characterized by greater complexity, would require compliance with established managerial standards within a set of prescribed ethical and professional norms but would allow managers wider discretion on procedural and administrative matters to achieve results. In other words, while officers in the first case are expected to comply with strict

Figure 6.1 Evolution of Government Procurement Methods and Strategies

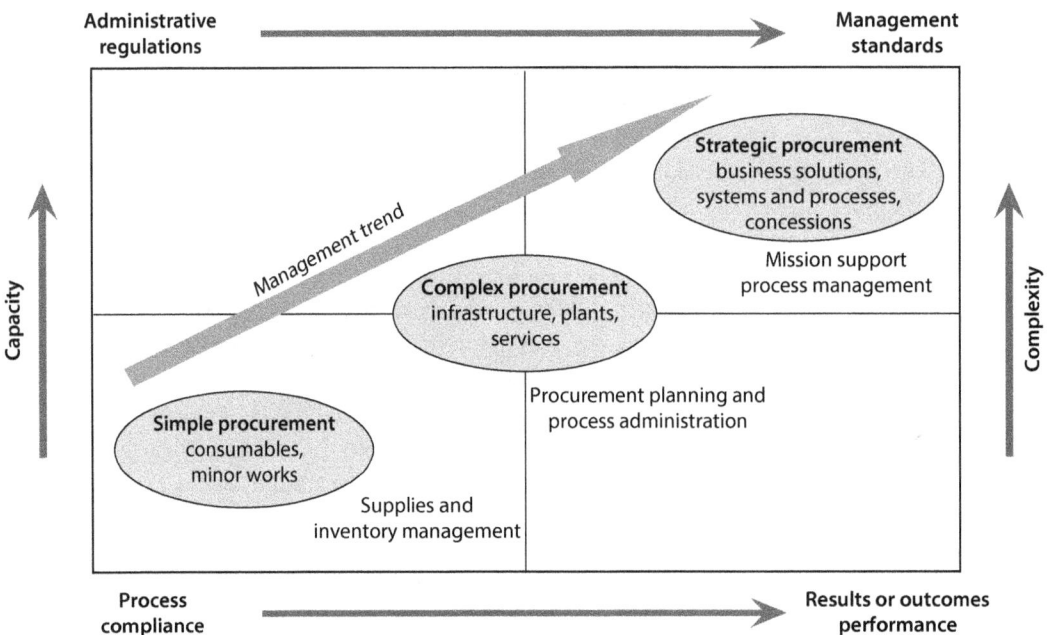

Source: Sanchez 2012.

formal procedures and have very limited discretion, in the second case they are expected to comply with ethical standards but have more procedural discretion to undertake analysis and exercise judgment to achieve project objectives. Similarly, while in the first case controls look at procedural matters, in the second case they focus to a greater extent on managerial performance and ethical behaviors. The complexity of modern procurement combined with increased emphasis on results requires greater capacity to make discretionary judgments based on contextual analysis.

Partly because of these new demands on procurement systems, public procurement is one of the fastest-changing government functions as both OECD and developing countries focus on the adaptation of procurement to new realities (see box 6.1). Moreover, the intense public interest in the fight against corruption and global concerns about fiscal efficiency have also created pressures for politicians and governments to address the need for more transparent and functional procurement systems.

Despite the various influences described in box 6.1, it is fair to say that procurement remains the least satisfactory aspect of most government systems, particularly in developing countries. Most developing countries inherited a colonial model of procurement that implemented a rule-bound, highly centralized process through national tender boards and stores or similar bodies. The successful adoption of even this rule-based model of procurement was uneven across countries. Procurement is particularly problematic in developing countries, because wherever the institutions and norms for public management are not well established, and wherever the civil service may be poorly trained and remunerated, compliance with rules tends to be weak and overall governance conditions poor.

However, as procurement expanded in volume and diversity, and as globalization changed technological specialization and the underlying market structures, centralized procurement became even less able to respond to the needs of the client agencies. The system often failed to perform because, in its rigidity, it could not adapt quickly to modern market conditions.

The response to this problem of outdated, ineffective procurement was to recommend an alternative institutional model for procurement administration. The 1994 UNCITRAL Model Law on the Procurement of Goods, Construction and Services was promoted across much of the world by international organizations such as the agencies of the United Nations and the World Bank. This model law—formally adopted by over 30 countries and influential on the procurement systems of many others—recommended the following:

- Centralized regulation of procurement at the national level, with decentralized procurement by the different agencies at the central or subnational levels under the responsibility of designated agency or district procurement authorities.
- A permanent administrative authority (usually the Ministry of Finance) to coordinate procurement policies with the overall goals of government.

Box 6.1 Influences on the Approach to Procurement

Important developments in the early 1990s triggered the change in perspective regarding the role of procurement beyond the conception of a mere administrative function into a strategic state sector function. These events forced governments to focus on procurement as they sought to adapt national systems to international trade agreements and to new business concerns. In addition, growing civil society interest in curbing corruption and the greater demands for accountability and results put politicians on notice about the importance of promoting and ensuring efficient and transparent procurement. Several events or developments during this period served as important drivers in reforming procurement:

- The General Agreement on Tariffs and Trade (GATT) and the Uruguay Round of multilateral trade negotiations within the GATT framework culminated with the signing in April 1994 of the Governments Procurement Agreement (GPA) and the creation of the World Trade Organization in 1995. The GPA introduced a multilateral framework for government procurement that aimed to achieve greater liberalization and expansion of world trade.
- In 1994, the United Nations Commission on International Trade Law (UNCITRAL) published the Model Law on Procurement of Goods, Construction and Services. This law was in response to the fact that in a number of countries the existing legislation governing procurement was felt to be inadequate and outdated, resulting in inefficiency and ineffectiveness in the procurement process, patterns of abuse, and the failure of governments to obtain value for money in the use of public funds.
- Amid increased public interest in government corruption and the creation, Transparency International was established in 1993.[a]
- In the mid-1990s, in response to these events, international development institutions shifted the focus of procurement due diligence from supervising borrower compliance with their policies and procedures to one of promoting systemic analysis, risk assessment, and policy advice on how to improve national systems.
- The technological impetus beginning in the early 1990s made available new tools for electronic procurement that revolutionized the way governments could do business.[b]
- The creation of the European Union (EU) in 1993 brought to the forefront the multiplicity of national procurement systems that were an impediment to free trade and forced governments to focus on aligning their national systems, which culminated in the EU procurement directives adopted in March 2004.
- In March 2006, all leading multilateral and bilateral development agencies, 91 countries, and several civil society organizations involved in development issued the Paris Declaration on Aid Effectiveness. The declaration committed institutions and countries to continuing and increasing efforts in harmonization, alignment, and managing for results. It also listed a set of monitorable actions and indicators to accelerate progress in these areas. As a result of the 2006 declaration, the OECD produced a standardized diagnostic tool to assess public procurement systems on the basis of an internationally accepted set of standards for good procurement that governments can use as a benchmarking and monitoring instrument.

Source: Sanchez 2012.
a. For more information about Transparency International and its Corruption Index, see the website, http://www.transparency.org.
b. The original 1994 UNCITRAL model law was recently replaced by an updated model law in 2011 that incorporates the issues of e-procurement, among other changes. For more information, see the UNCITRAL website: http://www.ppi-ebrd-uncitral.com/index.php/en/uncitral-model-law.

• A central independent regulatory agency responsible for formulating policies; issuing instruments for application of the regulations (such as instructions, manuals, and model or standard solicitation documents); monitoring procurement operations; and training and disseminating knowledge to procurement officers.

Although the expectation was that the new institutional model would be more effective and responsive to modern conditions and the needs of specific agencies, it significantly raised the bar in terms of capabilities. It required the executing agencies to have higher capacity and establish adequate oversight and ensure consistency of policies and procedures. As with all institutional change, this adaptation has not yet occurred, for complex reasons—one being that most of the central regulatory agencies created under the reforms generally lacked the technical and budgetary resources as well as the political influence necessary to meaningfully affect system performance.

Because of the shortage of resources, many procurement officers throughout the system remain ignorant of the new regulations and instruments, particularly at the subnational level. A background assessment of the impact of procurement system reforms came to this dismal conclusion "There is little or no information on evaluation of the impact of recently implemented reforms on efficiency, transparency, public trust in the system, or results. In fact, there is no methodology for this kind of evaluation, and there are few documented evaluations of progress in implementing action plans." (Sanchez 2012)

Although applied economic theory and legal theorists have provided a useful framework for thinking about the challenges of procurement, there is a gap between procurement theory and practice, and public management practitioners continue to struggle with designing and reforming procurement systems. The gap is particularly large in developing countries where capabilities significantly lag the needs of governments. In broad terms, the status of appropriate institutional arrangements for procurement and the capacity of governments to undertake effective procurement generally appears, at best, to be "work in progress," with most countries still far from achieving an effective system for procurement.

Why Procurement Is Integral to Public Investment

For the purpose of this volume, our interest is in procurement related to public investment expenditures specifically, which typically involve moderate to complex contractual features, as depicted in figure 6.1.

Most international development assistance is classified as capital expenditure and deployed to finance public investment projects, and it forms the bulk of investment spending in low-income countries. Countries also allocate substantial shares of revenue from booming natural resource sectors to investments intended to create critical development infrastructure.

If we were to be told then that the assets purchased through such spending were subject to fraud and corruption—that collusive cartels had inflated the costs of the assets or, worse still, replaced them with poor-quality substitutes or never delivered them at all—we would conclude that public investment was a wasteful expenditure with little or no impact on the growth prospects of the country.[2] Even more benign factors may contribute to the low value of public investment: for example, many countries consistently underspend the allocated capital budget, in part because of delays in the procurement process, and the delays then contribute to cost escalation and devaluation of benefits.

The scenarios just described and myriad other pitfalls can derail a public investment project, no matter how critical it may be. Whether the investment ultimately succeeds or fails hinges on the strengths or weaknesses of a government's procurement system. The most prevalent challenges might be characterized as classic principal-agent problems and industry-specific hindrances to fair competition.

Principal-Agent Problems

Government procurement of goods and works suffers from the fact that the resources are managed on behalf of absent principals—the citizens (and taxpayers in the donor country)—by agents (politicians and government bureaucrats) who may not fully represent the principals' best interests. Politicians claim to represent the electorate and to make well-considered decisions in the broad public interest. It is clear from international experience that, once elected, politicians have a strong financial incentive to exercise discretion in ways that strengthen their political benefits and often deviate from the public interest. A common strategy for incumbent political parties is to maintain a monopoly on political donations by threatening to revoke market privileges, including procurement contracts, from contractors who donate resources to opposition candidates. This is the first distortion created by the separation of the principal and the agent within a government agency undertaking procurement.

Another distortion—information asymmetry between the purchasing department and the contractor—creates a further class of problems that complicate procurement. Procurement processes are susceptible to a range of rent-extracting practices, all the more with complex contracts and limited competition. Because economic returns to capital investment projects are often large, contractors may offer bribes to be favored in the award of contracts and seek to corrupt government officials.

A considerable amount of attention, therefore, focuses on ensuring that procurement departments follow competitive and transparent processes; avoid conflicts of interest; and reflect adequate concern for efficient and effective procurement of goods, construction, and services of the required quality and quantity at the least cost. Inevitably, these objectives require a system for monitoring and oversight that identifies and sanctions corrupt behavior by government officials and firms and provides a check against corruption.

Thumbs on the Competitive Scales

A second set of issues emerges from the nature of the industry supplying the good or service and whether it is characterized by competition or by collusion. If an industry has barriers to entry that limit competition, or if firms behave collusively or fraudulently in any way, then even a well-managed procurement agency will find it difficult to contain costs and ensure quality.

In some cases, governments seek to achieve multiple, even laudable, objectives through procurement, such as promoting local industry through local content requirements. Unfortunately, such limitations may also lead to higher costs or lower quality. In addition, public procurement often has attracted organized cartels, and without a sound system of detecting and penalizing collusion and ensuring fair competition for the supply of goods and services to public agencies, the efficiency of public investment could be significantly reduced.

Add a weak government procurement management system to a monopolistic or collusive set of suppliers, often allied with rent-seeking political elites, and you have a formula for the worst possible outcomes. Where powerful cartels offer bureaucracies monetary inducements to steer government contracts their way, the interaction between a weak government and strong business interests can lead to high-cost procurement and wasteful allocation of public resources. When audit processes fail to identify such corrupt practices or where political influence is used to suppress the reporting of collusion or imposition of penalties, the corruption in the procurement process can become an entrenched problem.[3]

Real-World Costs

Public investment procurement is particularly prone to significant efficiency losses because it involves large, discrete contracts that can provide high payoffs to elites by means of poor accounting and collusion. Some examples will illustrate the nature of the problem more vividly:

- *Collusive environment combined with inadequate design and appraisal.* Turkey's public investment program at the end of the 1990s consisted of 5,321 projects with an estimated cost of $150 billion and an unfinished balance of $105 billion. Based on the approximate $5 billion allocated for all public investment in 2001 and projections of similar amounts in future years, the State Planning Organization estimated that the current portfolio would take over 20 years to complete. Despite a fairly capable cost-benefit analysis process, the procurement process proved to be problematic: projects that were put out for bid often cost, at completion, up to three times the costs estimated at appraisal (World Bank 2001). One reason for the cost escalation was the widespread use of change orders in design and construction contracts. Although inadequate design at the appraisal stage contributed to the problem, the procurement process and collusion were seen to be significant reasons for the observed cost escalation of investment.

- *Rampant cost overruns.* The Construction Sector Transparency Initiative (CoST 2011) found variations between final and initial contract prices of typically 10–50 percent—in some cases as high as 100–180 percent for selected agencies in Ethiopia, Guatemala, Malawi, the Philippines, Tanzania, the United

Kingdom, Vietnam, and Zambia. Even countries with well-developed public investment management (PIM) systems, such as the United Kingdom, have cost overruns of up to 15 percent. The disparity between initial and final costs most commonly pertain to inadequate project identification and design as well as inefficient procurement contracting and execution (CoST 2010). These findings suggest that there is a large scope for efficiency improvement in all PIM systems, but in low- and middle-income countries, the potential efficiency gains can be especially significant.

- *Low capacity in fragile countries.* Project design and procurement in politically fragile countries can be complicated by limited information, low private sector interest, and technical complexity. In one country, the rehabilitation of a power transmission line across 2,000 kilometers of jungle led to numerous failed efforts over 10 years before a contractor was competitively procured.

- *Poor procurement performance hampering development.* A recent review of about 500 projects funded by the World Bank across all regions concluded that unsatisfactory procurement performance significantly affected the development outcomes of projects, with those outcomes being three to five times more likely to be negative in cases with poor procurement performance. The sustainability of such projects was also adversely affected (World Bank 2014).

At Stake: The Value of Public Investment

The investment lending portfolio of an organization like the World Bank provides a broad view of the global procurement problem. In 2000–10, the World Bank lent, worldwide, close to $56 billion for road construction and maintenance—slightly less than 20 percent of the Bank's total lending over the past decade. The roads sector illustrates the difficulty of managing procurement in an important sector for development (Patterson and Chaudhuri 2007). In one country, the World Bank's appraisal process identified 36 areas at risk of corruption in the design, planning, award, and management of a roads contract and recommended monitoring 59 different indicators (World Bank 2006, 146–54). Among 29 cases of World Bank-funded projects that were reviewed because of allegations of misconduct in procurement, three broad types of misconduct were often noted: collusion, false documentation, and fraud in contract implementation, the latter occurring often with the aid of project managers.

As the examples in box 6.2 illustrate, public procurement systems are integral to PIM because they have a potentially significant impact on the cost-benefit calculus that justified the project. Poorly performing procurement systems diminish the value of public investments (often at tremendous current and long-term cost) and often impair the sustainability of the investment. Effort expended in selecting good projects and in ensuring adequate budgeting (among the subjects of earlier chapters in this volume) may be completely undermined by a weak system of public procurement.

Box 6.2 Collusion and Cartels in the Roads Sector

In June 2011, the World Bank Integrity Vice Presidency issued an investigative report that documented widespread fraud, corruption, and collusion that plague the roads sector worldwide. The following selected excerpts from that report (World Bank 2011a) show some glimpse of the scope of the problems and their costs to developing countries.

> In an investigation in Bangladesh, evidence showed that companies paid project officials up to 15 percent of the contract value in exchange for contract awards. A Kenyan informant said that "collusion was rife" in the nation's roads sector, an allegation later confirmed by the Kenyan Roads Authority and the Kenyan Anticorruption Commission (Government of Kenya 2004, 2007). After interviewing several firms and government officials in Cambodia, [World Bank Integrity Vice Presidency] (INT) investigators concluded that there were strong indications that "a well-established cartel," aided and abetted by government officials, controlled the award of roads contracts. In the Philippines, "Numerous witnesses independently informed INT investigators that a well-organized cartel, managed by contractors with support from government officials, improperly influenced [Department of Public Works and Highways] contract awards and set inflated prices on projects funded by the Bank and others" (World Bank 2011b, 3). One Indonesian respondent explained that "the Indonesian collusive system had been operating for 32 years, and many viewed the 'free market' system as counter to the cultural norm of consensus and cooperation," a statement consistent with reports by Indonesia's competition law authority (Soemardi 2010) and scholarly research (van Klinken and Aspinall 2011).

The INT report sought evidence of collusion in Bank-supported projects, and it also found well-documented examples of collusion in non-Bank projects.

> Staff of the Overseas Development Institute reported evidence of an industry-wide cartel to fix prices on roads contracts in Uganda (Booth and Golooba-Mutebi 2009). In Tanzania, a review by a former Prime Minister disclosed an industry-wide cartel in the roads sector (Government of the United Republic of Tanzania 1996). In 2005 Indian Deputy Government Secretary Sanjeet Singh told participants at an international conference that cartels in the roads sector operated in various Indian states (Singh 2005). A joint study by the Government of Nepal, the Asian Development Bank, the U.K.'s Department for International Development, and the World Bank concluded that in recent years no tender in the Nepalese construction industry had been free of collusion (Government of Nepal 2009). A statistical analysis of bids in road tenders by the Lithuanian competition agency strongly suggested collusion among firms there (Government of Lithuania 2008); a 2009 World Bank study of public procurement in Armenia noted widespread reports of collusion in tendering (World Bank 2009); and in 2005 the Slovakia Anti-Monopoly Office uncovered a cartel among road construction firms (OECD 2005). At the 9th Global Forum on Competition in 2010, the governments of Colombia, Peru, Pakistan, and Turkey all reported that cartels were operating in their roads sector (OECD 2010).

Cartels are active in the roads sector throughout the developed world as well. The United States is certainly no stranger to bid rigging in auctions for highway contracts, the federal prosecutions of which peaked in the 1980s. The OECD's own work attests to the

box continues next page

Box 6.2 Collusion and Cartels in the Roads Sector *(continued)*

persistence of collusion in road contracts. It has held no fewer than five conferences over the past decade and issued several papers on how to combat bid rigging and cartelization in the construction sector.

In 1992, the Dutch parliament concluded that the entire construction industry in the Netherlands was cartelized (Van den Huevel 2006); in 2000, the Swiss Competition Commission concluded that the market for road surfacing in the northeastern part of the country was controlled by a cartel (Hüschelrath, Leheyda, and Beschorner 2009); and in 2010, the *Konkurransetilsynet*, Norway's competition authority, fined two companies for colluding on highway bridge maintenance tenders (Government of Norway 2011).

Source: World Bank 2011a.

Table 6.1 Estimated Cost Savings in Public Infrastructure Procurement from a 10% Increase in Competition, by Global Region and Sector, 2011
Average percentage of costs saved, % of GDP

Region	Road[a]	Electricity[b]	Water	Sewerage[c]	Total
East Asia and Pacific	9	4	2	2	15
Europe and Central Asia	43	24	2	2	64
Latin America and the Caribbean	4	2	0	0	6
Middle East and North Africa	7	3	0	0	10
South Asia	41	7	2	2	46
Africa	11	2	4	4	19
Total	16	7	2	2	25

Source: Estache and Iimi 2011.
Note: GDP = gross domestic product.
a. Assuming a road length of 150 kilometers.
b. Assuming an installed capacity of 75 megawatts.
c. Assuming a treatment capacity of 50,000 cubic meters.

Estache and Iimi (2011) provide a highly relevant discussion of the state of knowledge regarding procurement and investment in infrastructure, drawing on the experience of both developed and developing countries. A robust principle that emerges, consistent with auction theory, is the value of competition to reduce cost and increase quality in procurement outcomes (Klemperer 2000; Krishna 2002). Although the data on the number of bidders for procurement contracts in various sectors are limited, the authors note that evidence from aid-financed projects suggests that the average number of bidders is higher in road contracts (about 6.2 per contract) than for water sector (5.2) or electricity (4.6) contracts. They estimate that a 10 percent increase in the number of bidders has the potential to reduce the procurement cost of infrastructure by 5–11 percent, with the larger elasticity applying to the water sector, the lower-bound estimate applying to the electricity sector, and the roads sector's elasticity estimated to reduce costs by about 9 percent (Estache and Iimi 2011, 49–54). Table 6.1 shows an estimate of cost savings due to more competitive procurement, by sector and region.

Procurement's Role in an Integrated PIM System

To be effective, procurement needs to be understood in the context of the broader functioning of the public sector and not as a self-standing system. Seen from a positive perspective, procurement systems that give the public sector access to private sector innovation and creativity can greatly enhance the returns to public investment and the benefits the nation derives from public projects. In a recent policy document on developing the capability of the civil service, the U.K. Government conveyed ideas that are essential to improve a national procurement system (see box 6.3).

While acknowledging the importance of the broad civil service ethos to any public management process, we focus here on developing a procurement approach as part of a PIM *system* that, while consistent with the three-part description in box 6.3, goes far beyond it.

Procurement is often mistakenly conceived as a technical contracting exercise that culminates in the signing of a contract by a successful bidder. This conceptualization of procurement has driven a deep focus on the *process* of contracting:

Box 6.3 The U.K. Civil Service and Procurement

In 2013, the U.K. Cabinet Office published a report titled "Meeting the Challenge of Change: A Capabilities Plan for the Civil Service," which emphasized the need to obtain better value by improving the procurement skills of all civil servants, "not just those deemed to be procurement specialists." An excerpt from that section follows:

> Value is obtained during all three phases of commercial engagement: preprocurement, procurement, and postcontract. Today we tend to overly focus on the procurement phase. All civil servants involved in policy development and delivery will need to do the following:
>
> - *Preprocurement:* Develop better skills to specify needs confidently, clearly, and concisely, while not being overly prescriptive, in advance of commencing a formal procurement. This will allow for meaningful, planned, and competitive engagement with the whole market.
> - *Procurement:* Understand the underlying economics and contracting aspects of suppliers' tenders including pricing techniques, margins, and open book arrangements, as well as basic contracting terms such as contract changes, intellectual property rights, and termination. Knowing how to negotiate a good deal, applying commercial judgment is as important as understanding the procurement process.
> - *Postcontract:* Understand and apply commercial techniques to ensure that suppliers deliver to meet our (contractual) expectations in order to maintain best value, and be able to negotiate with suppliers when they do not deliver, including competently and confidently handling disputes.
>
> In addition, we should be able to meet and deal confidently with senior representatives from large suppliers, understanding their personal, professional, and corporate drivers.

Source: HMG 2013, 7.

---

defining the steps in the process in great detail and the mechanisms to be used to determine the winning bid. Although these steps and mechanisms are important aspects of a good procurement system, they provide an incomplete perspective and create a potentially costly detachment from the full public investment process.

A more integrated and robust understanding of the procurement function stretches from project planning through selection of the appropriate procurement method, the contracting process, and contract management. Particularly for procurement of technically complex systems, procurement does not stop with the contract award but remains relevant during implementation and contract management.

Figure 6.2 illustrates the full scope of an integrated PIM system and highlights essential linkages and primary points of intersection with the budgeting and procurement processes. It identifies the key stages of procurement (planning, method selection, contract planning, tender evaluation and contract award, contract management, review and monitoring, and audit and reporting).[4] Each of these stages has linkages to associated aspects of PIM and budgeting that, if well managed, could lower costs and speed up project implementation.

Of course, the items listed under the "procurement" heading are not unique to capital investment projects; all types of government purchases involve planning, a mechanism for awarding contracts, and contract monitoring. Many of the technical aspects of procurement—rules about how to advertise, or the opening of bids, or bid evaluation—are also common across all forms of procurement.

Figure 6.2 PIM System Linkages

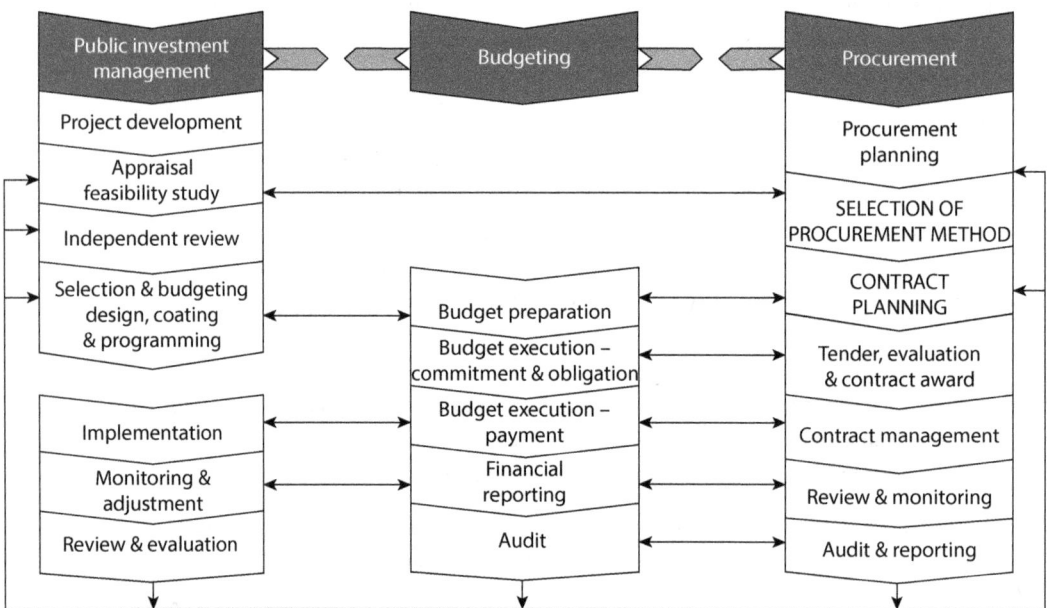

Source: Adapted from Biletska and Fozzard 2012.

Moreover, the spread of procurement laws shaped by the UNCITRAL Model Procurement Law over the past two decades (as further described in box 6.1) has created strong similarities in the substance of rules across countries.

However, as noted earlier, procurement for public investment projects raises distinct challenges (relative to procurement for standard goods). A major infrastructure project may require multiple contract awards for designs, separate contracts for construction, and yet others for technical supervision and oversight. Land acquisition is often problematic in countries where property rights are not clearly established and where legal systems are inefficient or overloaded. Each of these processes requires specific skills for the technical engineering, environmental, financial, and legal aspects of the project. In many cases, governments may also have to define technical standards for unique conditions. Because some problems manifest only during construction, governments also need to make ex post assessments and potentially resolve disputes with contractors. Warranties extend the need for contract and asset management well past the completion of the initial work and require continued attention.[5]

Unlike standard goods procurement, the limited scope to find private sector comparators for public goods such as national roads or an irrigation system or airports implies that governments must define technical standards and mechanisms to determine costs and quality ex ante and undertake complex monitoring and measurement to ensure adherence ex post. Value for money in capital investment procurement is also a much more difficult construct than in standard goods procurement—involving a determination of the extent to which the asset is fit for purpose and the total lifetime cost of the asset (a variable that is often not possible to determine without an analysis of the rate of depreciation).

Some of the complexity of public investment procurement can be better managed through a systematic and disciplined approach that links the project selection, design, budgeting, and procurement processes. Making better use of information from upstream PIM and budgeting can enhance key stages of procurement and project implementation and contribute to efficiency in public investment. The following subsections describe elements of the procurement process and the importance of their linkages to the PIM and budgeting processes as part of an integrated systems approach.

Procurement Planning

Good procurement planning that is derived from the investment project plan is a critical element in effective investment. Procurement planning should ideally be initiated in parallel with the project design and appraisal, and it may influence the budget plan estimates of the project cost by identifying a procurement method that offers the best prospect of achieving lowest cost for acceptable quality. But procurement planning is usually the weakest link between procurement and the PIM and budget systems, in part because it is not adequately recognized as an integral aspect of PIM. As a result, countries commonly underspend the budgetary allocation for capital investment. Ironically, when scarce resources are allocated to public projects with potentially high rates of return, a failure to synchronize procurement planning with budgeting leads to delays and low utilization of resources. Such delays can then contribute to cost escalation and further erode the efficiency of investment.

Government agencies in many countries typically do not develop detailed procurement plans for high-value, complex projects even though acquisition of such public investments is precisely an area where such plans have the most value added. Detailed plans can assist in determining an appropriate procurement method and, by more effectively managing multiple procurement contracts associated with acquisition of public infrastructure, achieve a better focus on procurement results.

The procurement process is often initiated only after funding for a public investment project is already allocated, allowing procurement staff little time to analyze needs, research the market, and develop specifications. Procurement planning often starts after a few months of the fiscal year have elapsed, and a contract may be awarded more than halfway through the fiscal year. Because budgets are generally appropriated annually, this delay is repeated every year and contributes to cumulative slippage in the implementation plan. It also undermines effective contract planning that takes market structure and supply chains into consideration, ensures appropriate contract design and methodology, and supports adequate costing and budgeting. Exceptions may be large capital investment projects with external financing[6]: feasibility studies for such projects are usually prepared with the involvement of procurement experts and consider alternative procurement options.

Upstream delays can also affect procurement. In many countries, project approval and budgetary resource allocation take a long time. For instance, in the United States, this process takes more than three years (Gansler 2002). Inadequate budget allocation poses another significant obstacle to efficient procurement planning, even for projects that are accurately costed. Additional complications are introduced for procurement planning when projects are fragmented with the aim of bypassing the scrutiny of economic appraisal.

Tender Evaluation and Contract Award

This stage in the public procurement process has a major impact on the efficiency of public investments, and in poor governance settings with weak capacity, this is also where a number of things can go wrong. Ensuring competitive selection and a fair market price remains a challenge in both low- and middle-income countries. Powerful vested interests often capture the tender evaluation process and influence the composition of an evaluation team, the evaluation criteria, the contractor selection and bidding methods, and the contract award. Complaint and appeals mechanisms in such cases are usually not effective. Governments often insist on domestic content in selection criteria when the capacity of domestic producers is limited. Yet a number of countries have made progress toward greater competition, including Albania, Mexico, Poland, Turkey, and others, where transparency and compliance with the procedures during the tender

---

Box 6.4 Elements of the Theory of Procurement

There is a rich literature on the applied economic theory of procurement (competitive markets and barriers to entry, information asymmetry, incentive economics, contract theory, and mechanism design). Much of the literature on procurement and regulation was sparked by seminal work by Jean-Jacques Laffont and Jean Tirole in the 1980s, who applied the perspective of informational asymmetries between buyers and sellers to better understand the problems of procurement and regulation. Laffont and Tirole (1993) describe the issues that complicate public procurement in terms of moral hazard, adverse selection, and nonverifiability.

Later on, Estache and limi (2011) succinctly describe the key ideas of the literature that provide the basis for decisions regarding whether an investment should be undertaken in-house or contracted out (contract theory); whether and how to unbundle construction and operation in investment projects; how to select contractors (auction theory); and whether to establish an ex post adjustment or an incentive contract.

While economics provides a strong analytical basis for designing procurement systems, a literature derived from legal theory provides a complementary basis for approaches to procurement. For example, Schooner (2002) provides a justification for key principles that provide a robust basis for the legal foundations of procurement in the United States. These include competition, systemic transparency, and procurement integrity, which are critical for the U.S. procurement system.

---

evaluation and contract award have significantly improved. On the other hand, as discussed in box 6.4, firms often enter into collusive agreements, which can impair efficiency and value for money.

The proliferation of procurement regulations in low- and middle-income countries also tends to become counterproductive, with adverse effects on efficiency and costs. Overregulation prompts contractors to specialize in bidding for work at a single agency or very few, which effectively leads to market segmentation and reduced competition. The volume of procurement regulations at the national level—excluding treaties, special acts, and guidelines—ranges between 158 and 508 in Latin American countries, 25 in Australia, and 83 in Canada, with the United Kingdom and New Zealand falling in between (Veiga Malta et al. 2011). Moreover, the rigidity of the established prohibitions on post-tender negotiations often impedes the ability of the purchasing agency to address strategic requirements of complex infrastructure procurement, such as adaptation of design and project schemes to the contract commitment (Krüger 2009).

The contract award stage in the procurement process also has significant implications for budgeting of public investments and overall fiscal sustainability. It is a widespread practice that contracts are signed without verification of budgetary resources. The lack of commitment control is a dysfunction of the public financial management system, undermining the ability of the procurement units to deliver efficient procurement outcomes. If the ministry of finance is not aware of the true amount of contractual commitments, there is no guarantee that it will be able to find sufficient resources when payments are due. Outstanding commitments for infrastructure projects can often reach a multiple of the infrastructure ministry's annual operating budget. The problem of "pending bills" also causes contractors to factor payment delays into their bids, further escalating the costs of public investment—a practice that, if left unaddressed, can undermine investment efficiency across the board. In other cases, procuring entities may deliberately understate the value of the contract to stay below a threshold for scrutiny by the ministry for finance or planning. But gaming the system in such a way can lead to problems downstream during project execution when contractors demand change orders that escalate the costs to their true level.

Contract Management

Contract management begins when a procurement contract is signed and ends when all the contracted services and products have been delivered, accepted, and paid for, and all associated contract paperwork and files have been archived. Good practice suggests that the management entity prepare a contract management plan that identifies the activities that project staff should perform or initiate to manage, track, amend, and close a contract. The plan's level of detail should be determined by the value and the risk associated with the contract.

Contract management involves supervising the contractor's performance, having qualified engineers or auditors verify completion and quality of planned phases of construction work, and authorizing payment tranches as per the contract terms. When the contractor requests a change order, a technical expert may need to assess the request on a timely basis, but the contract manager would need to follow a systematic procedure to ensure appropriate and transparent documentation and decision making.[7]

Without good contract management, payments can be delayed or payments may be authorized without verifying receipt of goods or services or progress of works. In extreme cases, the disbursement of funds may precede the commencement of a project, which may adversely affect the performance incentive of the contractor. As indicated earlier, upstream problems such as cash rationing or lack of commitment control can hinder the efforts of even a good contract manager. Deficiencies in the interaction between the procurement, PIM, and budgeting systems create a vicious cycle in which every broken link weakens another one, to the detriment of overall investment outcomes.

Large, complex projects always require adaptation and modification: Disputes arise over contract interpretation or how an unanticipated problem should be addressed. Problems may arise concerning land clearance or the collaboration between levels of government, and so forth. To handle such issues, contract management can either be proactive—anticipating problems and finding ways to resolve disputes before they escalate—or it can be bureaucratic and rigid, leaving people more concerned about avoiding blame for improper actions than about getting the project done. In India, for example, disputes have stopped work on approximately 10–15 percent of projects, and a massive amount of construction resources are trapped in projects that are not progressing (World Bank 2008). Effective contract management makes sure that physical and financial progress are aligned and on track, and figures out what to do in case they are not. It also makes sure that mechanisms for checking the quality of work are functioning properly and effectively.

At the most extreme, mechanisms for acquiring capital assets can become dissociated from PIM and budgets as governments turn to trading resources for investment, having contractors build assets with a promise of repayment, or relying excessively on government-to-government deals. Arrangements such as these are often popular in resource-rich, cash-poor nations that have little experience or capacity to execute stipulated procurement procedures in a manner that adds value. Capital "spending" in the Democratic Republic of Congo, the Lao People's Democratic Republic, and Mongolia, for example, have featured extensive use of such types of deals, often undertaken without the necessary transparency regarding the terms of the deal, much to the consternation of parliaments and development partners. It is important to note that such turnkey deals may sometimes be a rational choice in situations where governments lack the capacity to manage complex procurement and contract management, but such contracts still need to be negotiated transparently and with an eye to value for money.

Review and Monitoring

Monitoring the implementation of a contract, although treated separately here, is intrinsic to effective contract management. Contracts can include penalties for delays or underperformance, and such provisions require the contract manager to monitor and assess performance relative to the terms of the contract. Without consistent monitoring and periodic discussion with the contractor, projects are likely to go off-track, and any potentially corrective measures for delays or poor performance may come too late. A failure to review and manage contractors probably accounts for the widely noted tendency for large change orders and cost escalation. For instance, the Colombian government allowed contract modifications for roads concessions signed with various entities in 2008 for twice as much as the original contracted amounts; existing concessions were extended, and one was lengthened by 20 years with additional financing totaling four times the original amount (Veiga Malta et al. 2011).

Contracts are usually amended through change orders or, in extreme cases, renegotiation of the contract scope and provisions (Krüger 2009). Contract modifications are typically not captured in a financial management information system, so the financial implications of the change orders are not highlighted. Few countries have their e-procurement systems linked to the integrated financial management information system. Monitoring of the progress and quality of works is frequently a pro forma exercise. For instance, spot checks on sites in Mongolia and Peru are rare and their quality control marginal. Under these conditions, monitoring the implementation of contracts is weak, and significant cost overruns may be frequent with investment projects.

Audit and Reporting

Procurement audits play an important role in a well-functioning integrated procurement system. They not only address compliance with regulations and financial and operational integrity but also provide additional assurance that the procured goods and services can and will continuously perform according to acceptable standards. In addition, procurement audits can identify weaknesses in procurement processes and practices with a view to recommending necessary improvements.

In a well-functioning system, procurement audits are conducted periodically, covering different government agencies based on the risk management strategy. Reliable and full procurement reporting comprises all the information material to the procurement process, such as the tender evaluation, financial reports (including cost overruns with documentation explaining increases), reports on the physical progress and quality of works, and facility completion reports. Such reporting is fundamental for the efficient public investment and expenditure management that contains cost escalation and delivers value for money. Moreover, accurate recording and reporting of the finished infrastructure procurements makes it more likely that created assets are properly transferred to "owner" government agencies, are accounted for in the asset registry, and have an asset management plan.

Implications and Illustrations

From a diagnostic point of view, the approach described above provides a basis for diagnosing weaknesses in existing procurement systems and identifying the aspects that most critically affect the efficiency of public investment. However, it may strike the reader that the management capabilities for a fully integrated approach to procurement as a key aspect of PIM are quite demanding.

Building the capability of a broad class of civil servants to understand markets and industries, to negotiate and manage procurement contracts, and to exercise judgment that ensures good value for government is an achievable goal for advanced countries, but it is likely to be a long-term objective for most developing-country governments with limited capabilities.

Models for Reform

However, some examples offer a way to strengthen procurement for investment projects. Some countries have tried strategies that boost performance by supporting the ability of agencies to shape and manage complex procurements.

Strengthening Contract Monitoring and Oversight

The United Kingdom's Gateway review process was created to help agencies avoid the most common causes of project failure.[8] Under the auspices of the

Office of Government Commerce (OGC), Gateway reviews convene panels of knowledgeable, respected public and private sector representatives to provide guidance and advice at critical points to agencies managing large procurements. Six separate Gateway reviews are organized to examine the strategic assessment of each large project, the business justification for the project, the acquisition strategy, the contractual arrangements, the readiness of the agency to manage the asset once it is delivered, and a final review of the operation and the benefits received after delivery of the project.[9]

Although no definitive study has been conducted on the Gateway process's impact, the reviews are credited with contributing to significant savings in procurement and with creating a more informed approach across government to procurement of capital projects. One measure of its perceived success is the decision by the Government of New Zealand to adopt a similar practice for its major acquisitions.

Aligning Organizations around the Procurement Function

Although developed countries with higher capability may succeed with such approaches, there are ways to strengthen the link between procurement and project management that economize on limited capacity, which may offer developing countries some means to improve outcomes. In most countries, procurement is conducted by an enormous number of ministries and agencies that have a large number of other functions. The bureaucratic practices, civil service human resource policies, and official hierarchies that define these bodies often impede the type of decision making and output orientation that is essential for optimizing either the execution of procurement or the management of contracts. They also fail to consolidate limited capacity where they would be most effective. One way to improve on this is to create a state organization that is specifically designed to procure and manage large projects.

The South African National Roads Agency Ltd. (SANRAL) is a state organization consciously designed for the purpose of managing all aspects of a road network, including procurement and contracting.[10] Operating like a private sector firm, the agency was entrusted with responsibility for implementing the Government of South Africa's transportation policies in a commercially viable fashion. The agency structure supports a flat hierarchy, operating with a strong output orientation. Organizational structure and processes were designed to enhance the efficiency of operations and the effectiveness of project management. The tendering process was restructured to include an independent evaluation committee that brought together the project manager with representatives of the private sector. Integrating sophisticated market expertise in the review process enabled the agency to review a range of different proposals, expanding its ability to give contractors and consultants more freedom to propose innovative approaches. Staff were organized in expertise clusters to reduce hierarchy, promote technical excellence, and foster proactivity in risk and contract management.

The Power of Public Investment Management • http://dx.doi.org/10.1596/978-1-4648-0316-1

In part because of high-quality leadership, SANRAL has been largely success-ful. In the first decade of its existence, SANRAL more than doubled the size of the road network (from 7,000 kilometers to 16,000 kilometers) and prepared South Africa's infrastructure for the challenge of hosting the World Cup in 2010. Expansion of the road network took place at the same time that the financial model for building roads was changed, and the procurement process was recon-structed and enhanced.[11]

Part of SANRAL's success is derived from its organizational structure. Freed from traditional bureaucratic limitations, SANRAL was able to shape its procure-ment practices to meet its orientation toward performance.[12]

Marshaling Limited Capacity for Emergency Action

Modification of organizational arrangement for procurement has also been pur-sued in Papua New Guinea (PNG) for quite different reasons. In 1994, twin volcanoes erupted and rendered the central town of Rabaul uninhabitable. In response the Government of PNG established the Gazelle Restoration Agency (GRA) to act as the project implementation unit for all restoration work (World Bank 2010). Concentrating the limited technical expertise into one unit enabled the GRA to amass the necessary skills to effectively manage and execute pro-curement transactions and manage sophisticated contracts for relocating an entire town. Centralization of responsibility also provided donors and other aid providers with a focal point for support and capacity development.

Over the course of 10 years, the GRA oversaw the completion of 99 out of the 125 priority projects and initiated work on an additional 13 (while funding was still being sought for the remaining 13 undertakings). In a situation of severe capacity constraints and urgent need, centralizing responsibility into a single entity to manage project implementation proved to be a successful strategy for improving procurement performance.

Planning for Change

Another area to target for improving procurement is to anticipate the needs of large, complex public investment projects where contract modifications are highly likely. It would be important to ensure that the contract management includes an established process and performance metrics for effective monitoring of the project. Each public investment project must have an engineer assigned to supervise the physical progress and quality of works. Such an engineer signs off all work before payments are processed. The engineer is accountable for the delivery and quality of the project and thus should be vested with independence and authority to carry out this responsibility. But when significant change orders may be anticipated, it may be appropriate to retain a qualified technical expert or agency to offer timely advice on what contract changes are justified and how to keep costs and the completion schedule as close to original estimates as possible. Should the cost implications be very large, it may be necessary to reconsider the viability of the project.

The Republic of Korea, for instance, adopted the Total Project Cost Management System (TPCMS) in 1999 that enables the Budget Ministry to undertake continuous checks on project costs for large-scale procurements (Kim 2008). Although line ministries receive a contingency fund of up to 8 percent of total project costs to manage, the Ministry of Strategy and Finance (MOSF) must review all increases in total project costs. The TPCMS also institutes a triggering mechanism to ensure that projects remain feasible: An increase in project costs by over 20 percent triggers a reassessment of project feasibility (to prevent new money being thrown after bad). The TPCMS process also regularly checks the accuracy of the demand forecasts to ensure that no material changes would affect demand projections. A reduction in demand by over 30 percent triggers a reevaluation by MOSF of overall project feasibility. Since the application of the TPCMS, the percentage of projects with significant cost overruns has shrunk dramatically. From 1994 to 1998, more than 9 percent of projects registered increases of over 20 percent in their total costs. By 2002–04, that percentage had dropped to under 3 percent (Kim 2008).

Other pragmatic remedies may be within the reach of developing countries. For one, to begin procurement planning at the project design stage would enhance the efficiency of tendering and contracting once the project has been approved and budgeted. The benefits of such improved upstream preparation and coordination could be significant for major projects.

Conclusion

This chapter has underlined *the critical need to recognize procurement as a core aspect of a comprehensive approach to PIM* (and to good public management, more generally). This important linkage is often not acknowledged and even more rarely reflected in efforts to strengthen PIM. It also *set out a conceptual framework* for linking procurement to the process of PIM (particularly in the discussion surrounding figure 6.2) and *detailed the benefits* that coordinated management within this framework could achieve:

- Integrating the schematic features of a procurement process with PIM in a way that assesses the strengths and weaknesses of actual procurement and PIM arrangements in particular countries.
- Providing the key design principles for procurement reform to target and strengthen the weakest links.
- Aligning the procurement process with the growing interest in moving away from the older compliance-with-rules approach and toward a more modern, performance-based approach to procurement.

Achieving these benefits, however, does require a government to develop strong coordination and management capabilities to tailor reforms as well as to provide consistent political leadership of reforms.

Need to upgrade capacity substantially. Because the human resource and institutional capacities required are high, few countries currently do well in managing an approach to procurement that is integrated with PIM. Nevertheless, these capacities can be built up over time and activated through incremental reforms if motivated by good design principles and an end goal of efficient and effective investment. Focusing scarce managerial capacity on high-value projects may allow gradual progress rather than attempting to cover all public investment projects, many of which may be of low value.

Need for domestically tailored approaches to achieve reforms. It is worth emphasizing that the institutional arrangements should be intelligently adapted to domestic capability. Focusing on institutional functionality avoids the problem of "isomorphic mimicry," wherein blind imitation of developed-country institutional forms fails to achieve functional purpose in a developing-country context (Pritchett, Woolcock, and Andrews 2011).

Need for committed, credible leadership—both political and technical—to maneuver the institutional reform process. Procurement reforms, like most public sector reforms, rarely proceed according to a standard blueprint or plan. Being a deeply political process, reform requires both credible, authoritative political leadership and competent, motivated technical leadership. It is the combination of a reform pull from the top (through the adoption of new policies and practices) combined with a push from the bottom (through agencies and ministries developing practices that produce better outcomes) that ultimately yields sustained performance improvement. Sustained citizen engagement and interest in receiving public goods and services can motivate scrutiny and feedback that can limit waste and fraud in the procurement and investment process. Initiatives to improve the transparency of contracts can galvanize political and bureaucratic response and improve procurement processes and outcomes.

It is not that hard to point to new practices that have improved procurement outcomes in one or more jurisdictions. Introducing nontraditional forms of contracting (such as turnkey, performance, and other public-private partnerships) or increasing transparency around contract prices and input costs, or enhancing oversight of contract performance can all change the dynamics of the procurement process, and this list of innovations is by no means complete. However, the list of countries that have achieved sustained performance improvements in procurement across their PIM systems is much smaller.

Suffice it to say that the space between conceptualizing the dimensions of a well-integrated procurement system and establishing such a system is wide. Bridging that gap will require sustained effort to collect a stronger body of knowledge from experience across countries and sectors. This chapter is, we hope, a conceptual contribution toward building that body of knowledge.

Notes

1. The terminology for new approaches to procurement is not fully settled. An *electronic reverse auction* is an online, real-time dynamic auction between the purchasing organization and suppliers who compete against each other to win the contract by submitting successively lower-priced or better-ranked bids over a scheduled period.

A *framework agreement* between one or more contracting agencies and one or more suppliers or vendors establishes the terms (prices and the quantities envisaged) that will govern contracts to be awarded during a given period.

2. Poor procurement can also lead to fraud and waste in the purchase of office supplies, school textbooks, pharmaceutical products, and so on; thus the inefficiency can also affect the recurrent budget and undermine government services.

3. A range of literature discusses how political interests influence the procurement process and undermine investment outcomes (Tanzi and Dawoodi 1997; Pinto-Duschinsky 2002; Olken 2007, 2009; Olken and Pande 2012; Sacks et al. 2013). Golden and Min (2013) provide a broad review of distributive politics over 30 countries.

4. See Veiga Malta et al. (2011) for more detailed steps of the procurement process.

5. Many of these features can also be found in contracts for goods. Government purchasing of gasoline or computers often involves large sums of money, complex contractual terms, and advanced mechanisms to monitor contractual performance. We have emphasized distinctions between procurement in capital investment projects and simple procurement to highlight certain factors, but the more general point is this: the complexity of modern contracting implies that our perspective on all of our procurement needs to be revised.

6. However, even externally (donor) funded projects often cannot escape the limitations of poor procurement planning and budgeting.

7. Australia provides clear guidance on this process, including a checklist for considering requests for contract variation. To see the checklist and other parts of the Australian Government's "Better Practice Guide on Developing and Managing Contracts," refer to the website: http://www.anao.gov.au/html/Files/BPG%20HTML/Developing%20 and%20Managing%20Contracts/5_10.html.

8. A list of the most common causes of project failure in the United Kingdom, compiled by the National Audit Office and the Office of Government Commerce, highlights issues such as the lack of alignment between the organization and the project's strategic priorities, the absence of senior leadership, the lack of effective engagement with shareholders, and the lack of project management skills and experience dealing with supplier markets. See "Common Causes of Project Failure" at http://webarchive .nationalarchives.gov.uk/20110822131357/http://www.ogc.gov.uk/documents /Project_Failure.pdf.

9. For information about OGC Gateway Reviews, see http://webarchive.nationalarchives .gov.uk/20110822131357/http://www.ogc.gov.uk/what_is_ogc_gateway_review.asp. For information on the review process used in New Zealand, see Major Project Approval and Assurance Guidance, April 2011, at http://www.Hm-treasury.uk/d /major.projects.approvals.assurance.guidance.pdf.

10. For information on the South African Road Agency, Ltd. (SANRAL), see Bennet 2011.

11. The performance of SANRAL sets it apart from other African road agencies that were established at approximately the same time. For a comparison of the performance of different road agencies, see Pinard (2012).

12. The outstanding performance of SANRAL has not been shared by many of the road agencies that were established at around the same time. Road agencies can be found across the globe, but many of these bodies have been unable to establish independence from political control or to create organizations that function differently from more traditional ministries. The SANRAL experience demonstrates the possibility of

using organizational restructuring to generate improved procurement outcomes in capital projects, while the experience of other agencies cautions that such performance improvement is the exception rather than the rule.

Bibliography

Audet, Denis. 2002. "Government Procurement: A Synthesis Report." OECD *Journal on Budgeting* 2 (3): 149–94.

Bennet, Richard. 2011. "Increasing Transparency and Improving Project Management: South Africa's National Roads Agency, 1998–2011." Case study, Innovations for Successful Societies, Princeton University, Princeton, NJ. http://www.Princeton.edu /successfulsocieties.

Biletska, Nataliya, and Adrian Fozzard. 2012. "Integrating Procurement and Public Financial Management." Unpublished manuscript, World Bank, Washington, DC.

Booth, David, and Frederick Golooba-Mutebi. 2009. "Aiding Economic Growth in Africa: The Political Economy of Roads Reform in Uganda." Working Paper 307, Overseas Development Institute, London. http://www.odi.org.uk/resources/download/3829.pdf.

CoST (Construction Sector Transparency Initiative). 2010. *Report of the CoST International Advisory Group*. CoST International Secretariat, London.

———. 2011. *Report on Baseline Studies: International Comparison*. CoST International Secretariat, London. http://www.constructiontransparency.org/documentdownload .axd?documentresourceid=42.

Estache, Antonio, and Atsushi Iimi. 2011. *The Economics of Public Infrastructure Procurement in Developing Countries: Theory and Evidence*. London: Center for Economic Policy Research.

Gansler, Jacques. 2002. *A Vision of the Government as a World-Class Buyer: Major Procurement Issues for the Coming Decade*. Grant Report, New Ways to Manage Series, The PricewaterhouseCoopers Endowment for the Business of Government, Arlington, VA. http://www.businessofgovernment.org/sites/default/files/A%20Vision.pdf.

Golden, Miriam, and Brian Min. 2013. "Distributive Politics around the World." *Annual Review of Political Science* 16 (2013): 73–99. doi: 10.1146/annurev-polisci-052209 -121553.

Government of Kenya. 2004. *Proceedings of the First Kenya-South Africa Roundtable Discussion on Science & Technology Partnerships Related to Infrastructure*. Ministry of Planning and National Development, Nairobi, August 31–September 2.

———. 2007. *Examination Report into the Systems, Policies, Procedures, and Practices of the Roads Sub-Sector*. Kenyan Anti-Corruption Commission, Directorate of Preventive Services, Nairobi.

Government of Lithuania. 2008. "Lithuania." A statistical analysis of bids in road tenders by the Lithuanian competition agency. In *Policy Roundtables: Construction Industry 2008*, ed. by the OECD (Organisation for Economic Co-operation and Development) Competition Committee, 133–39. Paris: Directorate for Financial and Enterprise Affairs, OECD.

Government of Nepal. 2009. "A Review of Cases of Collusion and Intimidation in Public Procurement: A Way Forward to Mitigate Risks of Collusion and Intimidation." Joint study with the Asian Development Bank, the U.K. Department for International Development, and the World Bank, Government of Nepal, Katmandu.

Government of Norway. 2011. *Annual Report of Norwegian Competition Authority 2010*. Konkurransetilsynet (Norwegian Competition Authority), Oslo. http://www.konkurransetilsynet.no/en/2010/.

Government of the United Republic of Tanzania. 1996. *Report of the Presidential Commission in Inquiry against Corruption* (two vols.). Dar es Salaam.

HMG (Her Majesty's Government), United Kingdom. 2013. "Meeting the Challenge of Change: A Capabilities Plan for the Civil Service." Planning document, Civil Service Commission, Cabinet Office. http://engage.cabinetoffice.gov.uk/capabilities-plan/wp-content/uploads/sites/3/2013/04/Capabilities-Plan.pdf.

Hüschelrath, Kai, Nina Leheyda, and Patrick Beschorner. 2009. "Assessing the Effects of a Road-Surfacing Cartel in Switzerland." *Journal of Competition Law & Economics* 6 (2): 335–74.

Kim, Jay-Hyung. 2008. "Institutional Arrangements for Enhancing Public Investment Efficiency in Korea." Unpublished manuscript, Korean Development Institute, Seoul.

Klemperer, Paul, ed. 2000. *The Economic Theory of Auctions* (in two volumes). Cheltenham, U.K.: Edward Elgar.

Krishna, Vijay. 2002. *Auction Theory*, 2d ed. Burlington, MA: Academic Press.

Krüger, Kai. 2009. "Ban-On-Negotiations in Tender Procedures: Undermining the Best Value for Money." In *International Handbook of Public Procurement*, ed. by K. V. Thai. Boca Raton, FL: CRC Press.

Laffont, Jean-Jacques, and Jean Tirole. 1993. *A Theory of Incentives in Procurement and Regulation*. Cambridge, MA: MIT Press.

OECD (Organisation for Economic Co-operation and Development). 2005. "Cartel Agreement on Highway Construction." In *Annual Report on Competition Policy Developments in the Slovak Republic*, ed. by the OECD Competition Committee, 5–7. Paris: OECD. http://www.oecd.org/slovakia/37029727.pdf.

———. 2010. "9th OECD Global Forum on Competition." Paris, February 18–19. http://www.oecd.org/daf/competition/mergers/theroadtorecoveryunderconstructioncompetitionpolicyatwork.htm.

———. 2011. "Size of Public Procurement Market." In *Government at a Glance 2011*, OECD Publishing. http://dx.doi.org/10.1787/gov_glance-2011-46-en.

Olken, Benjamin A. 2007. "Monitoring Corruption: Evidence from a Field Experiment in Indonesia." *Journal of Political Economy* 115 (2): 200–49.

———. 2009. "Corruption Perceptions vs. Corruption Reality." *Journal of Public Economics* 93 (7): 950–64.

Olken, Benjamin A., and Rohini Pande. 2012. "Corruption in Developing Countries." *Annual Review of Economics* 4 (1): 479–509. doi: 10.1146/annurev-economics-080511-110917.

Patterson, William D. O., and Pinki Chaudhuri. 2007. "Making Inroads on Corruption in the Transport Sector through Control and Prevention." In *The Many Faces of Corruption: Tracking Vulnerabilities at the Sector Level*, ed. by J.Edgardo Campos, and SanjayPradhan, 159–90.Washington, DC: World Bank.

Pinard, Michael Ian. 2012. "Progress on Commercialized Road Management in Sub-Saharan Africa." Working Paper 92, Sub-Saharan Africa Transport Policy Program, World Bank, Washington, DC.

Pinto-Duschinsky, Michael. 2002. "Financing Politics: A Global View." *Journal of Democracy* 13 (4): 69–86.

Pritchett, Lant, Michael Woolcock, and Matthew Andrews. 2011. "Capability Traps: Techniques of Persistent Development Failure." Background paper for *The 2011 World Development Report: Conflict, Security and Development*. Washington, DC: World Bank.

Sacks, Audrey, Erman Rahman, Joel Turkewitz, Michael Buehler, Imad Saleh, and Ahsan Ali. 2013. "The Dynamics of Centralized Procurement Reform in a Decentralized State: Evidence and Lessons from Indonesia." Unpublished manuscript, World Bank, Washington, DC.

Sanchez, Alfonso. 2012. "Procurement." Background Paper, World Bank, Washington, DC.

Schooner, Steven A. 2002. "Desiderata: Objectives of a System of Government Contract Law." *Public Procurement Law Review* 11: 103.

Singh, Sanjeet. 2005. "Fighting Corruption in Developing Countries: Dimensions of the Problem in India." Paper presented at "Seminar on Good Governance, Institutional Integrity, and Human Resources Management for Road Administrations," World Road Association, Warsaw, Poland, October 20–22. http://publications.piarc.org/en /seminars/seminars_05/warsaw_October05.htm.

Soemardi, Tresna. 2010. "Interface between Competition Authorities, Competition Regulations, and Other Regulatory Frameworks and Institutions in Infrastructure Service". Report prepared for "Multiyear Expert Meeting on Services, Development and Trade: The Regulatory and Institutional Dimension," United Nations Conference on Trade and Development, Geneva,March 17–19.

Tanzi, Vito, and Hamid Dawoodi. 1997. "Corruption, Public Investment and Growth." Working Paper 97/139, International Monetary Fund, Washington, DC.

Van den Heuvel, Grat. 2006. "The Parliamentary Enquiry on Fraud in the Dutch Construction Industry: Collusion as Concept between Corruption and State-Corporate Crime." *Crime, Law & Social Change* 44 (2): 133–51.

van Klinken, Gerry, and Edward Aspinall. 2011. "Building Relations: Corruption, Competition, and Cooperation in the Construction Industry". In *The State and Illegality in Indonesia*, ed. by Edward Aspinall and Gerry van Klinken, 139–64. Leiden, The Netherlands: KITLV Press.

Veiga Malta, N. Joao, Paul Schapper, Oscar Calvo-Gonzales, and Diomedes Berroa. 2011."Old Rules, New Realities: Are Existing Public Procurement Systems Addressing Current and Future Needs?" Public Sector Study 66427, World Bank, Washington, DC.

World Bank. 2001. *Turkey: Public Expenditure and Institutional Review: Managing Budgetary Institutions for Effective Government*. Report 22530-TU, Washington, DC.

———. 2006. "Paraguay—Road Maintenance Project." Project Appraisal Document, Report 36421, World Bank, Washington, DC.

———. 2008. *Indian Road Construction Industry: Capacity Issues, Constraints, and Recommendations*. Report 46326-IN, South Asia Transport Unit. Washington, DC: World Bank.

———. 2009. *Republic of Armenia: Country Procurement Assessment Report*. Report 49975-AM. Washington, DC:World Bank.

———. 2010. "Building Capacity by Rebuilding Community Assets: Learning from the Gazelle Restoration Authority (GRA) Experience." Working Paper 68732, World Bank, Washington, DC.

———. 2011a. *Curbing Fraud, Corruption and Collusion in the Roads Sector*. Report of the World Bank Integrity Vice Presidency, Operations Policy and Country Services, World Bank, Washington, DC.

————. 2011b. *Redacted Report: National Roads Improvement and Management Program (Phase 1). Republic of the Philippines.* Report of the World Bank Integrity Vice Presidency, World Bank, Washington, DC.

————. 2014. *The World Bank and Public Procurement—An Independent Evaluation.* Report of the World Bank Independent Evaluation Group (IEG), World Bank, Washington, DC.

CHAPTER 7

Public Investment Management for Public-Private Partnerships

Motivation: Aligning Public-Private Partnerships with Traditional Public Investment

There are a variety of modalities for provision of public infrastructure. A wide range of parties and agencies participate in this process. Investment requirements should consider the full range of available public and private modalities and provisions. This is the case not only for central government but also for state-owned enterprises, subnational governments, and the private sector, particularly in the form of public-private partnership (PPP) programs.

As an attractive modality for public infrastructure provision, PPP programs have been widely discussed and developed since the 1990s. The United Kingdom outstrips the rest of the world in the number of PPP projects, although Australia, Brazil, Germany, India, the Republic of Korea, and South Africa as well as other developed and developing countries have also implemented many PPPs.

Definitions diverge regarding what constitutes a PPP, which leads to different figures regarding the number of PPPs.[1] As such, not all the figures are comparable, but those such as the following do give an indication of the wide extent to which countries use PPPs:

• Infrastructure projects constitute the largest sector by number of deals internationally, and PPP activity reached a peak during the 2003–07 period before slowing down because of the onset of the global financial crisis and recession (OECD 2010a). *Public Works Financing Newsletter*'s (*PWF's*)

Helpful comments have been received on various versions of this chapter from Paulo Belli, James Brumby, Martin Darcy, Jonas Frank, Ian Hawkesworth, Richard Hemming, Kirsten Hommann, Jens Kromann Kristensen, Peter Matthews, Rui Monteiro, and Anand Rajaram. An earlier version of the chapter was presented at a section of Jim Brumby, Kai Kaiser, and Jay-Hyung Kim (2013), "Public Investment Management and Public Private Partnerships," in *The International Handbook of Public Financial Management*, edited by Richard Allen, Richard Hemming, and Barry H. Potter.

"International Major Projects Survey" collected data about projects that represent various combinations of public and private sector risk taking with cumulative data since 1985 (*PWF* 2009, 2; reprinted from OECD 2010a). As of 2009, road PPPs represented almost half of all PPPs in value ($307 billion out of $645 billion) and a third in number (567 out of 1,747). Second is rail and third is water. The *PWF* database also confirms that Europe represents about half of all PPPs in value ($303 billion) and a third in number (642) (OECD 2010a).

- The Private Participation in Infrastructure (PPI) Project Database developed by the World Bank and the Public-Private Infrastructure Advisory Facility (PPIAF) represents the same trend of PPP project numbers and investments.[2] By number of projects and by investment commitments of the private sector in the transport, energy, and water and sewage sectors, PPI has been significantly increasing in the past decade although it has experienced a contraction since 2008 in the wake of the global financial crisis.

One key challenge for many governments is how to best justify PPP projects against the variety of other modalities. Unfortunately, most countries have been managing PPP projects separately from traditional government-financed and procured projects. Even if a government moves ahead with large-scale PPP projects, those projects have been mostly appraised, selected, and monitored separately from traditional projects. Governments have paid less attention to the careful appraisal and economic analysis of PPPs than to those of traditional projects, or, at most, considered them as a supplementary approach without any recognition that PPPs are inherently public investment projects that should be selected based on their capacity to produce an acceptable social and economic outcome. This disparity has undermined adequate public financial management (PFM) and created undue fiscal risks, causing fiscal concerns with respect to appropriate forms of accounting, reporting, budgeting, and other processes.

A project implemented through PPP should require the same level of public investment management (PIM) social and economic justification. To these ends, this chapter argues the necessity for a "unified framework" for integrating both traditional government project implementation and PPPs. The objective is to increase awareness of the need to integrate PPPs into the traditional PIM framework, identifying opportunities for strengthening the integration of PPPs into national PIM systems. The chapter characterizes PPP schemes through the lens of the eight "must-have" features of PIM as presented in figure 2.1, comparing PPP management with conventional PIM. It recognizes the challenge in adopting a unified framework in practice but also suggests starting points to handle PPPs under the umbrella of a unified framework.

The next section presents the rationale for employing PPP as an implementation method for public investment projects. Following that, the section titled "Why the Need for a Unified Framework?" describes the advantages of developing such a framework. In the section titled "Challenges to Having a Unified Framework in Practice," the eight must-have PIM features in PPPs are explicitly characterized one by one. Some features are similar to those addressed in conventional government PIM, while others need to be adapted to the specific requirements of the PPP methodology. The section presents challenges to having a unified framework in practice by running through the eight must-have PIM features in PPPs. The section titled "Future Work for the Unified Approach" contains the concluding remarks.

The Rationale for Public-Private Partnerships

Countries tend to promote PPP projects because (a) they anticipate attaining better value for money by taking advantage of the creativity and efficiency of the private sector, and (b) they lack the financial or human resources to carry out the projects themselves. These two rationales for PPPs are usually stated as enhancing efficiency (or better value for money) and easing fiscal constraints (or resource additionality).

The principal rationale should center on efficiency in general. However, the efficiency rationale is usually based on a number of assumptions that may or may not exist in a given country: competitive markets, effective identification and implementation, optimal transfer or share of risks, and the ability to prepare good projects and develop and agree on good contracts. The fiscal constraint rationale is also important because the lack of government financial resources, particularly in developing countries, can lead to inadequate investment in essential infrastructure, leading to low levels of public sector investment against gross domestic product (GDP) and constraining GDP growth. This low public investment may in turn impair the government's ability to pay off debt. Given the effect of additional infrastructure investment on the national economy, many countries have promoted PPP projects instead of cutting investment amounts when they face a lack of financial resources.

Although additional resources for PPPs can accelerate the establishment of new infrastructure, it is neither possible nor desirable to increase the amount of additional resources without limits. Building infrastructure facilities through additional resources for PPPs means that the government borrows from the private partner to fund its investment needs; in effect, the additional resources still need to be paid off in the medium and long term. It is not "free money." The government cannot increase the amount of future liability indefinitely. Insofar as the efficiency enhancement is not achieved, the additionality rationale cannot be sustainably increased and maintained.

From a fiscal point of view, therefore, a principal key to initiating PPP projects is to establish whether a government can maintain the same level of fiscal efficiency and sustainability through PPPs as through conventional means of implementation. Unfortunately, countries with limited experience in PPP projects, and even those *with* PPP experience, find it hard to calculate how much private involvement or government liability will be efficient and sustainable.

Why the Need for a Unified Framework?

Across the whole investment cycle for PPP and conventional public investment, there are different modalities for identifying investment procedure and achieving value for money. In conventional schemes, based on solid information on the condition and cost of public services, the government specifies the quality and quantity of the services required. In a PPP scheme, however, the government explicitly specifies the quality and quantity of the service it requires from the private partner.

The private partner may be responsible for the project design, construction, financing, operation, and management of a capital asset as well as the delivery of a service to the government or the public using that asset. Project risk is identified, priced, and allocated to the private company where appropriate through a payment mechanism and specific contract terms. Risk transfer to the private partner may improve value for the money, but only up to the point where it creates the incentive for the private partner to improve efficiency. It is almost never the case that all risks in a project are transferred to the private company. This point must be kept in mind when comparing PPPs and conventional implementing options.

Under these different modalities, a unified framework would provide several advantages:

- Ensuring consistent assessment and decision making
- Supporting optimal risk transfer
- Avoiding unmanaged fiscal risks while improving transparency

Ensuring Consistent Assessment and Decision Making

First of all, a unified framework helps to ensure that decisions on public investment projects are consistent in keeping value for money objective throughout the project cycle, even though objective decisions cannot be guaranteed. According to an OECD (2010b) survey, the value-for-money (VFM) objective is often blurred in practice, and the choice between a PPP and traditional procurement is skewed by factors other than value for money; government officials in many countries feel that the rules in place impede attaining the maximum value for money by creating incentives to prefer traditional procurement to PPPs. Various factors that may skew this choice and thereby undermine the pursuit of value for money include the following:

- The legal and institutional setup
- The range and complexity of the VFM tests to which PPPs and traditionally implemented infrastructure projects are subjected
- The roles in the procurement process of the parliament, the ministry of finance, the PPP unit, and the implementing entities
- The accounting standards applied to both PPPs and traditionally implemented infrastructure projects

Political preference for or against PPPs may also play a role in skewing choices and affecting outcomes. A unified framework has the potential to minimize subjective decisions concerning traditional versus PPP implementation.

Supporting Optimal Risk Transfer

Second, a unified framework helps to accomplish optimal risk transfer. It is important to note that all service delivery mechanisms—whether they are public, private, or partnership models—are exposed to risks. The key difference with PPPs is that a large part of their efficiency or value for money is derived from the effective identification, pricing, and transfer of risk from the public to the private sector. Failure by the government to mitigate these risks may not only have fiscal consequences for the government but also affect service delivery. Good risk management allocates risk to the party best able to manage it.

Designing the optimal level of risk sharing (including the respective level of fees versus subsidies) involves complex trade-offs, and the optimal contract may depend on the specific circumstances of the project (Engel, Fischer, and Galetovic 2007). With the addition of each activity to the responsibilities of the private partner, the question is whether the private partner is the best party to manage the specific risk involved with the additional activity.

If each project (whether conventional or PPP) is separately managed, the concept of optimal transfer from one to the other may not be ensured; it opens doors to inadequate risk shifting in different steps in the project cycle. A unified framework, therefore, might be considered one of the conditions for achieving optimal risk transfer in both conventional and PPP options.

Avoiding Unmanaged Fiscal Risks and Improving Transparency

Third, a unified framework may help to avoid unmanaged fiscal risks and to improve transparency in the PFM system. It could lead to the incorporation of all PPP fiscal commitments and risks into the government's routine fiscal screening and monitoring process. As such, it enables the government to effectively assess the real burden of PPP commitments and risks within a medium- and longer-term fiscal framework. The government, for example, is able to forecast the present value of the PPP commitments as a fraction of current GDP or current government revenue to get a sense of its future fiscal flexibility and vulnerability to shocks that affect the payments.

A unified scheme is useful for the public reporting of PPP commitments as well. There have been numerous debates in the past decade about whether to attempt to classify PPPs as either government or private assets.[3] There is a concern that such a binary approach to accounting and reporting—where PPP assets are recorded either on or off the government balance sheet—will inevitably tempt governments to tailor PPPs to meet the requirements for off-balance-sheet recording (Hemming 2008, 239)[4] and is likely to present parallel budgeting for PPPs. A unified framework may discourage parallel budgeting by reporting the known and potential future fiscal costs of PPPs in the traditional budget system.

By strengthening procedural controls on PPP commitments, the framework helps to improve overall transparency in the PFM system.

Challenges to Having a Unified Framework in Practice: Eight PIM Features in PPPs

This section will apply the eight must-have PIM features presented in chapter 2 to *the modality of PPPs* with a view toward applying a unified framework. The preceding section provided arguments on the usefulness for a unified framework, but one must recognize a series of incentive problems and practical implementation constraints that limit the possibility to swiftly apply such a framework in practice. This section therefore highlights the difficulties in applying a unified approach by running through the eight steps that correspond to the must-have PIM features for PPPs and discussing several entry points to move toward such a framework.

Step 1: Strategic Guidance for Screening and Planning PPPs

In conventional public investment, strategic guidance is critical to anchor government- and sector-level decision making. Such guidance is described in a national plan or medium- to long-term strategic document that establishes economywide development priorities at the highest decision-making levels.[5]

In contrast, in many countries, PPP projects are *not* formally included in the national development strategy or other medium- and long-term government investment planning. They are chosen without any integrated strategic guidance and coordination between conventional and PPP implementation methods. Instead they are mostly managed as stand-alone projects or initiatives. In most cases, planning instruments do not explicitly (a) provide any strategic guidance for PPP project identification or selection; (b) highlight the role of PPPs for economywide development priorities; or (c) describe why and how these projects might benefit a nation's social and economic development. Under such nonunified proceedings, PPPs can be more easily affected by politically driven decision making. Although most governments declare that PPPs should be selected only when this approach promises better value for money compared with conventional public investment, in practice there is often insufficient scrutiny to properly screen and plan all candidate PPPs.

Establishing strategic screening and planning guidance for potential PPPs should therefore be the starting point because it offers the following fundamental advantages:

- By listing eligible asset types in the PPP law or regulation, some governments can more directly signal where and in which sectors private capital is required to benefit the public.
- A certain level of restriction for a narrowly defined sector of candidate PPPs is useful: it facilitates the assessment based on a public sector comparator or a private finance initiative.

On the downside, one might well argue that such restrictions limit the flexible and innovative nature of PPPs. However, lack of guidance may open doors for politically driven projects. An explicit legal and regulatory framework, along with planning and proper guidance, facilitates the initiation of PPP projects because it concedes to the private sector the right for initiation or participation. Clearly, the enabling legislation also needs to allow for some flexibility to cover most circumstances.

A unified guidance for identification, appraisal, and selection of both PPP and conventional projects is arguably complex. It represents an ideal solution, but it is also clear that institutional arrangements in some countries, along with political conditions, might rule out a more comprehensive approach. In such a case, a more realistic and "second-best" solution may be to develop a separate and basic guidance for qualifying PPPs along the following minimum criteria:

- The project should be in accordance with the medium- to long-term national strategic plan for public investment in the country.
- The project should meet eligibility criteria and appraisal standards relative to other candidate PPP projects.

The first requirement is expected to help minimize distortion in prioritizing PPPs relative to conventional investments, whereas the second should help in prioritizing *among* PPPs.

Dealing with Unsolicited Proposals

An unsolicited proposal is one initiated by a private partner to undertake a PPP project rather than one submitted in response to a government request. This is the opposite of conventional proposals, which are solely initiated by the government. Most countries reserve the right only to the public sector to initiate PPP projects. However, some countries also allow unsolicited proposals. They require a specific treatment because it can be expected that more countries are likely to allow unsolicited proposals in order to reap further efficiency gains and additionality of resources. Unsolicited proposals allow governments to benefit from the creative knowledge and ideas of the private partner.

However, unsolicited proposals also create challenges that may increase the risk of mismatch in funding or prioritizing a government's strategic planning for infrastructure projects. Solicited PPP projects would be selected within the scope, sectors, and boundaries established by a national strategy and planning, but, by definition, unsolicited projects are not mainstreamed or included within such a national strategy. Accepting unsolicited projects, particularly if they are given preference and prevalence over already existing high-priority government projects, may cause distortion within the public investment portfolio.

To minimize these risks, specific eligibility criteria for unsolicited proposals should be developed and announced. The rules would assure that

- The unsolicited proposal is consistent or comparable with the existing national planning so that it may not distort planned priorities;

- It is creative and efficient enough to deliver extra value to the sector to compensate for possible costs of distortion; and
- If the project fails to meet the above two clearing rules, it should be rejected.

Step 2: A Unified Framework for Project Appraisal

Achieving the objectives of the project at the optimum "value for money" should be the driving force behind any project appraisal. In many countries, the VFM objective in project appraisal is sacrificed for other goals or even simply ignored. Conventional methods are applied to PPP projects as default modes without any careful VFM comparisons (OECD 2010b).[6]

Unfortunately, most countries still have not developed clear criteria to identify whether projects are either PPP or conventional candidates. Although PPP projects are often not numerous, they usually involve large sums of resources; as such, they are considered as special cases that create incentives for exceptions to established screening and eligibility criteria. It is important, therefore, to provide fiscal regulation for PPP project assessments with the same care applied to conventional implementation. A unified framework in appraisal would ensure achievement of this goal.

Countries that have a long history of PPP implementation have made efforts to establish a unified framework for project appraisal (further discussed in box 7.1), such as the following:

- In Australia and the United Kingdom, most PPP projects have been service-contract types that generate long-term government commitments, and there is a need to establish the same scale and quality of project preparation, appraisal, and screening processes for all forms of projects.
- In the United Kingdom, the government's guidance on appraisal and evaluation, known as *The Green Book*, provides a unified framework for the preparation and assessment of both conventional and PPP projects. It provides guidance for all central government agencies on how to conduct ex ante project appraisal and ex post project evaluation (HM Treasury 2011). *The Green Book* clearly states that public bodies need to carefully consider which implementation route is likely to be most efficient and effective, and it also contains principles to guide decision makers on how to undertake a project, including the degree of private sector involvement.
- In Australia, the state government of New South Wales delivers a unified scheme by first deciding whether the investment in a specific project is necessary ("decision to invest") through analytical methods such as cost-benefit analysis, then considers the procurement option ("method of financing") through VFM analysis. At that time, it compares VFM inherent in a conventional approach relative to making use of a PPP. This process can prevent the government from pursuing PPPs for motives other than VFM (NSW Government 2006).
- Korea is another case where a unified framework for project appraisal was established that required an option test using cost benefit and VFM analysis in considering a potential investment project.

Box 7.1 Project Appraisal Frameworks in the United Kingdom and Australia

The United Kingdom

The decision on the need for investment is made during the appraisal process, implemented by the proposing ministry. The economic study and the affordability study are thoroughly reviewed. When the project business case is approved, HM Treasury, through the Spending Review, makes the final decision on the project implementation.

The Green Book is the HM Treasury guidance that sets out a framework for the appraisal of all central government projects and programs (HM Treasury 2011). It clearly states that public bodies need to carefully consider which implementation method is likely to be most effective, and it also contains guidance to decision makers on how to undertake a project, including the degree of private sector involvement.

Among the stages of an assessment—broadly identified as justifying action, setting objectives, option appraisal, developing and implementing a solution, and evaluation—the option appraisal stage is often the most significant part of the analysis where values of the costs and benefits are identified and adjusted. In the ensuing solution development and implementation stage, implementation routes, including the role of the private sector, are considered. The outputs are presented in the form of business cases.

Business cases are the documents through which investment proposals are proposed, scrutinized, and, if approved, executed to ensure that the proposed project is affordable and offers value for money. A strategic outline case (essentially a prefeasibility study) establishes the need for investment, appraises the main options for service delivery, and issues a recommendation. The document entails preparation and appraisal of the wide range of options for achieving the project objectives, including service delivery options and funding options. The service delivery options range from in-house to outsourcing, from using the public sector to using the private sector, or a strategic combination of both (PPP). Regarding funding options, the choice of whether the required services may be provided on a PPP basis is carefully looked at.

To achieve better value for money for public spending, HM Treasury revised the project approval process, which has been effective since April 1, 2011. The Major Projects Authority, replacing the Major Projects Directorate in the Office of Government Commerce, has been established within the Cabinet Office's Efficiency and Reform Group.[a]

Australia

The decision on a capital investment consists of government approval of both the investment and the preferred implementation method. The procuring agency initially identifies infrastructure needs and analyzes the expected benefits of the investment. Government departments and agencies analyze implementation methodologies to determine the most appropriate method.

Departments and agencies undertake asset and infrastructure planning. It is generally advised that new infrastructure investments be planned only if the assets required for service delivery and resources are likely to be available. In the project assessment and procurement strategy stage, a business case is widely used, which addresses project objectives and scope, financial analysis, and risk analysis. The procurement strategy includes procurement

box continues next page

Box 7.1 Project Appraisal Frameworks in the United Kingdom and Australia *(continued)*

options and analysis and recommends to government the most appropriate method of implementation.

After short-listing delivery models and considering the suitability of various delivery methods, a validation and delivery-model options analysis is conducted. A preferred delivery model is selected after thorough analysis of the model that best achieves the requirements and objectives of the project and minimizes risks. The analysis includes determining (a) core versus noncore services (core services being those that government retains responsibility for delivering); (b) value for money, to see whether private sector involvement is likely to deliver the best value for money; and (c) market capability and appetite.

Infrastructure projects are delivered through a variety of delivery models that include PPPs; construct-only (lump-sum or fixed-price contract); design and construct; design, construct, and maintain; construction management; alliance contracting; or managing contractor model. The best delivery model is analyzed through suitability criteria and drivers of value.

Sources: Australian Government 2008; HM Treasury 2011.
a. In the United Kingdom, the Treasury withdrew the VFM quantitative tool on December 2012 when Private Finance 2 (PF2) was introduced. At the same time, the Treasury said it would update the existing VFM assessment guidance to reflect a wider choice of contracting options, including PF2, but this extended guidance is still under development (National Audit Office 2013).

Considering the experiences and lessons from Australia, Korea, and the United Kingdom, a standardized example for project appraisal in a unified framework could be composed of two phases: (a) decision to proceed and (b) decision to implement (see figure 7.1):

- *Decision to proceed (preliminary feasibility study)*: A preliminary feasibility study should be conducted to prepare for the decision to proceed and a full preparation in a later stage. Justifying the need for an intervention and setting the objectives for a project are crucial first steps. Cost-benefit analysis enables a feasibility assessment of the project from a national economy perspective and gives an early indication of whether a conventional or PPP approach might be feasible. The preliminary feasibility study not only assesses whether to proceed with the full project preparation but also pushes the government to invest in more detailed project preparation in advance.

- *Decision to implement (value for money [VFM] assessment)*: If the proposed project appears to be feasible, a VFM assessment would assess the implementation options—conventional versus PPP. Basically, government costs and project inputs of an often-known *public sector comparator* are compared against those of the projected risk-adjusted costs of a PPP alternative to assess whether the PPP might achieve better VFM. The VFM assessment provides a quantitative VFM comparison between the options and a justification for the decision on the implementation option. It also encourages project appraisers to consider risks early in the project life cycle and address risk transfer options in the bidding process.

Figure 7.1 Standard Example of a Unified Framework for Project Appraisal

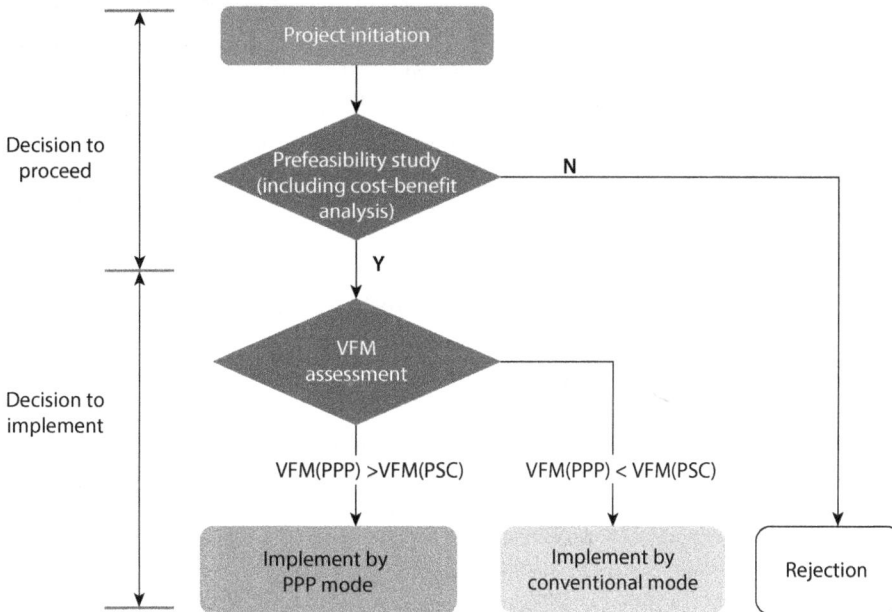

Note: PPP = public-private partnership; PSC = public sector comparator; VFM = value for money.

If the PPP option cannot demonstrate best VFM, the project is implemented by the conventional method, provided it fulfills all appraisal standards.

Step 3: Independent Review of the Appraisal

As described previously in chapter 2, an independent review is useful particularly for projects that are large, whose benefits are uncertain, or whose fiscal risks are too high. The so-called optimism bias—underestimation of costs and overestimation of benefits—is a well-known incentive problem, and an independent peer review can provide additional constraints to limit any undesirable effects. The function can be performed by the ministry of finance, a planning ministry, other specialized agency, or technical specialists outside the government. Clarity of specific responsibilities is important: a multiplicity of players with unclear accountabilities in independent reviews can overburden the appraisal system and weaken it.

In the case of PPPs, the role of independent peer reviews may be especially important given the role of dedicated PPP units.[7] Although OECD (2010a) and World Bank and PPIAF (2007) do not highlight the importance of the independent role, it is essential to clearly establish whether and from whom the dedicated unit should be independent.[8] The best value for money should be achieved when optimal risks, but not the highest risks, are transferred and shared among the public and the private partners. This is because risk transfer can increase value for money, but only up to the point where it creates the incentive for the private partner to improve efficiency. The more the evaluating entity is independent from a particular delivery method or agency, the more its judgment is likely to be unbiased, which favors and facilitates an *optimal* partnership between two parties.

The cases of Australia (Partnership Victoria); Korea (Public and Private Infrastructure Investment Management Center [PIMAC] at Korea Development Institute [KDI]); the Netherlands (former Dutch Kenniscentrum PPS); Portugal (former Parpublica SA)[9]; South Africa (National Treasury's PPP unit); and the United Kingdom (former Partnership UK or Infrastructure UK)[10] deliver some different rationales of good practices.[11] There are three emerging models for these units:

- *A new agency*: Australia (Partnership Victoria), Portugal (former Parpublica SA), and the United Kingdom (former Partnership UK)
- *A government think tank*: Korea (PIMAC at KDI) and the Netherlands (former Dutch Kenniscentrum PPS)
- *A body within a ministry such as the finance ministry*: South Africa (National Treasury's PPP unit) and the United Kingdom (Infrastructure UK)

These units are mostly declared to contribute to managing PPP policy and strategy, project analysis, transaction and contract management, monitoring, and enforcement. The models are not without the risk of conflict of interest: they are mandated to promote and improve PPP policy and projects for the direct interest of spending ministries and agencies, and, at the same time, they are supposed to be independent from the spending ministries and agencies as gatekeepers. However, the two roles of the unit—as a PPP promoter or a gatekeeper—may actually be in conflict with each other. A body responsible for promoting PPPs cannot really be seen to be independent of interest in the subject matter.

In light of these risks and possible conflicts of interest, the key recommendation is that there be strict independence from the direct interests of spending ministries and agencies.

Step 4: Transparent Accounting, Budgeting, and Safeguard Ceilings for Fiscal Commitment
Accounting and Reporting of PPPs
There is still no comprehensive and universally binding or accepted accounting standard for the treatment of PPPs in national budgets and international comparable statistics.[12] With the growing harmonization of accounting worldwide, steps have been steadily taken to offer guidance on the PPP accounting issue, but so far the guidance has been still too limited and its application in practice has been uneven.

The absence of clear and operationally relevant standards limits the enforcement of spending controls, and therefore PPP projects often circumvent spending ceilings and fiscal rules. Existing standards are also too lax, with no clear mechanism to prevent investment that would be considered public investment off the government's balance sheets. These circumventions include moving expenditures to future budgets, increasing government liabilities, and entering into guarantees to receive private financing but with taxpayers bearing the risk of future high costs and failure of the contract.

It is not surprising then, that European Union (EU) countries, for example, have previously turned to PPPs as a way to avoid the limits on public debt and budget deficits set under the EU's Stability and Growth Pact. Facing growing criticism of this loophole, governments of member states decided to set rules on accounting procedures for PPP projects (Eurostat 2004, 2012).[13]

Recent developments in international accounting and statistics standards, such as the International Financial Reporting Standards (IFRS) and the International Public Sector Accounting Standards (IPSAS), increasingly reduce the opportunities to use PPPs to distort fiscal realities, but these have not filtered through to actual practice and so do not as yet provide an effective response to the misuse of PPPs (see box 7.2).[14]

Budgeting PPPs

It is essential that the process of planning, appraising, and selecting public investment projects be linked appropriately to the budget cycle even though the project cycle may run along a different timetable. There is clearly a two-way relationship between the budget cycle and the project cycle. The keys to efficient investment are good decisions about the choice of investments; active management of the asset portfolio; and a budgetary process that ensures recurrent funding to operate and maintain existing assets.

The growing interest in PPPs has increased the need for clear rules for budgeting. Transparency is a key element in budgeting and good governance, and, therefore, IMF (2006) and OECD (2012) address the principle that budget documentation should transparently disclose all information possible regarding the costs (capital and recurrent), explicit liabilities, and contingent liabilities of PPPs. In countries with significant PPP programs, disclosure could be in the form of a budget statement on PPPs (see box 7.3). The information should include what and when the government will pay as well as full details of guarantees and contingent liabilities. The payment stream from the government under the PPP contract should be highlighted, particularly if it is loaded toward the outbound years.

Because PPP costs may be contingent or occur in the future, annual budget cycles may be insufficient. So, at a minimum, there needs to be a credible and practical budgeting approach for good PFM.

When governments provide up-front payments to PPP projects, the payments required are similar to those for traditional government-financed projects, and they can be built into annual budgets and the medium-term expenditure framework relatively easily. In some countries, such as India, special PPP funds from which such payments will be made are introduced as well.[15]

Safeguard Ceilings for PPP Fiscal Commitment

IMF (2006) recommends giving high priority to the institutional framework for PPPs—including disclosure requirements and, when appropriate, ceilings on government payments. As Irwin (2008) describes, setting a safeguard ceiling can create incentives for agencies to choose conventional implementation over a PPP even when a PPP might provide better value for money. Nonetheless, given the

Box 7.2 Recent Development of International Accounting and Statistics Standards for PPPs

The International Financial Reporting Standards (IFRS) Interpretations Committee (IFRIC) issued the IFRIC 12 "Service Concession Arrangements" published on November 30, 2006, and effective for annual periods beginning on or after January 1, 2008—to decrease the diversity of existing accounting practice for service concession arrangements (IFRIC 2006). No specific IFRS recognition and measurement guidance previously existed for these types of arrangements.

IFRIC 12 applies to those service concession arrangements in which the public sector (the grantor) controls or regulates the services provided with the infrastructure and their prices, and controls any significant residual interest in the infrastructure. In these circumstances, the operator does not recognize the infrastructure as its property if the infrastructure is existing infrastructure of the grantor or is infrastructure constructed or purchased by the operator as part of the service concession arrangement. The operator recognizes either a financial asset or an intangible asset, or both, at fair value as compensation for any construction services that it provides.

The International Public Sector Accounting Standards (IPSAS) are the accounting standards for public sector entities developed by the International Public Sector Accounting Standards Board (IPSASB). The accrual IPSAS are based on the IFRS, issued by the International Accounting Standards Board.

On October 31, 2011, the IPSASB finalized IPSAS 32, "Service Concession Arrangements: Grantor," effective for annual financial statements covering periods beginning on or after January 1, 2014. IPSAS 32 addresses the grantor's accounting using an approach that is consistent with that used for the operator's accounting in IFRIC 12. IPSAS 32 uses the principles in IFRIC 12 for determining which entity (the grantor or the operator) should recognize an asset in a service concession arrangement, to ensure that the grantor recognizes a service concession asset it controls. The aim of approval of the new standard is to enhance the transparency and accountability of public sector entities by ensuring that service concession arrangement assets and their related financing are reported. It is believed that this will close the gap on significant assets not being recognized by either the grantor or the operator.

Eurostat of the European Commission published on March 15, 2012, the revised *Manual on Government Deficit and Debt*, an application document complementary to the European System of Accounts (ESA95) (Eurostat 2012). The manual states that the core approach to be applied as a matter of principle in national accounts is the "risk and rewards" approach, which differs from the "control over the asset" approach adopted by the private sector accounting standard (IFRIC 12) and the international public sector accounting standard (IPSAS 32). According to the manual, it is not the role of statisticians to examine the economic and financial viability of projects or to provide detailed definition of PPPs because the expression applies to a wide range of arrangements. For the time being, therefore, the EU approach to accounting treatment of PPPs will use the method of examining existing risk and rewards.

Box 7.3 The IMF's Comprehensive Disclosure Requirements for PPPs

According to the International Monetary Fund's requirements, information on PPPs should be disclosed in budget documents and end-of-year financial reports. In countries with significant PPP programs, disclosure could be in the form of a statement on PPPs. In addition to an outline of the objectives of the current and planned PPP program and the capital value of PPP projects that are at an advanced stage of bidding, for each PPP project or group of similar projects, information should be provided on the following:

- Future payment obligations for the following periods: 1–5 years, 5–10 years, 10–20 years, and over 20 years
- Significant terms of the project agreement(s) that may affect the amount, timing, and certainty of future cash flows, valued to the extent feasible (for example, contingent liabilities, the period of a concession, the basis upon which renegotiation is determined)
- The nature and extent of rights to use specified assets (such as quantity, time period, or amount, as appropriate), obligations to provide or rights to expect provision of services, arrangements to receive specified assets at the end of the concession period, and renewal and termination options
- Whether the PPP assets (or any part thereof) are recognized as assets on the government's balance sheet and how the project affects the reported fiscal balance and public debt
- Whether the PPP assets (or any part thereof) are recognized as assets either on the balance sheet of any special purpose vehicle or in the private partner's financial statements[a]
- Any preferential financing for PPPs provided through government on-lending or public financial institutions
- Future expected or contingent government revenue, such as lease receipts, revenue or profit-sharing arrangements, or concession fees
- Any project financing or off-balance-sheet elements such as contingent liabilities provided by entities owned or controlled by the government
- Signed PPP contracts (which should be made publicly available) and major new contracts that have a short-term fiscal impact (which should be indicated in within-year fiscal reports)

Source: IMF 2006.

a. The disclosure of the private partner's accounting treatment has been suggested by Heald (2003). Although there is no question of enforcing symmetrical accounting treatment by the government and private partner, any lack of symmetry may point to areas worthy of scrutiny, especially if no part of the PPP asset is on either balance sheet.

---

difficulties in deciding whether a particular PPP commitment is affordable, limits or ceilings on aggregate PPP expenditure can be a helpful way to ensure that the government's total exposure to PPPs remains within manageable limits. Box 7.4 highlights some different approaches.

To practically implement a safeguard ceiling on government commitments to finance PPP projects, the following points should be carefully reviewed and answered in each country:

- What is an optimal or acceptable level of PPP expenditure for a safeguard ceiling?

Box 7.4 Recent Country Experiences with Fiscal Limits on PPPs

Indeed, several countries are endeavoring to establish some limits and regulations. In Hungary, the public finance law limits the total nominal value of multiyear commitments in PPPs to 3 percent of government revenue.[a] Following the financial crisis in 1998, the Brazilian government set a safeguard ceiling—the upper limit of the local governments' financial commitment to PPP projects—of up to 1 percent of the government revenue. It adopted a series of strict fiscal rules, including central government authority to withdraw support for a PPP project if the local government fails to comply with the standard on public financing.

The Korean government also examined and adopted the idea of a ceiling on the total governmental disbursement for PPP projects in 2008. It was recommended that the government set a safeguard limit to effectively manage aggregate fiscal commitment to PPPs. Under the recommendation, it is assumed that if the government maintained either a government payment ceiling for PPPs of 2 percent of the national budget expenditure or PPP investment at 10–15 percent of total public investment and managed the commitment in the medium and long term, this would ease the fiscal pressure when it comes to public financing commitments of PPP projects.[b, c]

a. Act 38 of 1992, Article 12, cited from Irwin (2008).
b. No specific guidelines or upper limits for PPPs exist in the United Kingdom, which controls an aggregate amount of annual government payment related to PPP (or Public Finance Initiative [PFI]) projects. A series of government documents and data in early 2000, however, implied that annual government payments for PFI have been maintained at about 2 percent of the total annual government budget. The U.K. government also seemed to watch the total amount of PFI projects based on a standard, such as the capital budget. PFI accounts for 10–15 percent of total public investment. (HM Treasury 2004, 2006).
c. For more information, see chapter 6 of Kim (2007).

- Is the ceiling mandatory or merely a guideline?
- What is an appropriate annual reporting format?
- How should the ceiling be reported to parliament, and should the ceiling be subject to parliament's approval?
- Is there any responsibility for publishing?

Step 5: Tightening PPP Project Implementation

During implementation of a PPP project, modifications to the original project plan need to be anticipated. Therefore the government should make sure that the indicators laid out in the project feasibility study, the business case, and the VFM analysis are not weakened or impaired during the process. VFM outcomes are contingent on effective management over contract terms. Poor contract management with the private partner can result in higher costs, wasted resources, and impaired performance. Hence PPPs require careful oversight and regular audits.

After the ex ante project appraisal and selection stages, a competitive bidding process (while not the only possible way of selection) is essential to ensure VFM and optimal allocation of risk between the public and the private sector.[16] Tender documents should be formulated based on the results of the project appraisal so that minimum requirements to achieve the project objectives and

VFM are satisfied. The final PPP contract terms and conditions resulting from nego-tiation with the private sector should reflect the ex ante VFM. This aspect needs regular checking throughout the preparation and tender stages of the project.

In practice, there are often changes to the project cost in the course of the procurement process. In the case of cost overrun, reassessment of feasibility and VFM is recommended at least for large projects; this would enable the govern-ment to recheck the impact of changes in project contents or the business case as well as to scrutinize the adequacy of the cost increase. In Korea, for instance, the reassessment study of feasibility (RSF) is mandatory and requested by the central budget authority on a project where a total project cost increase of more than 20 percent is proposed over the estimate at a previous phase of the project.[17]

It is useful to develop and announce standard implementation guidelines for deciding procurement strategy, managing bid processes, developing model proj-ect agreement and standard clauses, issuing guidelines for output specification, managing contracts, and so forth. These guidelines provide both public procurers and private companies with a basic understanding and clarity on how individual PPP projects have been developed and procured under a unified framework, which reduces project risks and uncertainty. It is also important to provide public officers in charge of implementing and managing PPP projects with capacity-building and training programs on how to develop and procure PPP projects.[18]

Step 6: Project Adjustment by Refinancing and Renegotiation

The main focus of PPP project management has been on the ex ante stage, meaning "good" project appraisal and initiation. As projects enter into the implementation phase, efficiency of project management and renegotiation acquire importance. It is essential to clearly understand the process of PPP project adjustment, particu-larly regarding the two distinct cases of refinancing and renegotiation.[19]

Refinancing a PPP Project

Refinancing of a PPP project is the process of changing the project company's equity structure, investment share, or debt financing conditions. Upon comple-tion of construction, private construction companies generally want to exit the project by selling their shares. Also, shareholders want to convert a part of their equity into subordinated debt upon completion of construction. Because signifi-cantly less risk is present after the construction and commissioning stages have been completed, the premium paid for that risk (reflected in the margins on the finance) should also be less. This is one of the major reasons for refinancing maturing PPP projects.

Under the terms of many PPP project agreements, the competent authority may expect to share the refinancing benefits equally with the project company. The refinancing benefit is measured as the increase in investors' expected inter-nal rate of return in the postrefinancing financial model against the base case financial model. Several governments have already introduced rules for how refinancing benefits will be treated. The public authority and the concessionaire may split the benefit 50-50 or in other alternate ways.[20]

The Power of Public Investment Management • http://dx.doi.org/10.1596/978-1-4648-0316-1

Renegotiating a PPP Project

Renegotiation means an adjustment or change in the project agreement between two or more parties in a PPP. Terms and conditions in the project agreement can be renegotiated when the project agreement allows it. This might be foreseen, for example, when policies related to the project or the project scope change. Renegotiation is possible when the government wants to rebalance the use of facilities among government facilities and PPP facilities. The government and public authorities are supposed to pursue renegotiation in the interest of the public and users. The request for renegotiation is not restricted to public authorities. The concessionaire can also request changes to the project agreement. Guasch (2004, 19) argues that renegotiation can be a positive instrument when it addresses the inherently incomplete nature of PPP contracts, while particularly opportunistic renegotiation can reduce or eliminate the expected benefits of competitive bidding.

Some guidelines for effective renegotiations include the following:

- Renegotiation requires agreement among the public and the private partners along with their financiers.
- Renegotiation takes into account the original project agreement.
- Many countries (the EU countries, in particular) have strict rules on adding to the original scope or scale of the project without changing the nature of the original tender process.
- Ex ante value for money should not be negatively affected whenever renegotiation is made.
- The government should consider compensating the private partner only when conditions change because of discretionary public policy actions.
- Careful consideration is needed regarding any shifts in the project risk profile. The financier of the project will equally want to be sure that its own rewards are not diluted through a renegotiation.
- Any renegotiation process should be made transparently and subject to the law.

Step 7: Better Service Delivery through Better Operation and Maintenance

By definition, a large portion of value for money in PPPs should be created by more efficient management of the delivery of the services and operation and maintenance of the assets. PPP project monitoring is managed by the relevant public authority, and the management structure is stipulated in each project agreement. To achieve the value for money envisaged at the signing of the project agreement, both the government and the private partner need to make sure that the planned allocation of responsibilities is clear and that risks are optimally shared and balanced.

Throughout the term of the contract, the following is assumed:

- The government is responsible for monitoring contract compliance and service performance by the private partner and for ensuring that all contracted payments are paid appropriately.

- The private partner is likely to monitor compliance by the government to ensure its responsibilities under the contract.
- Both parties are responsible for mitigating risks in operation and maintenance.

Each public authority manages projects by following the protocols stipulated in the project agreements and receiving project progress reports. Public authorities typically receive monthly reports from the private project company and may submit the results to the central PPP unit or the central budget authority. It is recommended that the authority input detailed information about PPP projects in a database. The main components of this database might include financial status, project progress, and fiscal support-related matters. The database can be used to develop better PPP policy and implementation at hand and in the future.

A good thing about PPPs is that PPP projects easily use a satisfaction survey and performance evaluation to assure service quality control. Performance checks and evaluation are conducted as specified in the standard performance quality requirement. The purpose of the performance evaluation is to check and assess whether service delivery outputs and outcomes are in accordance with the project agreement and output specification. Deductions can be applied to the payments from government to private partner for poor performance to promote private sector accountability and incentivize better operational performance. The facility operation performance is evaluated regularly, and if the agreed-upon service availability levels are not met, a deduction is applied to the government payments. If the level of service (content and quality) falls short of what the project agreement stipulates, a certain percentage can be deducted from the agreed-upon government payment.

Step 8: PPP Project Ex Post Evaluation: Does PPP Provide Better Value for Money?

Chapter 2 argues that a basic completion review should apply to all projects in a systematic way. That review comprises an examination by a responsible agency or line ministry to assess whether the project was completed within the original (and amended) budget and time frame; whether the outputs were delivered as specified; and whether the original objectives of the project have or are being achieved. As a supplement, the supreme audit institution should periodically conduct a compliance audit of a sample of investment projects. Good practice suggests that the project design should build in the evaluation criteria and that learning from such ex post evaluations should be used to improve future project design and implementation. OECD (2012) recommends that the supreme audit institution (a) maintain sufficient capacity to give a clear verdict on whether the project ultimately represented value for money; (b) suggest possible improvements to the regulatory PPP framework of the preparation and procurement processes; and (c) make available overall lessons regarding the use of PPPs and investments.[21]

Unfortunately, the evaluation of PPP projects is extremely difficult because of both the conceptual slipperiness and the large number of disciplines involved—economics, accounting, law, political science, engineering, and

Box 7.5 The Challenge of Ex Post Evaluation in PPP Projects

Although Australia and the United Kingdom have already produced substantial evidence of
better VFM in some cases, Hodge (2010, 95) concludes that empirical tests of the VFM of PPP
projects are not conclusive: the real VFM performance of PPPs remains empirically open.[a]

Related to the mixed evaluation results and real VFM performance, it is important to recognize that, in most countries, PPPs have proved popular for many bad reasons as well as good.
Boardman and Vining (2010, 162–64) note that governments like PPPs because they postpone
government cash outlays, allow the cost of the projects to be placed off-budget, improve
government net cash flow, reduce the transparency of government finances, transfer risks to
the private sector, and reduce exposure to political risk. They also allow governments to
announce and initiate projects for political kudos without having to be too concerned with
future affordability. Any problems can be inherited by future governments and taxpayers.

a. Irwin (2012) even argues that the benefits of PPPs may be illusory.

so on—that need to be brought together and reconciled (Allen 2012). Many
important technical areas, such as developing an international accounting standard for PPPs and an appropriate legal framework, have not been fully resolved.
Hodge (2010, 93) explains why different reviewers often see the same results
differently. Evaluation has also proved difficult in practice because of the inherently political nature of the decision-making process, which acts as a distorting
lens (see box 7.5).

One way to evaluate PPPs, nonetheless, is to explicitly trace out evidence of
cost savings and efficiency gain as well as evidence of PPP contribution to the
national economy, as follows:

- *From a microeconomic point of view*, the efficiency of PPP projects could be
  measured and analyzed to review whether gradual improvements, compared
  with the cases of conventionally implemented projects, have been made in the
  efficiency of costs, toll rates, and economic rates of return.

- *From a macroeonomic point of view*, the PPP contribution to the national economy could be analyzed. The impact of PPP projects could be diagnosed as to
  whether they have ripple effects on the national economy through several
  channels: economic growth resulting from the inflow of private capital;
  increased social welfare resulting from the timely delivery of social services;
  and the early realization of social benefits. Despite such expansion in private
  investment through PPPs, it is not easy to measure and present private investment's contribution to economic growth.[22]

Despite these challenges, the ex post evaluation of PPPs should be more rigor-
ously managed within a comprehensive framework of analysis, applying both
micro- and macroeconomic points of view. Multidisciplinary approaches and

comparative studies, combining PPPs and conventional financing, are strongly recommended. Because it is not always clear whether the PPP is a good route, the cost and benefit of PPP initiation should be reviewed objectively within a unified PIM framework.

Future Work for the Unified Approach

Because the scale of PPP investment and related government commitments (both explicit and contingent) have rapidly increased in the world, the need for a unified framework is increasing as well. Too often, PPP investment has been treated separately from publicly financed investment and has not come under direct regulation as government expenditure. Because large parts of future government obligations on PPPs are long-term commitments such as government payments for service purchase-type projects and guarantee payments in some cases, it is important to examine whether a government can maintain the same level of fiscal soundness and sustainability for both conventional and PPP financing in a unified framework.

This chapter pointed out the importance of a unified framework for comparably and effectively appraising and analyzing both conventional and PPP forms of implementation. But to make this a win-win situation, an optimal partnership between both parties needs to be fostered. This is arguably challenging in practice because it requires reconciliation of the public interest with private interest. Such reconciliation is more likely found when the bias for one form of implementation or another is mitigated or eliminated.

Future work is needed to help governments put in place the unified approach for public investment that enables them to select the public investment option that delivers the best value for money, whether by traditional budget financing or PPP. An immediate task to make the unified approach viable is to provide further diagnostic tools that would synthesize and deepen guidance on systematic assessments for PPPs in and jointly with PIM systems. Such tools, while aligned with the Public Expenditure and Financial Accountability (PEFA) assessment tool of the conventional PIM framework,[23] would need to develop new indicators and means of verification to assess the performance of PPP systems, processes, and institutions.[24]

Notes

1. There exists no standard definition of what constitutes a public-private partnership (PPP). The World Bank and Public-Private Infrastructure Advisory Facility (PPIAF) (2012) define a PPP as "a long-term contract between a private party and a government agency, for providing a public asset or service, in which the private party bears significant risk and management responsibility." The Organisation for Economic Co-operation and Development (OECD) (2008) defines a PPP as "an agreement between the government and one or more private partners according to which the private partners deliver the service in such a manner that the service delivery objectives of the government are aligned with the profit objectives of the private partners

and where the effectiveness of the alignment depends on a sufficient transfer of risk to the private partners." HM Treasury (2008) of the United Kingdom defines a PPP as "arrangements typified by joint working between the public and private sectors. In their broadest sense they can cover all types of collaboration across the private-public sector interface involving collaborative working together and risk sharing to deliver policies, services and infrastructure."

2. The World Bank and PPIAF database (http://www.ppiaf.org/) provides good information for PPP projects. The database includes data on a wide spectrum of private participation in infrastructure (PPI).

3. For further discussion on PPP reporting and accounting, see the next section under "Step 4."

4. Hemming (2008) argues that a binary approach could result in governments accepting bids from private partners prepared to accept more risk, irrespective of the cost to government of having them do so, which would defeat the objective of using PPPs to achieve value for money. By the same token, projects that offer good value for money may be of little interest to the government given that they have to be recorded on the balance sheet. In other words, bad PPPs could end up driving out good ones.

5. This is the document that sets priorities for government investments in the national strategic guidance and planning. In practice, such documents are not always followed and are subject to political influence. Many countries at least provide national guidance and planning for prioritizing traditional government investments.

6. The OECD recommendation seems to highlight that the traditional procurement mode should not remain the default mode (OECD 2010b).

7. In managing PPPs, arguments exist both for and against the establishment of a dedicated PPP unit. OECD (2010a) points out that these arguments center on the separation of policy formulation and project implementation, the pooling of expertise and experience within the government, the standardization of procurement procedures, the appropriate budgetary consideration of projects, and the demonstration of political commitment and trust. World Bank and PPIAF (2012) also reviews establishment of a PPP unit.

8. World Bank and PPIAF (2007) defines a dedicated PPP unit as any organization designed to promote or improve PPPs that has a lasting mandate to manage multiple PPPs' transactions in response to government failures including poor procurement incentives, lack of coordination, lack of skills, high transaction costs, lack of information, and so on. OECD (2010a) defines a dedicated PPP unit as any organization set up with full or partial aid of the government to ensure that necessary capacity to create, support, and evaluate multiple PPP agreements is made available and clustered together within government. The reference to "multiple" PPPs is an important distinction to differentiate a dedicated government PPP unit from a dedicated PPP project unit, which may be located in government organizations to support the management of an individual project. The definition of OECD (2010a) seems more oriented toward supporting the role of independence.

9. The Portuguese government established a PPP Unit in Parpublica SA in 2003, but, with a concern that technical support was too dispersed within the public sector, Parpublica's role as the main PPP unit was ceased and in 2012 the Ministry of Finance established UTAP under its direct authority. See EPEC (2014).

10. The former Partnership UK as a new agency was abolished, and the Infrastructure UK as a regulatory body within HM Treasury of the United Kingdom was formed separately with a different mandate since 2010.

11. OECD (2010a) presents a good survey of institutional and governance structures of dedicated PPP units.

12. However, there exists an example of government financial statistics as a form of PPP reporting. The Eurostat standards, widely accepted in European Commission countries under the European System of Integrated Economic Accounts (ESA95) standards, are reporting following the standards of the International Monetary Fund's Government Finance Statistics Manual 2001 (IMF 2001). At present, the standards do not ensure useful reporting of PPP commitments in long-term purchase contracts.

13. According to the accounting rules announced by Eurostat in 2004 and restated in 2012, the assets (or debts) involved in a long-term PPP contract between a government unit and a nongovernment unit can be considered as nongovernment assets (or debts) only if there is strong evidence that the nongovernment partner is bearing most of the risks attached to the asset (or debts) all over the contract (Eurostat 2004, 2012). The rules state that in such cases where government revenues exceed 50 percent of government payments to the private partner in a PPP project, the project should remain on the balance sheet of the government and not be classified as a PPP.

14. Accounting treatment of PPPs has historically been based on "risk and reward" criteria, but recently IFRS and IPSAS argued for "control" criteria. The "risk and reward" criteria, adopted by Eurostat, highlight the responsibility of the party that bears the project risk and reward, while the "control" criteria claim the responsibility of the party that controls the decision. The assets (or debts), whose risks are mostly borne by the nongovernment unit, can be considered as government assets (or debts) only if the government controls the decision on who bears the risks. See IFRIC 12 "Service Concession Arrangements" (IFRIC 2006) and the IPSAS ED 43 (IPSAS 2010).

15. In July 2005, the Cabinet Committee on Economic Affairs established India's Viability Gap Fund (VGF) program through its approval of the "Scheme for Financial Support to Public Private Partnerships in Infrastructure." The primary objective of India's VGF program is to attract more private investment in infrastructure by making PPP projects financially viable. The scheme is funded by the Government through its budgetary resources, with budget provisions made on an annual basis linked to likely demand for disbursements during the year. In the first year a budgetary provision of US$40 million was made. The scheme also provides for a revolving fund to be kept at the disposal of the Empowered Committee to ensure liquidity of the VGF, and replenished as needed. In any given year, the scheme provides for a cap on the value of projects approved equivalent to ten times the budget provisions for VGF in the annual plan—to ensure continuing liquidity and preventing bunching of disbursement requests as far as possible. This cap can be modified if the Ministry of Finance considers necessary. In practice, the cap has not been binding, and the total VGF support during any year has been based on the estimated requirement for disbursals during the coming year. Source: Ministry of Finance, Government of India (2013), Scheme for Support to Public Private Partnerships in Infrastructure. See World Bank and the PPIAF (forthcoming).

16. The relevant authority—either a central or a local government agency—forms a tender evaluation team, and, in general, the evaluation is conducted with prequalification and evaluation of technical and financial or price elements. One preferred bidder is selected for negotiation based on the result of the evaluation, and the second preferred bidder is invited to negotiate only if the negotiation with the first preferred bidder has failed. Under EU rules, a Competitive Dialogue procedure can be conducted where the procuring agency negotiates with more than one bidder simultaneously.

17. The mandatory reassessment study of feasibility (RSF) in the Republic of Korea, declared in the National Finance Law, has proven to be effective in discouraging unnecessary cost-increase requests by spending ministries and agencies. They are more likely to quit requesting higher cost increases (more than 20 percent) than to let the projects be reassessed at a zero-base.

18. Public officers in every country are well acquainted with traditional procurement policy and projects but not necessarily with their PPP counterparts. Therefore, PPP capacity-building and training programs are strongly recommended.

19. Among various issues of ex post monitoring, performance management, refinancing, and renegotiation, issues of refinancing and renegotiation are unique to the PPP route, whereas the remaining issues (of ex post monitoring and performance management) pertain to both PPP and traditional procurement projects. Traditional procurements, in general, hardly ever have refinancing and renegotiation issues.

20. The United Kingdom's HM Treasury introduced into its standard PFI contracts a 50-50 split of any refinancing gain (HM Treasury 2003), but this was subsequently revised up to a 70-30 split in favor of the government in the wake of the global financial crisis in the late 2000s.

21. OECD (2012) encourages the supreme audit institution to assume an important role in examining whether the risks involved in PPPs are managed effectively. The supreme audit institution's reports to the parliament can keep the public informed about the service that they receive and disseminate best practice.

22. According to a study by Rhee and Lee (2007) in Korea, the promotion of PPP projects results in a decline in fiscal investment by the government, implying a crowding-out effect of PPPs on public investment, and therefore PPP promotion does not have a significant effect on total investment.

23. See further discussions about the existing framework of Public Expenditure and Financial Accountability (PEFA) for conventional public investment at http://www.pefa.org.

24. To assess the performance of PPPs in a unified framework, a new "PIM for PPP" diagnostic framework with the PEFA-type indicators and means of verification was developed by the World Bank (World Bank forthcoming).

References

Allen, R. 2012. "Review *of International Handbook on Public-Private Partnerships*, Graeme A. Hodge, Carsten Greve, and Anthony E. Boardman, eds. Cheltenham: Edward Elgar, 2010." *Governance* 25 (3): 521–23.

Australian Government. 2008. *National PPP Guidelines Overview*. Canberra: Infrastructure Australia.

Boardman, A. E. and A. R. Vining. 2010. "Assessing the Economic Worth of Public-Private Partnerships." In *International Handbook on Public-Private Partnerships*, ed. by G. A. Hodge, C. Greve, and A. E. Boardman, 159–86. Cheltenham, UK: Edward Elgar.

Brumby, J., K. Kaiser, and J.-H. Kim 2013. "Public Investment Management and Public Private Partnerships." In *The International Handbook of Public Financial Management*, ed. by R. Allen, R. Hemming, and B. H. Potter.

Engel, E., R. Fischer, and A. Galetovic. 2007. "The Basic Public Finance of Public-Private Partnerships." Working Paper 13284, National Bureau of Economic Research, Cambridge, MA.

EPEC. 2014. *Portugal: PPP Units and Related Institutional Framework*. European PPP Expertise Center.

Eurostat. 2004. "New Decision of Eurostat on Deficit and Debt: Treatment of Public-Private Partnerships." News Release 18. February 11.

———. 2012. *Manual on Government Deficit and Debt: Implementation of ESA95*. 2012 Edition. Luxembourg: Eurostat.

Guasch, J. L. 2004. *Granting and Renegotiating Infrastructure Concessions: Doing It Right*. World Bank Institute (WBI) Development Studies. Washington, DC: World Bank.

Heald, D. 2003. "Value for Money Tests and Accounting Treatment in PFI Schemes." *Accounting, Auditing, and Accountability Journal* 16 (3): 342–71.

Hemming, R. 2008. "PPPs: Some Accounting and Reporting Issues." In *Public Investment and Public-Private Partnerships: Addressing Infrastructure Challenges and Managing Fiscal Risks*, ed. by G. Schwartz, A. Corbacho, and K. Funke, 235–44. New York: International Monetary Fund; Hampshire, U.K.: Palgrave Macmillan.

HM Treasury, United Kingdom. 2003. *PFI: Meeting the Investment Challenge*. London: HMSO.

———. 2004. *Standardization of PFI Contracts Version 3*. HM Treasury guidance on PFI project issues, HMSO, London.

———. 2006. "PFI: Strengthening Long-Term Partnerships." HM Treasury guidance document, HMSO, London.

———. 2008. "Infrastructure Procurement: Delivering Long-Term Value." HM Treasury guidance document, HMSO, London.

———. 2011. *The Green Book: Appraisal and Evaluation in Central Government*. London: HMSO.

Hodge, G. A. 2010. "Reviewing Public-Private Partnerships: Some Thoughts on Evaluation." In *International Handbook on Public-Private Partnerships*, ed. by G. A. Hodge, C. Greve, and A. E. Boardman, 81–112. Cheltenham, U.K.: Edward Elgar.

IFRIC (International Financial Reporting Interpretations Committee). 2006. "IFRIC 12 Service Concession Arrangements." Interpretation document, IFRIC, London.

IMF (International Monetary Fund). 2001. *Government Finance Statistics Manual*. Washington, DC: IMF.

———. 2006. "Public-Private Partnerships, Government Guarantees, and Fiscal Risk." Special Issues Paper, Fiscal Affairs Department, IMF, Washington, DC.

IPSAS (International Public Sector Accounting Standards). 2010. "IPSAS ED (Exposure Draft) 43 Service Concession Arrangements." Accounting standards document, IPSAS Board, New York.

Irwin, T. 2008. "Controlling Spending Commitments in PPPs." In *Public Investment and Public-Private Partnerships*, ed. by G. Schwartz, A. Corbacho, and K. Funke, 105–17. New York: International Monetary Fund; Hampshire, U.K.: Palgrave Macmillan.

———. 2012. *Accounting Devices and Fiscal Illusions*. Staff Discussion Note, International Monetary Fund, Washington, DC.

Kim, J.-H., ed. 2007. *Performance Evaluation and Best Practice of Public-Private Partnerships*. Seoul: Korea Development Institute.

Ministry of Finance, Government of India. 2013. *Scheme for Support to Public Private Partnership in Infrastructure*, New Delhi.

National Audit Office, United Kingdom. 2013. *Review of the VFM assessment process for PFI*. United Kingdom.

NSW (New South Wales) Government. 2006. *Working with Government: Guidelines for Privately Financed Projects*. Sydney, Australia: NSW Government.

OECD (Organization for Economic Co-operation and Development). 2008. *Public-Private Partnerships: In Pursuit of Risk Sharing and Value for Money*. Paris: OECD.

———. 2010a. *Dedicated Public-Private Partnership Units: A Survey of Institutional and Governance Structures*. Paris: OECD.

———. 2010b. "How to Attain Value for Money: Comparing PPP and Traditional Infrastructure Public Procurement." Working paper, OECD, Paris.

———. 2012. "Recommendation of the Council on Principles for Public Governance of Public-Private Partnerships." Public Governance recommendation document, OECD, Paris.

PWF (Public Works Financing). 2009. *Public Works Financing Newsletter*. Vol. 242.

Rhee, C. and H. Lee. 2007. "Public-Private Partnerships in Infrastructure and Macroeconomy: The Experience of Korea." In *Performance Evaluation and Best Practice of Public-Private Partnerships*, ed. by J.-H. Kim, 51–85. Seoul: Korea Development Institute.

World Bank. Forthcoming. *Public Investment Management for Public-Private Partnerships: Analytical Framework and Assessment Tool*. World Bank report. Washington, DC: World Bank.

World Bank and the PPIAF (Public-Private Infrastructure Advisory Facility). 2007. *Public-Private Partnership Units: Lessons for their Design and Use in Infrastructure*. World Bank and PPIAF report. Washington, DC: World Bank.

———. 2012. *Public-Private Partnerships Reference Guide, Version 1.0*. Washington, DC: World Bank.

———. Forthcoming. *Public-Private Partnerships Reference Guide Version 2.0*. Washington, DC: World Bank.

Environmental Benefits Statement

The World Bank Group is committed to reducing its environmental footprint. In support of this commitment, the Publishing and Knowledge Division leverages electronic publishing options and print-on-demand technology, which is located in regional hubs worldwide. Together, these initiatives enable print runs to be lowered and shipping distances decreased, resulting in reduced paper consumption, chemical use, greenhouse gas emissions, and waste.

The Publishing and Knowledge Division follows the recommended standards for paper use set by the Green Press Initiative. Whenever possible, books are printed on 50 percent to 100 percent postconsumer recycled paper, and at least 50 percent of the fiber in our book paper is either unbleached or bleached using Totally Chlorine Free (TCF), Processed Chlorine Free (PCF), or Enhanced Elemental Chlorine Free (EECF) processes.

More information about the Bank's environmental philosophy can be found at http://crinfo.worldbank.org/wbcrinfo/node/4.

green press
INITIATIVE

www.ingramcontent.com/pod-product-compliance
Lightning Source LLC
Chambersburg PA
CBHW080545220326
41599CB00032B/6371